SHOPPING FOR FAITH

SHOPPING FOR FAITH

American Religion in the New Millennium

Richard Cimino and Don Lattin

o

Jossey-Bass Publishers
San Francisco

Jossey-Bass books and products are available through most
bookstores. To contact Jossey-Bass directly, call (888) 378-2537,
fax to (800) 605-2665, or visit our website at
www.josseybass.com.

Substantial discounts on bulk quantities of Jossey-Bass books
are available to corporations, professional associations, and
other organizations. For details and discount information, contact the special sales department at Jossey-Bass.

For sales outside the United States, please contact your local
Simon & Schuster International Office.

 Manufactured in the United States of America on Lyons Falls
Turin Book. This paper is acid-free and 100 percent totally
chlorine-free.

Library of Congress Cataloging-in-Publication Data

Cimino, Richard P.
  Shopping for faith: American religion in the new millennium /
Richard Cimino and Don Lattin. — 1st ed.
      p. cm.
  Includes bibliographical references and index.
  ISBN 0-7879-4170-0 (alk. paper)
    1. Christianity—United States—20th century. 2. Christianity—
United States—Forecasting. 3. United
States—Religion—Forecasting. I. Lattin, Don, II. Title.
  BR526.C565 1998   200'.973'01—ddc21   98-19707
CD-ROM ISBN 0-7879-4673-7

FIRST EDITION

HB Printing   10 9 8 7 6 5 4 3 2 1

CONTENTS

PART THREE
Searching for Common Culture

PREFACE

SHOPPING FOR FAITH charts the many directions of American religion, calling on the analysis of scholars and the stories of everyday people. Our goal is to provide a tour of today's spiritual marketplace and forecast the future of faith in the coming century. We will document

- How consumerism will shape all religious practice—from conservative evangelical worship to the wildest New Age workshop
- How personal spiritual experience will replace religious doctrine as the driving force in tomorrow's free market of belief
- How the baby boomers and Generation X will rediscover traditional faith
- How megachurches and small groups will provide new homes for spiritual seekers
- How secular spirituality will change the way Americans work, play, and express their sexuality
- How science, medicine, and the media will find religion
- How religious groups will play a greater role in social service and community development
- How new religious movements and apocalyptic groups will attract followers in the new millennium

Shopping for Faith examines the three major areas of religious life: individual spirituality and belief, religious institutions, and the interaction between religion and society. Each chapter contains a series of forecasts about the future shape of religion and spirituality. Each forecast—in bold type to make it easier to find—begins with a vignette to illustrate that trend. These stories are drawn from interviews with people we have met during our many years of monitoring the American religious scene. To protect their confidentiality and changing circumstances, we have changed the names of some people—those we identify with only a first name. For the same reason, the names of some individual congregations have also been changed.

Futurist treatments of religion often focus on the big questions—what will religion look like in the future? Will we be more religious? Which religions and theologies will become dominant? When the *Futurist* magazine in 1994 asked several futurologists what was on the horizon in religion, they did not waste any time on details. One observer forecasted a new United Nations of religions in which religious representatives would gather in "perpetual spiritual-parliamentary sessions in order to advance the knowledge of God or the Transcendent for the whole human family." Others saw the rise of a "mature whole-earth theology" and a "fully integrated male/female world theology." These forecasts were far from disinterested observations.

Our methods for chronicling religious trends include firsthand reporting and research, as well as a review of recent journalistic accounts and scholarly studies on religion in America. The best way to predict the future is to project current trends. Of course, no one knows exactly where American religion is headed. War, natural disasters, or a major economic depression—especially when accompanied by a powerful new spiritual movement or charismatic leader—can send shock waves through the religious terrain.

We draw our map of the religious future with many travelers in mind. Our summaries of scholarly work and religious forecasts provide useful information for clergy and laity, students and professors, journalists, or anyone interested in what others believe and in what difference beliefs make in their lives. There is a growing body of research on American religion, but it is often scattered among different disciplines and shrouded in "academese." We hope the stories we tell will provide information and inspiration for ordinary Americans negotiating the twists and turns of the spiritual path.

Think of the three parts of this book as three concentric circles. Each circle encloses the other and then radiates outward—starting with the individual, moving on to the institution, and concluding with society. Our book looks at how religion may be lived and believed in the future, not how it *should* be practiced. We are not pushing a particular religious agenda and believe the growing pluralism in American religion makes this an important book for our time.

CD-ROM

We've tried to make our book a timely and topical study of American religion, and the shiny little disk in the back of the book helps us realize that goal in an extraordinary way. Included with each copy of *Shopping for Faith* is a CD-ROM containing an electronic version of the book's entire text, with links to resources on the World Wide Web. With the click of a mouse, readers can follow links from key terms in the text to related sites and current news stories that are researched and maintained by TheLinkLibrary.com.

This innovative technology allows readers to get more information on some of the religious groups and spiritual movements discussed in *Shopping for Faith*. Detailed information and installation instructions for the CD, including customer support numbers, are on page 239.

The Authors

As coauthors, we approach the American religious landscape from different perspectives. Our book is the culmination of three decades of work chronicling the personal stories and social context of today's spiritual scene.

RICHARD CIMINO lives in New York and is the editor of *Religion Watch*, a newsletter monitoring trends and research in contemporary religion. He holds a bachelor's degree in journalism from New York University and a master's in sociology from Fordham University. Richard is also the author of *Against the Stream: The Adoption of Traditional Christian Faiths by Young Adults*.

DON LATTIN lives in California. He is the religion writer for the *San Francisco Chronicle*, and over the past two decades has interviewed thousands of Americans about their religious heritage and spiritual search. He has won numerous awards for his religion reporting, and was a fellow at the Program in Religious Studies for Journalists at the University of North Carolina at Chapel Hill. He has also taught religion reporting at the graduate school of journalism at the University of California at Berkeley, where he earned a degree in sociology.

Acknowledgments

We thank Sarah Polster, Darren Hall, and Carol Brown at Jossey-Bass for their help putting together this book. Richard Cimino would like to thank Michael Cuneo and Erling Jorstad for their helpful comments and criticisms on parts of the manuscript. The same gratitude goes to his parents for their assistance during this long project. Don Lattin would like to thank the *San Francisco Chronicle* for providing a sabbatical from daily journalism and for permission to use material originally published in the newspaper. He is also grateful for assistance offered by three good friends—Antonia Lattin, Aimee Chitayat, and George Paul Csicsery—and for inspiration provided by Laura Thomas.

August 1998

RICHARD CIMINO
North Bellmore, New York

DON LATTIN
Berkeley, California

SHOPPING FOR FAITH

INTRODUCTION:
BELIEF IN AMERICA

SIX AMERICANS SIT AROUND A TABLE—an aging rabbi, a Mormon businessman, a meditating nurse, a Mexican janitor, a skeptical writer, and a twelve-year-old girl. They all believe in God.

Fine, we ask, but what sort of God? How do they envision the divine?

"God cannot be defined," says the rabbi. "This confusion we have about God is one reason Jews have a harder time being believers than Catholics or Protestants. We don't know who it is, what it is, where it is. We don't know."

"God is a glorified man," says the Mormon businessman. "When we pray to God, we're not praying to a bunch of air, or some spirit floating around the universe. We are praying to our father, literally our father."

"God is both formless and form," says the meditating nurse. "I used to think he was this big fluffy thing with a beard. I knew there was something other than me, but I didn't know what it was. If God is everywhere, how can he have a form?"

"God loves us," says the janitor. "God gave us life."

"God has a deep announcer's voice," says the writer. "It's probably Charlton Heston."

"God is everybody," says the girl. "Everybody helps everybody else see God."

o

Americans believe in God. Around 95 percent of us, the pollsters say, believe in God or a universal life spirit. Those numbers have changed very little over the past fifty years. Sociologists tell us that overall attendance at religious congregations has remained about the same over the last forty years. Although the baby boom generation may attend fewer religious services than their parents did, recent research suggests that Americans are actually more religious now than in the nation's early years. These beliefs and practices have persisted despite gloomy theological forecasts of the "death of God," and countless commentators bemoaning the rise of secularism and disbelief in American culture.[1]

Americans believe in a personal God who is in control of the world, judges humanity, and performs miracles. Far fewer view God as a life force or spirit. In the 1990s, nine adults in ten said they believe in a heaven, whereas three in four believed in hell. Gallup polls report that one-third of Americans have had a profound spiritual experience, sudden or gradual, that has transformed their lives.[2]

Americans are, for the most part, Christian. According to a survey of 113,000 Americans by the City University of New York, an overwhelming 86 percent consider themselves Christian. Jews represent 2 percent, whereas Muslims, Buddhists, and Hindus have smaller representations.[3] Figures were even smaller for followers of nonconventional religions, such as the New Age movement. This study was significant because it allowed people to identify their own religious affiliation. Researchers reasoned that self-identification would provide a better picture of affiliation than denominational membership records, since many members no longer identify with the faith of their birth. Many immigrants from the non-Christian nations of Asia or the Islamic world are Christian, either because they converted after immigration or came to the United States for religious freedom. Though exotic religions like Islam and Buddhism get lots of media attention, Christianity's predominance in the United States is unlikely to be challenged by any other faith.

This stability of American belief makes our task—charting the future of religion—easier than one might think. Using the past as our guide, we can predict that the religious convictions of Americans will remain fairly stable well into the next millennium. So why, you may ask, are we writing this book? Because everything *except* the basic beliefs of Americans are in flux. There will be major changes in how these beliefs are expressed and interpreted by different social groups and traditions. New ways will be found to apply these beliefs to wider social issues. Historic shifts will occur in how these beliefs are blended with other religious perspectives. Although the New Age movement and Eastern mysticism have relatively few formal adherents, best-selling books on spiritualism and mysticism show that Americans love to "mix and match" religion.

What about those dire forecasts of growing secularization in American society? What about those theologians predicting the demise of religion? God did not die, but the religious denominations employing many of those liberal theologians show few vital signs. There was a dip in church attendance in the 1960s, but those forecasters were too quick to link the modernization of society with the decline of religious faith. According to some of the latest research, Americans are getting more religious. Pew Research Center reported in December 1997 that 71 percent of Americans say they "never doubt the existence of God," up 11 percent from a similar survey in 1987.[4]

These numbers do little to support the "secularization thesis" of the 1960s, those predictions of a progressive and irreversible decline in religion. Social scientists pointed to the emptying cathedrals of Europe and the dramatic decline of such mainstream U.S. denominations as the Episcopal Church and the Presbyterian Church (U.S.A.) as evidence for their theory. Religious institutions were seen as gradually retreating from their public role, especially in areas such as education, welfare, community standards, and social values. An optimistic view of the growing role of science, technology, and psychology, and their potential for enhancing human progress, seemed to rule out older notions of reality based on the supernatural.

Dismissing religion's role in the modern world could be done only by overlooking the places where faith survived and flourished. Secularists failed to notice that more conservative religious bodies grew while more liberal mainline churches declined. While Europe was increasingly secular, at least on the surface, other parts of the world, such as the Middle East, Latin America, and the Arab world, experienced a religious resurgence by the 1970s. Some argued that this growth in traditional faith was religion's last gasp—simply a reaction to the inexorable march of secularism. They were wrong.

Over the past two decades, conservative and traditional faith has increased its social and political influence. Islamic activism in the Middle East and North Africa, as well as the political activism of American evangelicals, illustrates how religion in the 1990s became far more than a private matter between believers and their God.

Secularization has occurred within certain American institutions. Some professions, such as the media, psychiatry, academia, and entertainment, have lower levels of religious commitment and practice than those found among business people or blue-collar workers. Sociologist Peter Berger has said that America often appears as secular as Sweden at the top, but more like India in the profuse religious expression of the people. Since "knowledge class" professionals produce much of the culture's media, someone watching television or reading newspapers can easily think that America is more secular than it really is.

Religious bodies that dismantled much of their theological identity, by putting more emphasis on social issues or psychological needs, can also be seen as secularized. This is especially the case in groups that have removed practices that once generated a sense of commitment and identity for their members, such as tithing or a literal view of the Bible.

Yet as the new millennium unfolds, the spiritual divide in American society will not separate atheists and believers as much as people with different religious sensibilities. In its first issue of 1998, the *New Yorker* magazine published the results of a national poll that divided the U.S. population into three groups. "Main Street" represented the overall adult population. "Easy Street" was the name for individuals making more than $100,000 a year. "High Street" identified the third group, those "cultural elites" who subscribe to the *New Yorker*. Asked, "Do you believe that your religion is 'true' in a way that other religions and spiritual traditions are not?" residents of Main Street said yes nearly twice as often as those on Easy Street, and more than three times as often as the people on High Street.[5]

Even those in professions once considered secular show growing interest in spiritual matters. Entertainers are unlikely to be pillars of traditional churches, but many have expressed a wide range of spiritual interests—from Scientology to the mystical Jewish teachings of the Kabbalah. In a similar way, social workers and psychologists show rising personal and professional interest in spirituality and see it as a way to address client needs.

One way to gauge America's elusive spiritual stirrings is to study the best-seller list. Phyllis Tickle, the former religion editor of *Publishers Weekly*, notes that many individuals are hesitant to express nonconventional religious beliefs and often begin their spiritual search in the private realm of books.[6] And the book market tells us that Americans have an insatiable appetite for religion and spirituality. According to the Association of American Publishers, the sales of books in the Bible, religion, and spirituality category shot up 59 percent between 1992 and 1994.

Many commentators see the American interest in spirituality as stemming from a host of current social problems. The exponential growth of technology and the resulting uncertainty about the future, we're told, make people search for an anchor of meaning in an unstable world. Some observers see a fragmented society and declining respect for government inspiring the search for another kind of authority. Others point to the possibility of nuclear and biochemical war, or the devastation brought on by AIDS, or the disintegration of families to explain the contemporary search for the sacred. Although these factors may all contribute to a spiritual resurgence, Americans have always faced tragedy and social dislocation. Any upsurge in spirituality is not a unique response to social problems but simply the latest rumblings beneath America's remarkably stable religious terrain.

As a new millennium dawns, one way to understand American religion and chart its future is to see the world of faith like any other product or service in the U.S. economy. Today's diverse religious landscape has been compared to a busy marketplace where competition thrives and seekers shop.

Many Americans say they want to become "more spiritual" but have little interest in "organized religion." Nevertheless, many of today's spiritual seekers do get involved in religion that is organized; it's just organized differently, or may be another religion. They may wind up meditating at a local Zen Buddhist center, find themselves at a Promise Keepers rally for evangelical men, or seek out a class in Jewish mysticism. We live in a post-denominational era, and the denominations that realize that fact are the ones that will thrive in the new millennium.

Some things do not change. Now, as before, the spiritual quest is often a search for community, a longing for belonging. It can also inspire greater social conscience. Religious individuals of all varieties tend to be more involved in community life. More and more religious congregations find themselves at the forefront of community development, providing charity and social service in an increasingly privatized world. Religious Americans are also involved in politics, both on the left and the right.

Nevertheless, for many Americans spirituality has become a private affair. Rather than gathering in religious congregations, millions of seekers curl up at home with the latest self-help book or inspirational tome. Instead of coming together Saturday at the synagogue or Sunday at church, they pray and meditate in their own private temples. Private religion and our dizzying array of spiritual choices can put us all in "little boxes," isolated from one another. We hope that our book will provide windows of understanding in this compartmentalized world, giving us all a better idea of what inspires our neighbors and gives meaning to their lives.

PART ONE

SEARCHING FOR SELF AND SPIRIT

THE DIVORCE BETWEEN SPIRITUALITY AND RELIGION

Spiritual Seekers, True Believers

Steve and Julie, a young California couple with two small children, looked back six years to the time in their lives when they first decided to go "church shopping."

Julie was born into a military family in the deep South in the early 1970s. Her parents sent her to the local Southern Baptist Sunday school, and to Bible class on Wednesday nights. When she was ten, Julie's dad was transferred to California and the family pulled up their roots. One of the torn roots was religion. Julie stopped going to church when her family moved to the Golden State.

Steve had no church to leave. He was born in Southern California in the early 1970s and raised in a loving, middle-class, "unchurched" family. His grandfather had been a conservative Methodist minister in the Midwest, but Steve's father was a "preacher's kid" who moved to California in the 1960s and left organized religion behind. Steve's mother was half Jewish, half Protestant, but as an adult had no particular interest in either faith.

When Steve and Julie met in high school, church was the last thing on their minds. Partying was high on the list. "I wasn't really living life like I should, but I still remember praying," Julie said. "One day I asked Steve if he believed in God, and he said he didn't think so. That seemed so weird to me."

Their life together took a dramatic change when Julie became pregnant and at age twenty the couple found themselves with a son. "Having a kid changed everything," Julie recalled. "It made me think how I wanted my kids to grow up, and what I wanted them to believe. I decided I had to learn more so I could teach them."

As an experiment, Steve and Julie went to the Protestant church down the street from their apartment. They were the youngest people at the service. No one talked to them. They didn't go back.

Steve started asking his friends and family questions about religion. His uncle gave him a book about Buddhism. A guy at work invited him to a Baha'i service, and he dragged Julie along.

"That freaked me out," she said. "I mean, they were nice people, but thinking Steve would get into that just freaked me out. It made me start to think about what I believed."

Julie was the child of Southern Baptists, but the couple felt little loyalty to that denomination. Steve certainly wasn't going to join the local Methodist church just because his grandfather was a minister in that faith. Their decision on what congregation to join had little to do with doctrine, and lots to do with the kind of music played, child care offered, and the feel of Sunday worship. They shopped for a church like they would shop for a car, looking for something comfortable and practical.

They were also looking for someone to marry them.

"We were both out looking for a church, messed up, and had no idea what we were doing," Julie recalled. "I guess the low point was when I went to see this one Baptist preacher. I told him I grew up in the Baptist Church. He asked me about Steve. I said he was kind of Methodist, kind of Jewish, kind of nothing. This preacher told us we shouldn't get married because we were of different faiths. Can you believe it! Here I am, twenty years old, an unwed mother, and he says we shouldn't get married! It was embarrassing. I felt ashamed. I just ran out of his church."

Amazingly, that experience did not sour Steve and Julie on church shopping. They soon found a church that accepted them for who they were, welcomed them into the fold, and helped them down the Christian path.

We'll get back to their story several more times in our book, when we talk about how Americans settle into a religious congregation, and how they grow in their faith, applying their beliefs to the world around them. But let's first consider the story of Miriam, a single woman old enough to be Julie's mother. Born in the middle of the baby boomer generation, Miriam is someone who may never settle into a religious congregation, a seeker who may never "find it."

Her first memory of organized religion is a bitter one, from when her parents sent her to Hebrew school in Brooklyn. This is how Miriam, the granddaughter of a Sephardic rabbi, remembers one of the first prayers she learned in school: "Blessed art thou, O Lord our God, who hath not made me a woman."

"Talk about invalidation," she steams. "I got that totally distorted conditioning of the Jewish religion that God is a vengeful God, to be feared."

Miriam's old ideas about God and spirituality were blown away one weekend in college, when she swallowed a dose of LSD on a lonely mountaintop. "Until then, I thought of God as an entity that existed someplace else, separate from creation," she recalled. "That LSD trip gave me my first experience of divinity inside my own being. It was absolutely orgasmic, as if every cell was thrilled."

Her curiosity sparked, Miriam began reading books on Buddhism and Taoism, and others written by Ram Dass, the bearded and beaded icon of 1960s counter-culture. Her spiritual journey continued with a correspondence course with the Self-Realization Fellowship of Swami Paramahansa Yogananada. That was followed by what Miriam calls her "Christian era," when this Jewish girl from Brooklyn joined a metaphysical Christian sect in San Francisco.

Two years later, Miriam traveled to India, changed her name, and became a follower of Bhagwan Shree Rajneesh, the Indian guru who would later move to America and start a controversial commune in rural Oregon.

"There was lots of criticism from people saying I was just jumping from one group to another," Miriam admits. "But this is all beyond the mind's consideration. It's the energetic link between you and the divine."

o

America has always been a spiritual melting pot, a place where believers claim the right to invent new theologies, to grow their own religion. It says so in the first line of the First Amendment of the Constitution and has been noted by social commentators throughout U.S. history.

In the new millennium, there will be a growing gap between personal spirituality and religious institutions. Religious beliefs and spirituality have traditionally been viewed as the province of churches, temples, synagogues, and mosques. Yet spirituality and religious faith are increasingly viewed as individual, private matters with few connections to congregation and community. Gallup polls show that seven in ten Americans believe that one can be religious without going to church. Clergy and denominational leaders dolefully note rampant individualism even among members of their own congregations. They are particularly concerned about the growing number of "seekers"—those who have dropped out or never became institutionally involved, despite a keen personal interest in spirituality.

Most of the world's religions began with individuals and their perceived encounter with the sacred. All faiths, no matter how communal and collective they eventually become, are based on revelations that were initially directed toward individuals, whether it was God giving the Ten Commandments to Moses, Jesus starting his ministry with a small group of followers, Allah revealing the Koran to Mohammed, or Buddha gaining enlightenment and bringing his teaching to others. It is only after these individual encounters that followers gather to decipher and apply the teachings, institutions are built, and successors are chosen to pass the word along to future generations.

For millennia, religious groups fought to keep spiritual energy contained within a community of faith. Mystics and saints have always clashed with religious institutions when their experiences of spiritual ecstasy transcend established rules and regulations. But North America, especially the United States, may be unique. It is a highly religious *and* strongly individualistic society. Though the country is dotted with communal faiths, and congregation attendance is higher than in other Western societies, the Protestant notion that there should be no mediator between the individual and God runs deep in the American soul.

This split between institutional religious life and private spirituality is especially clear today. The 1960s, which brought the sexual revolution and the breakdown of millions of American families, were also the turning point in this bitter divorce between religion and spirituality. It was the decade that brought no-fault divorce and no-fault religion. Sociologist Phillip Hammond asserts that what happened during the 1960s and 1970s was more than just another form of American religious populism. Though membership in religious congregations has long been voluntary, family ties, peer pressure, and social status traditionally impinged on Americans' religious freedom. The social revolution of "the sixties" elevated the values of free choice and experimentation in the religious marketplace.[1]

Most studies of American baby boomers show declining church attendance and less adherence to church teachings. In a major study of baby boomers' religion, sociologist Wade Clark Roof found that, as children, the baby boom generation was as religiously active as preceding generations. By their early twenties, however, only around one in four boomers was involved in organized religion. This does not mean that most baby boomers became agnostics or atheists. Rather, they adopted a religion tailored to individual preferences and experiences. Roof's survey found that baby boomers view "being alone and meditating" as far more important than "worshiping with others." They are drawn to experiential spirituality, which "places primacy not on reason, not even on belief systems, but rather on a mystical experiential stance."[2]

This divorce between religion and spirituality will be experienced differently in various parts of the nation. Regional differences have not been completely flattened out by the mass media and nationwide franchises, especially in American religion. In a study of the four U.S. regions represented by the states of North Carolina (the South), Massachusetts (New England), Ohio (the Midwest), and California (the Far West), Phillip Hammond finds that North Carolina has the least amount of religious individualism, while Massachusetts and California have the most.[3] Gallup polls also show the East and West Coasts as incubators of religious individualism. The West Coast ranks high in unchurched people, but continually shows a higher percentage of individuals pursuing spiritual practices such as meditation.

○

Let's linger for a moment along one stretch of the West Coast, the breathtaking Big Sur coastline in central California, and visit two places that speak volumes about religion and spirituality in the new millennium.

Immaculate Heart Hermitage, a Roman Catholic monastery, chapel, and retreat house, is perched on a bluff a thousand feet above the Pacific Ocean. From here, the sea is an ever-present source of inspiration, its moods changing with the weather and the tides. Sometimes, when the fog rolls in and rests at the cliffs below, the monastery sits above the clouds, nestled celestially in the lap of the Santa Lucia Mountains.

Solitude is the central experience of the laypeople who come here for spiritual retreat, and for the twenty-five Camaldolese monks who live here all year round. The monks live in twenty-five cinder-block cottages, or "cells," aligned in four rows behind the chapel. Five times a day, starting before sunrise with morning vigils, the monks don white robes and come together in the chapel for praise, prayer, meditation, and Holy Communion.

Several of the monks are true recluses, living in tiny cabins and trailers hidden in the woods behind the compound. Their home is a forest of redwood, oak, and madrone that reaches back into the hills, where all that can be heard are the sounds of streams tumbling to the sea, spraying ferns and gray-green boulders with cool mist.

Anne, one of a dozen guests staying in private rooms in the Immaculate Heart guest house, pauses on her way to evening vespers. She works in San Francisco, a four-hour drive up the coast, as a busy executive with a major clothing company. "My job takes a lot out of me," she says. "If it weren't for this, I probably wouldn't even take a vacation. I live by myself and can find quiet time at home, but there's something about the collective silence here that is amazingly different. Most of the day, we keep silent, and that's very freeing. It lets us slow down, to be in a beautiful place and listen to God's will."

The sun sets and a deep orange glow melts into a distant fog bank. Warning bells sound for evening vespers. Fifteen monks carrying hymn books walk quietly into the monastery's central chapel. They come together in song—sweet and strong. They and the retreatants file into the chapel rotunda for a half hour of silent contemplation. In the center of the rotunda, beneath a single cross hanging from the ceiling, two small candles illuminate the Blessed Sacrament, which sits atop a plain white table.

After the service, it is dark outside, the sea a silver shield under the moon. It is so quiet that the soft crunch of pebbles under your feet makes soft echoes into the hills. To preserve the stillness, you walk softer, feeling every step.

"Surprising things happen in solitude," explains the Reverend Robert Hale, who first came to Immaculate Heart in 1959, when he was a senior in college and thinking about becoming a monk. "Some people who come here get terrified and leave after the first night. People lead such distracted lives of job, family, television. Many are not aware of how many problems and conflicts, how much unresolved grief, dwells inside them. Others are delighted when they get here, connecting with the prayer, silence, and meditation. It's like coming home to their deepest center, to a God who loves them."[4]

About fifteen miles up the coast from Immaculate Heart Hermitage is another spot that helps us tell the story of religion and spirituality in America. Back in 1962, Michael Murphy and a Stanford University classmate, the late Richard Price, started an experiment at an old hot-springs resort at Big Sur. They called it Esalen, and it became ground zero of the "human potential movement" of the 1960s and 1970s, a blend of spirituality, psychology, massage, and mysticism. "There was an explosion of imitators, many of them right down to the letterhead we used," Murphy recalls. "About five of them made it through the 1980s. Now, it's starting all over again. It's like a second pulse. It's a social invention that's here to stay—a new kind of learning center." At Esalen Institute, today's offerings range from "mind brainwave training" to t'ai chi with Chungliang Al Huang. To many visitors, the place may seem more like a hedonistic mecca than a spiritual retreat. As they have for nearly four decades, naked retreatants soak in the silky radiance of natural hot springs that pour into stone pools cut into the side of the Big Sur cliffs. Nearby, masseuses offer nude body work under a brilliant California sun.

In some ways, Immaculate Heart Hermitage and Esalen Institute seem worlds apart. One is a place of solitude and tradition, the other a center of constant experimentation. If there is anyone who can bring these two worlds together, it's a monk we know named Brother David.

Monk, mystic, and spiritual teacher, Brother David Steindl-Rast divides his time between Immaculate Heart and Esalen, a modern-day circuit rider along one of the world's most spectacular stretches of coastline. Interlocutor in the dialogue between Catholicism and the New Age, Brother David's message blends Christianity, mysticism, and humanistic psychology.

"There is something happening in our time, and one of the most significant shifts is in the realm of religion," he says. "The emphasis is moving from the institution to personal experience. It is happening in people's individual lives on a very large scale, and it is absolutely irreversible. After 2,000 years, the institution has become so rigid and ossified it is collapsing under its own weight."

Brother David is something of an enigma to the Roman Catholic Church. One of the institution's sharpest critics, he is also a man who has brought thousands of lapsed Catholics back into the fold. Born in Vienna in 1926, he has, through his books and lectures, reenvisioned some of the key elements of Christianity in a way that provides new meaning for many Catholics unable to find a place in the institutional church. Prayerfulness becomes mindfulness, an awareness and gratitude for what life brings. Jesus is seen not as a messianic prophet who will return to judge but as a teacher of wisdom.

"When Jesus used scripture from the Hebrew Bible, it was not like the teachers of his time who laboriously interpreted from the text—like the church does today," he says. "Jesus talked about experience, about daily life. That was such an enormous change in the history of religion—especially in a culture like that in Israel, where the idea of God was so strongly theistic."

Brother David is a slim man, with a crew cut, angular features, and a close-cropped graying beard. His expression turns serious, almost dour, when he begins to reflect, then softens and brightens with the flow of conversation. Still, Brother David sees a need for tradition and ritual, and warns that many of today's spiritual seekers "get so enamored with the search that there is nothing more than finding."

A rugged simplicity in Brother David's garb speaks of a backwoods hermit. He walks down the long road leading from Immaculate Heart chapel to the coast. It is the first clear day after a long rain, and despite the chill in the air, he is wearing sandals with no socks. A black and well-worn religious vest, tied at the side of his waist, identifies him as a monk.

"When I talk about a shift to 'personal experience,' I don't mean 'private,'" he says. "'Personal' is defined in terms of your relations—it is community-related and community-imbedded. You become a person more deeply through your relations to other persons, your relationship to a community. There is great suffering for people who don't find this community."[5]

VARIETIES OF SPIRITUALITY

Experiencing Religion

At an Assemblies of God congregation, Pentecostal worshipers stretch their arms heavenward, bodies gently swaying, eyes closed, and lips slightly open. They radiate a sensual, almost contagious religious passion. They lay on hands and say that people are healed. They utter strange sounds and call them miraculous. They offer soulful testimonies of a tortured past and proclaim themselves "born again."

At a New Age seminar, seventy-five psychospiritual explorers lie flat on their backs on a hotel ballroom floor. Under dim lights they listen to a deafening, three-hour soundtrack of hypnotic drumming, sacred music, and other evocative sounds. After a prolonged session of deep, rapid breathing, many fall into a trance. Some lie quietly on their mats, seemingly asleep. Others let out ecstatic moans as they imagine cosmic realms and wave their arms in blissful, circular motions. Some let out demonic, blood-curdling screams as they relive scenes of childhood abuse or painful "past lives." Others curl up into a fetal position for a "rebirthing" experience.

At first glance, the conservative Christians at the Pentecostal church and the aging hippies at the New Age happening appear to have little in common. Look a little closer, however, and you may see the same great awakening of experiential spirituality.

Sandra came all the way from the Midwest to Eugene, Oregon, for the rebirthing and past-lives workshop. She had no prior experience with meditation or yoga, but was amazed to find herself "going into ancient yogic postures." Lying on her mat, listening to the drumming, she felt "wonderful, wild laughter coming out of me. I had this deep, profound joy and felt myself in complete rapport with the drumming. I knew what the drummer was saying."

William has been attending the Assemblies of God church since the Holy Spirit descended on him six months ago at an altar call. "I was being anointed with oil and praying with the pastor when I started feeling light," he recalled. "Suddenly, I was on the ground. I noticed there were words coming out of my mouth, kind of like babbling out loud. It's hard to put into words now. I had been really stressed out, and was just washed clean. I went in feeling broken, and came out feeling renewed."

Not surprisingly, Assemblies of God leaders do not encourage comparisons between the spiritual experiences at that New Age workshop and their Sunday morning service. "I guess both groups feel a desire for supernatural intervention," said one Pentecostal pastor, "but our one authority is the Bible. And the Bible tells us that every spirit is not of Christ. A lot of New Age thinking is a mixture of Eastern religions. In my view, some of it is classic demonic possession. There are many spirits in the world, and some of them are very deceptive."

———— o ————

In one sense, all spirituality is based on one's experience. Spirituality, more than any other component of religion, is intuitive, more emotional than intellectual. **As denominational doctrine becomes less relevant to many Americans, the experiential elements of religion and spirituality will become more important** to seekers like Sandra and believers like William.

In the past, spirituality was tied to a comprehensive belief system that valued intellectual agreement, authority, and tradition, along with personal faith experience. The modern emphasis on choice and the importance of the individual has often been translated into the view that beliefs and doctrine must be in sync with one's life experiences. An individual moved by experiential religion is not going to take the clergy's word that a particular belief is true. Though the breakdown of church authority can be traced back to the Protestant Reformation and the Enlightenment, spirituality has never been as centered around the individual as it is today. This tendency to judge spiritual truth by human experience will help us understand the varieties and cacophonies of American spirituality in the new millennium.

Theologian Harvey Cox places the "born-again" Christians and the New Age "rebirthers" on the same spiritual page. "Their psychology is quite similar—a retrieval of primal spirituality," Cox said in an interview. "There are a lot of similarities in the way they try to tap into the experience of awe and wonder with visions, healing, dreams, and trance. Both encourage you to be in touch with your own experience and talk about it—to offer personal testimony."

Cox sees the turn to experiential spirituality as a worldwide phenomenon, active in all major faiths. All traditions include movements that view the direct encounter with the sacred as a key dimension of faith. Such encounters can be experienced as transcendent, distinct from human experience, pointing to God or another reality. But for many seekers unattached to religious institutions, spiritual states are experienced as immanent, as an indwelling of spirit in humanity, nature, and the world. Since these movements are based on individual experience, they do not usually command the allegiance of more "rationalist" or doctrine-based groups. Cox sees this "experientialism" as a radical personal piety whereby seekers are "constantly compiling his or her own collage of symbols and practices in the light of what coheres with their own changing experiences."[1]

Religions that emphasize their experiential and mystical dimensions rather than their moral, social, or doctrinal sides have growing followings, although they are not necessarily showing institutional growth. For instance, Buddhism attracts a growing number of seekers for its mystical and contemplative spirituality, but it finds far less institutional success. In other words, people are more likely to experiment—read books on Buddhism and meditate at home—than join the local Zen center. Pentecostalism and other forms of charismatic Christianity attract both seekers and devoted members. These movements stand out from other forms of Christianity through their emphasis on a direct encounter with the Holy Spirit and their downplaying of creeds.

Though the growing tendency to separate faith from institutional belonging encourages experiential spirituality, this is not an entirely new thing. Religious commentators Phyllis Tickle and Harold Bloom see echoes of ancient Gnostic controversies in today's spiritual scene.[2] Gnosticism was condemned as an ancient Christian heresy because followers claimed spiritual truths based on secret knowledge and experience rather than on creeds and scripture. There is a growing, if disconnected and unorganized, Gnostic movement in the United States. More important, these currents have unconsciously influenced the Christian and Jewish faiths. Most Americans have never heard of Gnosticism, yet according to Tickle, "almost all America's contemporary god-talkers—Jews, Christians and Muslims, Buddhist, Hindus, and Baha'is alike—have some fairly basic Gnostic sympathies and even some outright beliefs."[3] Today's experiential spirituality shares with Gnosticism a need to know God personally without the intermediaries of church, congregation, priests, and scripture. The Gnostic factor can be found in the growth of occult and esoteric teachings and movements, where access to supernatural secrets are available through individual initiation and experience rather than through publicly revealed texts or doctrine. This new interest in Gnosticism is also seen in best-selling books by James Redfield *(The Celestine Prophesy)* and Marianne Williamson, one of many popularizers of *A Course in Miracles,* a volu-minous spiritual text and self-help book compiled by two New York psy-chologists, Helen Schucman and William Thetford, between 1965 and 1972. It can also be seen in the public's fascination with the Dead Sea Scrolls, in Elaine Pagel's work *The Gnostic Gospels,* and in the search for the historical Jesus.

Turning East

Mark and Jennifer were twenty-two years old, eager to see the world, and very much in love. They never intended to become Buddhists, let alone take vows to become a Buddhist monk and nun, when they went off to Europe together in the summer of 1994.

They met in high school in upstate New York. Neither of their parents had given them any formal religious upbringing. Jennifer's mother was something of a hippie, living for a while in the forest with a group of other families. Mom meditated, practiced a little yoga, but never pushed it on her daughter. Mark's parents didn't go to church or synagogue either, although they were interested in the teachings of Rudolf Steiner, the late Austro-German mystic, and sent their son to the local Waldorf School.

One of Mark's friends gave him a book by Vietnamese Zen Master Thich Nhat Hanh, entitled *Peace Is Every Step.* He was touched by its simple, yet deep, message, and decided that when he and his girlfriend were in Europe they would visit Plum Village, Thich Nhat Hanh's Bud-dhist community in southwestern France. "We wanted to follow a spiri-tual path," Jennifer said. "We wanted to go to India, but my Mom didn't want us to go. France was closer and safer."

At a one-week introductory meditation retreat, they fell in love with Plum Village, with the old stone buildings, the Vietnamese children play-ing in the fields, and the calm peaceful feeling radiating from the brown-robed monks and nuns. They returned to the United States to make money as fast as they could so they could return to Plum Village for a longer stay.

When they returned, they started talking about following in the foot-steps of the monks and nuns. Jennifer went to live with nuns, and Mark moved in with the monks, about a mile and a half away. They only saw each other a couple of times a week. "It was a very difficult transition from being in love to developing true love. We went from planning on having a family together to becoming a monk and a nun," Mark said. "I felt tremendous anxiety, but came to realize that all my resistance was rooted in my attachments and desires. When I saw that my love wasn't allowing her to be free, or allowing me to be free, we realized we really didn't have such a healthy relationship."

In the summer of 1996, under a full moon, they and three other novices took their vows as Buddhist celibates, becoming Brother Mark and Sister Jennifer.

"Something in my heart just opened, and I saw that the most wonderful thing in the world was to let go of everything in life except the Buddhist teachings," Jennifer said. "It came from somewhere very deep inside."

o

In the new millennium, spiritual seekers like Mark and Jennifer will continue to turn to the East for spiritual direction and inspiration, even though relatively few will formally adopt these Eastern religions as monks, nuns, or formal lay practitioners.

Rising interest in Eastern faiths like Buddhism, Taoism, Hinduism, and Sufism is part of the broader move toward experiential spirituality. Eastern spirituality is grounded in what could be called "heart knowledge," rather than "head knowledge," of the sacred. The practice of Eastern forms of mysticism, such as meditation, does not require the same kind of loyalty to an exclusive belief system as Christianity or Islam often does. In the new millennium, many practitioners of Eastern meditation techniques will continue to see themselves as Christians, Jews, or "none of the above."

Brother Mark and Sister Jennifer are the second generation of the latest "East-meets-West" phenomenon to sweep North America. American intellectuals, artists, and writers, from Henry David Thoreau to Jack Kerouac, have long been drawn to the East for spiritual inspiration. In the 1960s, the interest took on a wider appeal, especially for the younger generations. A new influx of Eastern religious leaders, partly brought on by the liberalization in the U.S. immigration laws and by the greater number of Asians practicing Buddhism and Hinduism, gave greater visibility to these minority religions.

Sociologist Peter Berger points to various encounters that Christianity has had with different cultures, and to how these encounters changed and challenged Western faith and culture. The first encounter was with the Greco-Roman world, the second with Islam, and the third with modernity. Berger writes that we are "now on the edge of a fourth weighty constellation, this time with the religious traditions of southern and eastern Asia."[4]

However one interprets the appeal of Buddhism, there is rising interest in this and other ancient Eastern paths. Book publishing shows many passing fads, from angels to crystals. But the interest in Buddhism and Eastern mysticism has remained relatively consistent among Americans. Aiding the flowering of Buddhism in the United States are the large number of celebrities and intellectuals, from Richard Gere to Martin Scorcese, taking up Buddhist practices and reflecting that fascination in film and other forms of pop culture. There is also a strongly experiential and psychotherapeutic thrust to the Buddhist spirituality in the West. This new Americanized and largely Caucasian expression of Buddhism is very different from the more ceremonial, nonmystical religion of Asian Buddhists. As one Japanese-American Buddhist leader quipped, "White practitioners practice intensive psychotherapy on their cushions in a life-or-death struggle with the ego, whereas Asian Buddhists just seem to smile and eat together."

In a different way, the turn East can also be seen in Christianity and Islam. Western Christians and others look to Eastern Orthodox and Coptic spirituality for their rich mystical traditions. Many Catholics and Protestants draw upon the spiritual resources of Orthodoxy—such as the use of icons, fasting, elements of the liturgy, and monasticism—but only a minority will fully embrace this faith's rigorous demands and exclusive claims of religious truth. Sufism, the mystical branch of Islam, has been strongly divorced from its Muslim matrix in the United States, and is therefore finding a growing following among seekers. As Sufism grows closer to its Muslim foundations, it will be interesting to see whether seekers who may initially have been drawn to this spirituality through new translations of the Sufi poet Rumi find themselves on the road to Islam.[5]

Claiming Spiritual Roots

For Rabbi Josef, the journey back to mainstream Judaism was a long, strange trip. As a dedicated student of Zen meditation, Josef studied with Buddhist masters in Japan and served as the director of a California Zen center before rediscovering his Jewish roots.

"Authentic Judaism was originally presented as a deep spiritual path," he said. "But the presentation of Judaism most people in America received was a denatured and despiritualized version. We have to rediscover the sense of spirituality that was lost in Judaism."

Today, as the spiritual leader of a growing Conservative-movement synagogue, Rabbi Josef borrows the techniques of Zen Buddhism, such as increasing awareness in the present moment, but places his teaching in a Jewish context. "I don't practice Buddhism anymore," he said. "I don't bow to Buddha."

Instead, he is helping to revive interest in Jewish mysticism, in Jewish meditation. In 1997, hundreds of people of all ages filled his synagogue for a conference on Kabbalah and other forms of experiential Judaism. Kabbalah is an ancient, esoteric form of Jewish worship that has seen other revivals over the centuries. One of the most influential mystical texts in Judaism, the Book of Splendor, was written by Moses de Leon, a thirteenth-century Spanish Kabbalist. Its central image is the Tree of Life, which shows the descent of the divine into the material world. Through righteous living, contemplation, and meditation, Kabbalists mystically ascend the Tree of Life, passing through stages such as Endurance, Loving-kindness, Wisdom, and Humility.

Many Jewish women are also rediscovering their faith's mystical heritage. Claire, a woman attending the Kabbalah conference at Rabbi Josef's synagogue, recalled how she drifted away from Jewish practice, uncomfortable with the "patriarchy, sexism, and God language in the Orthodox world." Now, she encourages her women friends to take another look at Judaism. "We have a wonderful mystical tradition in Judaism," she said. "It's up to us to take from it what is wonderful and good."

_____ o _____

This "pick and choose" approach to faith, the desire to "take from it what is wonderful and good," will continue in the coming century. The same consumeristic and experiential approach popularized via Eastern mysticism will be brought to the traditional spiritual teachings of the West.

This search for roots is fueled by a sense of dislocation, of lost heritage, a yearning to go home. Although American religion is often characterized by practicality and innovation, the interest in tradition may reflect the pragmatic view that beliefs and spiritual practices that have stood the test of time may serve one better than the latest fad.

Among American seekers, the desire to unearth one's spiritual roots are more likely to involve Western sources of spirituality than those from the East. The search for roots encompasses the revived interest in Celtic mysticism, various forms of paganism, goddess spirituality, and American Indian shamanism, as well as orthodox Jewish, Islamic, and Christian faiths. Spiritual seekers today can pick and choose spiritual teachings and writings from the Middle Ages via the local bookstore or the Internet. Although these spiritual currents may fade with time, their ongoing appeal illuminates a long-lasting spiritual search.

Best-selling spirituality books in the 1990s included several on "ancient wisdom," including that of the Roman Catholic Church. The publication of the *Catechism of the Roman Catholic Church* was at first considered an unlikely best-seller, particularly since it was first marketed with clergy in mind. The skyrocketing sales of the book point to a desire for American Catholics to measure their own views of their faith against a more ancient and universal standard. Even as Protestant seekers remain critical of some Catholic teachings, there is a widespread interest in pre-Reformation spirituality, whether it is expressed in the popularity of Gregorian chant or at retreats featuring contemplative prayer.

Catholicism preserved its monastic tradition when most Protestants discarded it, and provides a ready-made source of spirituality for many Americans. Increasingly, however, monasteries and spiritual centers are diversifying their offerings to reach a pluralistic audience, including Zen teachings and other forms of East-West syncretism. The retracing of religious history to find spiritual sustenance can also be seen in the popularity of pilgrimages to sacred places and shrines among both Americans and secular Europeans.

There is rising interest in Celtic spirituality among both Christians and non-Christians. Conservative Christians receive new energy from the early Celt's simplicity of prayer and harmonious living with creation, as well as the transcendent majesty of their God. Celtic spirituality has also been popular among liberal Christian and neo-pagan groups hoping to revive an indigenous, earthy spirituality.

Starhawk, the popular pagan writer, notes that Halloween had its roots in an old Celtic feast marking the onset of winter. It has always been a way to express the fear of death ritually, to get through the long, cold nights of winter. "We celebrate the turn of the wheel of the year into darkness," said Starhawk, who marks the occasion with a dance and trance ceremony sponsored by the Reclaiming Collective, her witch's coven. "Witches have always gathered at this holy time, to mourn and release the newly dead."[6]

Neo-pagans often gravitate to the gods and goddesses and related spiritual practices of their own ethnic backgrounds. African Americans and Latinos have shown a similar interest in recovering spiritual insights from their African or Latin heritage, often as supplements to their Christian or Islamic faith.

In San Francisco, there were efforts in the late 1990s to put more of a spiritual and ethnic focus on the Latino celebration of *El Dia de los Muertos,* the Day of the Dead. It had been increasingly mixed up with the partying and commercialism of Halloween. "Partying doesn't bother me, but the loss of spirit does. Everything has become so commercialized, even in Mexico," said one Latina organizer of the celebration. "We want to bring together all colors, nationalities, and spiritual persuasions. Death is something we all share."

Mix-and-Match Spirituality

Rap music and pulsing techno-tribal rhythms blast out of a warehouse in the San Francisco Bay Area. Casual passersby assume that it's just another rave—local teenagers and college students blowing their minds on "ecstasy" or the latest designer drug, dancing like fools into a sweaty state of altered consciousness. Bodies are swaying and minds are expanding in this space, but this is no ordinary party. What's happening in this space is church, with the Reverend Matthew Fox, high priest of mix-and-match religion, presiding.

It's the Sunday night Techno Cosmic Mass, a worship service that gives new meaning to the word *eclectic*. There's African drumming, strobe lights, candles, video monitors, t'ai chi, gospel music, aboriginal prayers, and Celtic blessings. Father Fox sits before a circular flower-bedecked altar in the center of the warehouse with his three co-celebrants, a local rabbi, a black preacher, and a Jungian psychologist. Some 350 souls are here tonight. They're handed bright yellow church programs that explain what happens in the warehouse of wonder. It's too dark inside to read the programs, but this is what they say: "The Techno Cosmic Mass is a radical new way of worshiping which blends Western liturgical tradition with ecstatic music and dance, urban shamanism, multimedia imagery, and Eastern and indigenous spiritual elements to create a multicultural, intergenerational, and ecumenical form of worship."

Once again, Matt Fox is going where no priest has gone before. This mix of rave and religion is just the latest stop in the magical mystery tour of Father Fox, the *enfant terrible* of organized religion. Expelled from the Dominican order in 1992, Fox joined the Episcopal Church two years later, but now calls himself a "postdenominational priest." His battles with Rome began a few years after the 1983 publication of his book *Original Blessing,* which attacked the church for its emphasis on redemption and original sin. His theology is called "creation spirituality," and celebrates the joys of nature, sexuality, music, and dance. And it has found an eager audience among lapsed Catholics of the baby-boom generation. His rave Masses are a bid to attract a younger crowd to his feel-good theology, to push the liturgical envelope.

"We don't have a lot of time to fiddle around with whether we're in this denomination or that one," Fox says. "I challenge you to find any twenty-year-old who can tell the difference between a Presbyterian, a Lutheran, a Methodist, an Episcopalian and a Roman Catholic. And who cares?

"Rituals like the Techno Cosmic Mass are a playing out of myth, putting the myth in our hearts and our bodies. A big part of rave culture is the community thing—there's a big yearning for community there. The word *community,* or *communio* in Latin, means sharing a common task working together. It's not just feeling one with each other. It's doing something. This yearning for community is very heartfelt, and we're trying to break through that with multicultural, multireligious events. Learning from each other's stories."[7]

Back at the rave Mass, a rap singer paces back and forth before the altar, belting out a staccato hymn with edge.

> One life, one breath, on Earth, one revelation,
> We all share creation: the common denomination.
> So I bow to the Tao and thank Brahmin.
> We all have creation in common.[8]

Matt Fox beams: "Is this the postdenominational age, or what? Let's dance our diversity!"

Among those dancing to diversity is Cindy, a forty-three-year-old white woman who quit her job in Southern California to study with Fox. Raised in the Roman Catholic Church, she left the church at age eighteen, bored by the worship and disaffected by the church's refusal to ordain women. "I did the seeker route to the East, explored Native American spirituality, but none of that fit for me," she said. "I was yearning for community and a place where I could worship with like-minded people. I don't think I'm ever going to find a Catholic church where I can dance with reckless abandon in the middle of the Mass."

---
o

Demographically located in the middle of the baby-boom generation, Cindy is one of many "recovering Catholics" who have turned to Matthew Fox and other purveyors of "syncretistic" spirituality. **This tendency to mix elements of different traditions into new hybrid forms will continue in the new millennium, as seekers separated from their religious heritage search out new expressions of faith.**

In today's marketplace of religion, fewer Americans feel social pressure to stay within the confines of their religious heritage. Brand-name religion is on the wane. The wide range of spiritual texts and self-help books comprise an endless menu of spiritual teachings that can be selected and combined to suit individual needs. Most people, however, don't have the time and fortitude to construct their own religion from scratch, so they rely on "prepackaged" expressions like Father Fox's Techno Cosmic Mass.

Of course, the most infamous example of syncretized spirituality is the New Age movement. While few people actually identify their religious affiliation as "New Age," this reluctance to label themselves goes hand in hand with the diffuse and loose-fitting nature of the movement. Participants may have a primary religious affiliation, and then draw various practices and teachings from the movement. Although New Age terminology, practices, and personalities may be faddish, its eclectic spirituality will endure in the new millennium.

As with any well-publicized trend, the New Age movement was judged to be over just a few years after it was discovered by the media in the late 1970s and early 1980s. Purists in the New Age vanguard disassociated themselves from crowds of initiates climbing on the bandwagon. While the diffuse nature of the New Age movement makes it hard to define, these unconventional spiritual stirrings have their roots in Eastern religions, occultism, neo-paganism, feminism, political activism, indigenous faiths, human potential teachings, new forms of psychotherapy, and environmentalism. Even its basic philosophy sends seemingly conflicting messages. While the movement stresses spiritual individualism, calling for individuals to discover their own path, it also proclaims a "world is one" communalism.

New Age trends follow the demographic journey of the baby-boom generation. Its predecessor, the human potential movement, was influenced by the use of hallucinogens—a practice that faded as its practitioners settled down to raise a family and pursue a career. During the 1980s, the New Age expressed itself in natural mystical experiences from channeling to meditation. When the baby boomers reached middle age in the 1990s, the emphasis again shifted, this time to social concerns, technology, environmentalism, and holistic healing. This intense interest in the spirituality of health, healing, and aging will continue as the baby boomers encounter frailty and death. The fact that the New Age is so closely tied to the baby-boom generation guarantees that it will continue to be a force in the coming decades.

But will the upbeat New Age message of higher consciousness and global transformation find a hearing among younger generations? Despite heroic efforts, Matthew Fox has had trouble attracting younger worshipers to his creation spirituality raves. Critic Carl Raschke is not surprised. He calls the New Age movement "a large-scale generational psychodrama that seems unintelligible to those both younger and older. . . . It is a massive working out of issues, as the therapists would say, of issues that never were worked out and perhaps can never be worked out. Yet it is America's burden for the foreseeable future."[9]

Secular Spirituality

Hundreds of disgruntled therapists, spiritual seekers, and other soulful explorers stood outside the packed ballroom of a Washington, D.C., hotel, trying to keep their cool. They wanted to get into a weekend conference on "Nourishing the Soul," but all 2,500 tickets were sold out. Some 1,500 people were turned away from the event, which featured two mainstays of the best-seller list: Thomas Moore (*Care of the Soul* and *Soulmates*) and M. Scott Peck (*The Road Less Traveled* and *Denial of the Soul*).

It was midway through the 1990s, which may go down in the publishing world as "the decade of soul." Moore kicked it off with his 1992 megabest-seller *Care of the Soul*. Within four years there were 322 book titles and annotations with "soul" listed in *Books in Print*—nearly four times the number in 1990. The Florida-based publisher, Health Communications, served up *Chicken Soup for the Soul* and quickly sold five million copies.[10]

Conference sponsor Anne Simpkinson, publisher of *Common Boundary* magazine, was amazed at the response to her Washington weekend. "People can define 'soul' in their own way," she said. "We are trying to open a space for inner exploration, and soul is a piece of that. There's an absolute hunger out there for people wanting to nourish their inner life."[11]

○

In the new millennium, spirituality and the search for "soul" will continue crossing the border from the religious to the secular side of life. The separation of spirituality from religious institutions and congregations gives the modern spiritual quest a "free-floating" quality that can easily attach itself to a wide range of "secular" activities and social movements.

The imprint of the New Age movement is evident in much of the literature of secular spirituality. The New Age tendency to "spiritualize" nature is seen among many of today's spiritual writers. Often, *spiritual* is defined in a sense even more diffuse than in the New Age movement. Wade Clark Roof has written that baby boomers often view self-expression, such as in "finding one's true self," and empathy with others as spiritual values in themselves.[12] Thus, wherever one finds one's "true self," whether it be in sports, work, hobbies, or sexuality, can become a place where sacredness and the "soul" are discovered. If spirituality can be translated into a search for one's true self and for other human values— creativity, love, trust, openness, personal fulfillment—where does God come into the picture? The answer is not always clear when examining the beliefs of Americans today.

Though most Americans believe in God, a *Newsweek* poll estimated that only 60 percent "think a person needs to believe in God in order to experience the sacred." Twenty-six percent of those polled said that they obtained a "sense of the sacred during sex."[13] Gallup polls have found that such a high proportion of Americans claim to pray that this activity must also include those who consider themselves atheists and agnostics. Artists and musicians claim that they experience something sacred in their creative work. Many Americans over the past three decades have experimented with psychedelic drugs such as LSD and "ecstasy," and many report feeling a profound sense of the sacred in their experience.

Some fear that if everything is "spiritual," then nothing really is. In one sense, the new secular spirituality is nothing new; mysticism in all faiths has been based on the interior search for contact with the sacred, including connections through human experiences and nature. Psychologist Mihaly Csikszentmihalyi writes that all humans have experiences of "flow," or profound experiences of human enjoyment and transcendence.[14] Such states are often characterized by the experience of "losing oneself" in an enjoyable activity, whether it is playing a game or listening to music.

Peter Van Ness notes that a secular spirituality is found in politics, as activists place a spiritual value on building a sense of community and social justice; in the natural environment, where nature is viewed as sacred in and of itself; in sexuality, where erotic energies are seen as connecting humans to each other and the cosmos; in sports, which fulfill one's "self-actualization" through training; and the arts, where creativity is seen as a spiritual value.

Joe Holland writes that "postmodern" spirituality sees the spiritual as "embodied" within the human body itself, nature, and society. This emphasis on the embodiment of spirituality can be interpreted as either the loss of transcendence or the resurgence of the sacred, but it is nevertheless a major factor behind the new secular spirituality.[15]

In the new millennium, aging will become a well-traveled path to secular spirituality, especially as baby boomers enter this phase of life. Recent studies show that although religious involvement tends to drop off as individuals age, belief and spirituality take on a new dimension as elders review their lives and seek meaning in the face of suffering and loss. They seek "spiritual reintegration" before death, to transform loneliness into the joy of solitude and a catalyst for renewed spirituality.[16]

Self-help and empowerment are central to the formation of secular spiritualities. The first self-help programs were based on a generic religiosity, as seen in Alcoholics Anonymous's invoking of the "higher power." The expanding self-help literature has maintained this spiritual dimension. Tickle writes that the growth of self-help thinking has "tilted our interest in spirituality toward its practical uses, in itself a substantive shift in paradigms." The relation of self-help to secular spirituality is even more direct, since, as Tickle adds, "much contemporary American spirituality is a recostumed and refurbished form of self-help that seeks more the well-being of its subject than any contemplation of the sacred."[17]

Psychotherapeutic insights and theories inform much of the new secular spirituality. This is especially the case with Jungian thought, which deals with spirituality and myth in everyday life. There has been a popularization of Jungian thought and anthropological views of religion that attempt to extract the common "myths" embedded in the different religious traditions. Mythologist Joseph Campbell played a pivotal role through his books and Bill Moyer's television series "The Power of Myth" in 1988. Campbell's theories on the universality of religious symbols reached many viewers who felt disconnected from denominations and other traditional forms of religious experience. The integration of psychology and spiritual development is a trend that is only likely to grow in the future.

Common Boundary magazine produced a 1994 directory of resources and programs integrating spirituality and psychology that provides a dizzying menu of choices: mind-body studies, somatic therapy, polarity therapy, Reiki, psychosynthesis, shamanic counseling, and mythopoetic music therapy.[18]

As many mental illnesses are increasingly viewed as medical problems best treated through drugs or short-term practical therapies, other forms of psychotherapy—even traditional Freudian psychoanalysis—have reemphasized their humanistic traditions as they provide guidance in achieving personal growth and meaning. Many such therapies, freed from a medicalized understanding of their work, have taken the next step of fusing personal growth to a spiritual framework, thereby redefining such concepts as "soul" and "spirit."

3

BRINGING SPIRIT TO LIFE

Gender Spirituality

It's Sunday night at the Scottish Rite Temple, and 750 men have been at it for nearly seven hours. They've chanted, screamed, shaken their fists, pounded on conga drums. They've read poetry, told stories, searched for meaning in the myths of the ancients. Huge murals of Zarathustra, Solomon, and King Minos stare down from the temple walls, which shake from the stomping of men. There's not a single female in this raucous sea of maleness. No one worries about frightening the ladies.

They roar a ballsy African chant with a Latin, back-beat rhythm. Gesturing violently, one half of the mob stomp toward the other, chanting: *Benne' Benne' go Blao—Benne' Benne' go Blae!* Shifting direction and shaking their fists, the other side answers with equal aggression: *Da Da Da Da mon ado—Da moon Dow!* As the testosterone levels rise, the sounds coming from the Scottish Rite Temple sound more like the Sunday roar of NFL football.

Poet Robert Bly, the inspiration behind this gathering of men, calls out from the stage, trying to calm things down. He asks each of the men to turn to the man next to him, knee touching knee, hand on the other's heart, and ask him whether there was something he resents about his father. Before long, the packed temple fills with the murmuring sound of 375 pairs of men opening up, a quiet conversation punctuated with an occasional sob or heart-felt roar.

Michael, a graduate student in political science at the University of California, first heard about Bly when a friend gave him an audio tape of one of his lectures on men. After searching his soul and his checking account, Michael decided to pay the $75 admission price and attend the all-day workshop. "There's been so much focus on the women's movement and what it means to be a woman in the man's world. Finally there's a focus on men," he said. "I grew up with a serious, no-nonsense father. Bly touches on what has been seen as our feminine side, our caring side."

Five years later, in the spring of 1995, there's another gathering of men down the California coast at the Los Angeles Coliseum. This one is one hundred times larger and unapologetically Christian, but many of the issues are the same.

High in the upper deck of the Coliseum, Nick talks about life before he was "born again," growing up in a broken family of nonbelievers. "My father lived in a different town," he yells over the crowd. "I didn't have a father figure, so I had no role model to . . ."

His story is interrupted—not by drunken Raider fans—but by the right-eous roar of 72,548 men fueled by dueling doses of testosterone and Christian piety. "We love Jesus! Yes we do!" one side of the stadium chants. "We love Jesus! How about you?" their brethren bark back.

Nick, an expectant father and Southern Baptist, tries to finish his story, yelling over the Coliseum crowd. "You see, I'm the first Christian in my family, so I had no role model to show me how to be a Christian man. Here, I can have fellowship with 70,000 Christian men."

Fellowship was found through Promise Keepers, the evangelical men's movement that—depending on whom you choose to believe—is a spirit-filled revival of Christian faith and family, or a sexist, homophobic erup-tion of the religious right. Rubbing shoulders at the Coliseum were an eclectic assortment of men—a hat-waving, hand-clapping, hymn-hollering collection of middle-aged businessmen in T-shirts, blue-collar men in base-ball caps, and delegations from groups like the Christian Surfing Associ-ation and the Soldiers for Jesus motorcycle gang. They paid $55 a ticket, which bought them sixteen hours of lectures, prayer, two box lunches, and upbeat Christian music.

"These are exciting days," said speaker Raul Reis, gazing out over the expanse of Christian masculinity. "These are not days to be wimps. They are days to be strong men."

Ed Cole, a Dallas pastor and leader of the Christian Men's Network, touched on the main theme sounded from Promise Keepers' podiums— the need for disciplined families headed by strong men. "Many of our fathers did not teach us well," said Cole. "The core issue in America today is fatherlessness."

○

Social changes around gender are increasingly reflected across the spiri-tual spectrum. Feminism, gay rights, men's movements, changes in fam-ily structure, and the loss of traditional gender roles all figure into the growth of gender spirituality. **In the new millennium, religious crusades like Promise Keepers may lose some of their fervor, but gender spirituality will have an even broader impact as it is integrated into mainstream religion.**

Promise Keepers was one of the signature spiritual movements of the 1990s, reaching its peak with a 1997 gathering of more than a half million men in Washington, D.C.

Though the men's movement of the 1990s began with New Age overtones, it exploded when it hit the evangelical world. Promise Keepers itself may have seen its greatest days. In early 1998, eight years after its founding, leaders of the Denver-based group announced that declining attendance at stadium events had caused a financial crisis, causing the organization to lay off all 345 of its staff members.[1] Nevertheless, the broader evangelical men's movement will continue to have an impact on church and society. Critics of the movement see Promise Keepers as a reaction to feminism, or a clever strategy for recruiting foot soldiers into the religious right. Yet the movement is not monolithic, nor is it primarily political. In a review of books by evangelical men's movement leaders, William Lockhart found that the literature does not simply display a return to traditionalism in family and theology; rather, the books are similar to other expressions of the men's movement. They seek to assert masculinity by using archetypes drawn from psychology and to help men build egalitarian relationships with women. They help men communicate and keep families together. Lockhart writes that the movement provides "room for evangelical men to maintain evangelical distinctives yet also cope with changing social realities."[2]

Two years before the Promise Keepers rally, hundreds of thousands of African-American men gathered in Washington for the Million Man March. Both marches sought to galvanize men to greater responsibility and commitment to their families and communities. Although the leadership of Louis Farrakhan of the Nation of Islam sparked controversy, the Million Man March showed how spirituality also drives the African-American version of the men's movement. Churches with little sympathy for Farrakhan's race-based teachings took part because of their growing realization that many black men are alienated from their congregations and communities. They realized that Farrakhan's unorthodox brand of Islam has successfully reached black males—especially inner-city youth—with its message of self-sufficiency and spiritual self-esteem. The effort to reconcile masculinity and Christian spirituality has since become a major emphasis in black churches.

Just as the men's movement seeks to instill a new kind of masculinity, feminist-inspired spirituality draws connections between women's lives and the sacred.

Books on women's spirituality are very popular. *In the Womb of God* by Celeste Schroeder and *Sister to Sister* by Susan Johnson Cook suggest that women's experiences of the sacred are significantly different from those of men. They draw on women's stages of life—the menstrual cycle and menopause, childbirth, and the role of care giving. They see a spiritual element in everyday activities of homemaking, such as decorating interior space, food preparation, and in fostering relationships.[3]

Women's spirituality finds many expressions; it can be deeply conservative or radically innovative. The flourishing spirituality surrounding the Virgin Mary views the mother of Christ as a model of receptivity and commitment toward God. Feminist spirituality, or the goddess movement, centers on the sacredness of the female experience and the empowerment of women.

Goddess spirituality easily finds its place in the eclectic marketplace of American religion, drawing on Judaism, Christianity, political feminism, psychotherapy, paganism, and the New Age. As with many forms of contemporary spirituality, it is based less on the transcendence of God and more on the nearness of the sacred to human experience.

Proponents of goddess spirituality claim to revive deities and culture predating the Judeo-Christian tradition. In the process, they often reconstruct ancient texts and history. Although some historians question the accuracy of these retrievals, goddess movement leaders seek to show that matriarchal culture was displaced by patriarchy and a hardening of spiritual outlook. Within mainline churches and synagogues, there is a strong feminist movement inspired by goddess literature actively promoting female imagery for God. A key question in the new millennium will be what effect these revisionist theories will have upon women in mainstream Christian and Jewish religion.

Goddess spirituality made headlines following a controversial church-financed conference for Christian feminists in Minneapolis called "Re-Imagining 1993." Reports soon emerged about some rather unorthodox prayers and rituals held in the name of "Sophia." It was an ecumenical gathering that attracted a crowd of two thousand women and eighty-five men, including leading staff members of the mainline Presbyterian and Methodist denominations.

"Our maker Sophia, we are women in your image," the women intoned. "With the hot blood of our wombs we give form to new life. . . . With nectar between our thighs we invite a lover . . . with our warm body fluids we remind the world of its pleasures and sensations."

Heresy and paganism, declared the *Presbyterian Layman*, the watchdog newspaper of evangelicals within the relatively liberal Presbyterian

Church (U.S.A.). "They (Christian feminists) seem determined to take the church back to the period when multiple goddesses were worshiped, where sex outside the covenant of marriage was declared a religious rite of passage, where children were regularly sacrificed, and where everyone did what was right in her own eyes."[4]

Sophia is Greek for "wisdom," and in many Biblical references, such as in the first nine chapters of Proverbs, Sophia is personified as a feminine spirit of wisdom. Mystics have long envisioned her as a primordial female power that gave birth to the male spirit. Her rediscovery by growing numbers of Christian women is part of the flowering of feminist theology in American churches and seminaries today.

When they first heard about Sophia, the folks at United Methodist headquarters in Nashville didn't know what everyone was so upset about. "I've worked for the church all these years, and I'd never heard of Sophia," said the chief spokesman for the United Methodist Church. "We thought she was the waitress down at the corner diner."[5]

New forms of gender spirituality are also emerging from the gay and lesbian community. Many women in the goddess movement are lesbian or bisexual, and the AIDS crisis has sparked a spiritual revival among homosexual men. Alienated by religious institutions that have long viewed them as immoral deviants, many gays and lesbians are finding spiritual sustenance in their own community, and in their own experience, flocking to gay churches, synagogues, and upbeat New Age congregations where the words *sin* and *judgment* rarely pass the pastor's lips.

Spiritual teachers popular in the gay community include those following *A Course in Miracles* and other forms of metaphysical Christianity, neopaganism, and the writings of Ram Dass, Stephen Levine, and Elizabeth Kübler-Ross. Many people with AIDS have worked to reconcile themselves with their Judeo-Christian heritage, reviving interest in faith healing and certain Roman Catholic rites such as anointing the sick and dying with oil. Countless others have been drawn to an eclectic assortment of meditation and visualization techniques, positive-thinking workshops, and New Age spiritualists.

Spirituality at Work

Spirituality is not the first thing that comes to mind when one thinks of a big-city newspaper. Other images arise—gruff editors shouting across rows of cluttered desks; reporters guzzling coffee, smoking cigarettes, and smashing down telephones as they fight a tight deadline; ink-stained alcoholics escaping to the corner bar for a quick drink between editions.

Well, forget those old-fashioned ideas about newspaper offices. At one major metropolitan daily, reporters have grown accustomed to computer messages flashing across the top of their screens announcing, "Stress-relieving massages are now being offered in the third-floor conference room." Moans of ecstasy are soon heard from journalists sitting in high-tech massage chairs, having their neck and shoulders rubbed by a certi-fied masseuse. Then there are the yoga classes, offered at noon in the basement meeting room. Tables are pushed aside, lights are dimmed, and a dozen employees sit cross-legged on little mats.

"Focus on your breath," the teacher softly suggests.

Judith, who both teaches the class and works at the newspaper, says it can be hard to change gears in the middle of the day.

"Everybody has been on the phone, running around here and there, and then we ask them to drop all that and create an atmosphere of calm," she says. "It's amazing, but it works. Some have done yoga before. Others are newcomers. One guy asked me about meditation classes and I gave him the number of a local ashram."

Occasionally, one even hears the sounds of quiet chanting drifting from a remodeled basement where mighty presses once roared.

"Ommm . . . Ommm . . . Ommm. . . ."

–––––––––––– o ––––––––––––

Newspapers were not the only companies to get spiritual in the 1990s. **In the coming century, more corporations will try to address the spir-itual and emotional needs of their employees, though concerns about productivity and religious freedom may get in the way.**

Those promoting workplace spirituality say the goal is to motivate and inspire workers, to help employees balance work with the rest of life. Boston University business professor Laura Nash calls it the "feminiza-tion" of the corporation, not to indicate the number of women in man-agement, but to denote a kinder, gentler capitalism that seeks to "empower employees in every aspect of performance."[6]

Seminars incorporating visualization and meditation have become some-thing of a corporate fad. "Soul committees," convened to deal with spiri-tual issues in work, are now found in several companies, including Lotus Development Corp, AT&T, and Boeing. At the World Bank in Washing-ton, D.C., a "Spiritual Unfoldment Society" meets every Wednesday at lunchtime. Fifty to eighty people meet to discuss a variety of spiritual topics ranging from attaining "soul connection" to reincarnation. There are also regular conferences, Web sites, newsletters, and a growing indus-try of workplace consultants. Worker spirituality is also hot in publishing circles. From 1994 to 1997, for instance, approximately fifty books were published on the topic.

Spirituality resonates deeply with many employees. For example, a 1995 survey of workers by *Personnel Journal* found that 70 percent think spirituality has a place at work. But only 27 percent said their organizations have private, quiet areas where workers can go for reflection and solitude; 56 percent say they pray, chant, listen to New Age music, or play meditation tapes at work to help relieve stress.[7]

Most workplace programs avoid explicitly religious or spiritual language, preferring terminology like "empowerment" or "energy" or "stress reduction." In a study of how people integrate spiritual principles with work, spirituality and business consultant Judi Neil found that most workers keep their spirituality secret for fear of being seen as impractical or as "New Agers." But as employees find co-workers with similar interests, they begin to support one another in spiritual growth, and become more outspoken.

Critics argue that companies are peddling "spirituality lite," putting Band-Aids on abusive corporate practices and masking the cut-throat downsizing of the 1980s and 1990s. Proponents of the "spirit at work" movement insist they are challenging, rather than affirming, conventional management.

As in the wider culture, there are many definitions for "soul" and "spirituality" in the workplace. Some see values like trust, openness, cooperation, environmental awareness, and community responsibility as primary signs of workplace spirituality. In this context, "spirit" refers to human spirit and creativity rather than a supernatural entity. Nash asks how far corporations can go in instilling spirituality in their workers. "Can a company alone provide real meaning to a Generation X employee who is 'beyond God?'"

Others worry about companies forcing employees to participate in spiritual workshops. Whereas consultants and business leaders may not view these programs as religious, employees might. Professionals may see a retreat modeled after Native American council meetings or "vision quests" as a pragmatic way to help participants view their work in more meaningful ways. A devout Mormon, however, may see participation in the retreat as disloyal to his faith. These conflicts are most likely to arise over the contested boundary between spirituality and psychology, especially where meditation, visualization, and relaxation techniques are employed.

Such conflicts are likely to intensify in the new millennium. Growing numbers of companies and employers are applying faith and spirituality—from evangelical Protestant to American Muslim—to their work. A survey conducted by the National Federation on Independent Business of 800 company owners found that 43 percent identified themselves as evangelical or born-again Christian.[8] Whatever their personal beliefs, employers will find that the most effective and least contentious way to integrate spirituality and business is through programs flexible enough for participants to make room for their own faith traditions and spiritual inclinations, while avoiding practices they may find objectionable.

God and Pop Culture

It was Christmas 1996, and angels were everywhere. Holiday offerings from Hollywood included a flock of all-too-human angels—including John Travolta in *Michael* and Denzel Washington in *The Preacher's Wife*.

This, of course, is well-worn territory. *The Preacher's Wife* was an updated version of the 1947 film *The Bishop's Wife,* in which Cary Grant arrives from heaven to soften a clergyman's heart. And all Christmas movies and angelic vehicles are measured against *It's a Wonderful Life,* when an angel named Clarence descends to inspire and redeem a suicidal Jimmy Stewart.

In the 1990s, however, these cheery Hollywood cherubs were more than just a seasonal bubble of holiday sentiment. On television, *Touched by an Angel* was one of the most watched programs of the decade. Millions of American Catholics might skip Sunday Mass, but they wouldn't miss the Sunday night episode of *Touched by an Angel.*

Angel books piled high in bookstores across the country, not to mention angel calendars, angel candles, and crystal angel statues. Newspapers and magazines wrote story after story on the angel craze. Angels had become the safe, all-purpose, nonthreatening symbol of pop religion. It seemed like everyone—Christians, Jews, Muslims, New Agers, even atheists—loved angels.

"It's a subject that's very pleasing to people," said Elliot Abbott, executive producer of *The Preacher's Wife*. "People are touched by the magic of it, the optimism of it."[9]

○

Religion has always been expressed through popular culture, and recent themes in music, television, and film reflect the secular supermarket of American spirituality. **As the entertainment media becomes the primary conveyor of common culture, it will compete with religious groups as the main bearer of spiritual and religious insight, no matter how mundane and homogenized those revelations may be.**

If angels were the symbol of pop religion in the 1990s, "soul" and "spirit" were the sound bites. It may have reached a low point when an actor playing the owner of a truck in a TV commercial praised Detroit's latest four-wheel-drive vehicle, calling the driving experience "a spiritual thing."

Critics complain that popular culture vulgarizes and trivializes spirituality, marketing it to satisfy consumer tastes. Writer Phyllis Tickle counters that the popular media can "democratize theology" by bringing "god-talk" into everyday life.[10]

Story-telling to convey spiritual themes is also popular among spiritual leaders who turn to fiction writing. Frank Peretti's novels depicting spiritual warfare, and fiction by Pat Robertson and Charles Colson, show the new interest among evangelicals. Writers and publishers associated with the New Age movement, such as Starhawk, Natalie Goldberg, and Deepak Chopra, view fiction as a natural medium for their work. Fiction and New Age spirituality are a good fit. Both easily draw on myth, mysticism, and emotion. Romance novels have also been gradually featuring religious, often evangelical Christian, themes and characters.

In the 1990s, Hollywood released many films with nontraditional religious stories—from the New Age themes of *Ghost* to Buddhist-inspired films like *Kundun* and *Seven Years in Tibet*. Other movies point to a less noticed trend of films depicting spirituality in a nonreligious context. *A River Runs Through It* conveyed the spirituality of fly fishing and the "interconnectedness" of humans with the rest of nature. *Fearless* revolved around one man's near-death experience. Careful watchers of another Travolta film, *Phenomenon,* saw vestiges of Scientology when the actor's character is hit by a flash of light and suddenly becomes "clear," assuming supernatural powers and awesome intelligence. Even the 1993 movie *Groundhog Day* was reportedly informed by the esoteric philosophy of George Gurdjieff, showing an individual awakening to his "true self."

According to a 1996 report by the Center for the Study of Social and Political Change, the film industry has veered away from traditional religious themes but continues to be fascinated by the spiritual and the supernatural. The study analyzed the content of hundreds of popular films from 1946 to 1990 and found that the favorable portrayal of traditional religious characters and institutions declined with each decade. As traditional religious themes waned, there were increasing depictions of alternative sources of spirituality.[11]

Nevertheless, traditional religion still finds its way onto film, if only because its mysterious and colorful rituals provide great visual backdrops. For instance, the portrayal of the Catholic Church in many films—especially of the horror and thriller genres—features dark churches, nuns and priests in traditional garb, statues, candles, and pre-Vatican II imagery. This may also help explain why the colorful and exotic world of Tibetan Buddhism resonates with Martin Scorcese, Bernardo Bertolucci, and other movie makers.

Music, especially rock, pulses with secular spirituality. *New York Times* writer Guy Garcia writes that U2, Snoop Doggy Dogg, and Peter Gabriel "express a spiritual yearning that harks back, consciously or not, to rock's gospel roots and a generational groping for more eternal values. Not since the peace and love era of the 1960s, when spiritual transcendence was celebrated by the likes of Bob Dylan, the Beatles, and Joni Mitchell, have religious themes been so conspicuously prevalent in pop.

"The spiritual slant in today's music is anything but a Sunday school endorsement of organized religion," he adds. "Instead of urging people to go back to church, or to pray, the message is resolutely iconoclastic. The songs seem to say that in a godless society the only recourse is to make a personal appeal to the divine."[12]

Even in the world of alternative rock, better known for sacrilege than spirituality, Biblical themes and Christian messages find expression. Sixteen Horsepower, an alternative band from Denver, draws on Biblical imagery in its 1997 debut album *Sackcloth 'n' Ashes*. Much more than contemporary Christian music, the religion of alternative rockers is heavy on realism, and raises doubts while longing for renewed faith and hope.

Pop culture generates its own religious icons. Fans of the Grateful Dead rock band, the TV show *Star Trek,* and Elvis Presley often display a religious fervor toward their idols. Elvis, "The King," is the ultimate example. Researcher John Strausbaugh found fans who venerate Elvis, pray to Elvis, see Elvis in visions, claim Elvis has effected miraculous cures, revere relics associated with Elvis, and do good works in the name of Elvis. Strausbaugh calls it recreational religion—or "an infusion of religious fervor and faith into the pursuit of an avocation one intensely enjoys."[13]

Peace Between Science and Spirituality

Fritjof Capra, author of the *Tao of Physics,* stood behind the pulpit at the First Unitarian Church and posed a question to a congregation of 200 scientists, mystics, and assorted truth seekers.

"Why do we see objects in the everyday world?" asked Capra, who had just told his audience that, according to both physicists and mystics, what is really out there is "a continuous dance of energy."

"Why do we see this glass of water as separate from this table?"

Capra was born in Austria and earned his doctorate in theoretical physics from the University of Vienna. He wrote his best-seller in 1975 and launched a new kind of thinking about science and spirituality.

Both mystics and physicists, he notes, conduct research into "the essential nature of all things." Although mystics explore this realm through quiet meditation, and physicists conduct their experiments with colossal atom smashers and complex mathematical equations, they sometimes produce remarkably similar findings. One famous example is the nature of light, which has paradoxically been found to consist of both waves and particles, depending on how the experiment is conducted.

It all sounds a bit like the profound mystical experience Capra had on a central California beach in 1969, an event that helped inspire the *Tao of Physics*.

"As I sat on that beach, my former experiences came to life," he recalls. "I saw cascades of energy coming down from outer space, in which particles were created and destroyed in rhythmic pulses. I saw the atoms of the elements and those of my body participating in this cosmic dance of energy. I felt its rhythm and I heard its sound."[14]

In the 1990s, the coming together of science and spirituality went far beyond the realms of fringe science, visions on a beach, and the free-thinking sanctuaries of Unitarian Universalism. It took 350 years, but the Vatican finally admitted it was wrong.

Back in 1633, Galileo was condemned by the Roman Catholic Church, arrested, and had his books burned for concluding that the Earth moves around the sun. Pope John Paul II admitted the church was wrong on October 31, 1992, formally lifting the edict of the Inquisition against the brilliant Italian astronomer and physicist.

Four years later, in another rapprochement with science, the pope gave his blessing to Charles Darwin, proclaiming that "fresh knowledge leads to recognition of the theory of evolution as more than just a hypothesis."

To many, the rulings were so long overdue they were laughable. To others, they marked a turning point in the centuries-old clash between science and religion.

"The Holy Father recognizes science as a depository of values on the same plane as those of the faith," said Antonio Zichicihi, a noted Italian nuclear physicist. "The third millennium will set the stage for a grand alliance between faith and Galilean science."[15]

○

Galileo's scientific revolution and Darwin's theory of evolution seemed to put science and religion forever into warring camps—one waving the banner of faith, the other marching to the certainty of fact.

In the new millennium, peace may finally come to science and religion. Battles will continue to flare, especially over bioethics and the brave new world of genetic engineering. But the search for spiritual truth and the quest to understand the cosmos are converging. Science is no longer seen as an obstacle to most spiritual seekers and religious believers, but as another way to explore different philosophies, spiritualities, and worldviews.

Philosopher Ken Wilber sees their coming together as one of the most important events in our times. "Science is clearly one of the most profound methods that humans have yet devised for discovering truth," he writes, "while religion remains the single greatest force for generating meaning."[16]

Signs of a science-religion truce are everywhere. Colleges and universities across the U.S. and around the world have inaugurated hundreds of new courses, conferences, and workshops on the interplay between science and religion. Funding by the Templeton Foundation, started by philanthropist and financier John Templeton, has significantly contributed to the dialogue at the college level. The philanthropic foundation gave grants in 1996 to set up 300 college-level courses on science and religion. New books on the subject come out each year.

This interaction is not just a one-way street in which theologians lead the charge. Many scientists are in the forefront of the exploration of new theories of religion and their impact on biology, psychology, physics, and cosmology. For example, "creation theology," which holds that God's creation of the universe is an ongoing process and that humans are "co-creators," was developed by both scientists and theologians. This is not the same thing as "creationist" theology, the more fundamentalist view that God set forth about 6,000 years ago to create the Earth in six days. Creation theology, and especially creation spirituality, is a more mystical expression that gives scientists a place at the table.

Recent scientific theories around the "new physics" and "chaos theory" also give many scientists and spiritualists something to talk about. These theories in physics argue that the systems of the universe are unpredictable and are open to rapid change. They see the various parts of the universe as interrelated and always evolving. God's work of creation, in other words, continues today. These ideas also mesh with the philosophy of the New Age, and the "paradigm shift" outlined by Thomas Kuhn, a historian of science who described how people make models of the universe to direct their interpretation of events. This has led to the idea that we cannot separate the way we look at things from our understanding of "reality." Central to New Age philosophy is the idea of a "wholeness paradigm" emphasizing the interconnectedness of all beings. This worldview is seen as replacing the old model associated with Isaac Newton, who saw the universe as a huge mechanical system that operated according to immutable laws.

Meanwhile, some biologists point to an "ever-increasing diversity of new life forms" as evidence of an "open-ended universe," where unpredictability is the rule. A scientist and Anglican priest, the Reverend Arthur Peacocke, reconciles all this with the theory that God may have created the world using chance but "loaded the dice in favor of life." These concepts, he notes, have a way of filtering down to religious congregations and everyday life. Since creation is still taking place, humans are called to "cooperate with God's intentions" and serve as "co-creators." This may lead Christians toward a more "positive assessment of civilization and technology" and inspire greater ecological concern.

Of course, many scientists question the speculative flourish spiritual writers bring to this melding of mysticism and empiricism. But Kevin Sharpe, editor of the *Science and Spirit News,* says new theories in biology and physics have had a "powerful effect in theology and in breaking down the determinism in science which has opposed religion." At the same time, these theories "soften the ground" so that all faiths—New Age, Eastern religions, and Christianity—benefit from a new encounter with science.

Another arena where science and spirituality intersect is in technology and computer science. Computer breakthroughs such as the Internet spawn new spiritual concepts. Psychologist Jean Houston sees the Internet as a material expression of spiritual connections already present among humans. "What's happening here is an electronic neurosphere that is going to change philosophy, theology, the way we think about ourselves—I mean literally a global mind field that is spawning a new culture."[17] Artificial intelligence also emerges at the crossroads of science and religion. Scientist and theologian Philip Clayton writes that the creation of computer intelligence systems, including advanced robotics, will force theologians and believers to redefine the concepts of "soul" and "created in the image of God." As technology takes on human attributes, Clayton ventures that our image of God may even have to be modified.[18]

Sometimes, science follows in the tracks of spirituality. Take the Gaia theory, birthed in New Age circles. This theory originally held that the planet, or "Mother Earth," is alive and acts with a sense of purpose to maintain the conditions of life. Eventually scientists trimmed much of the spiritual overlay from the theory, replacing the view that the earth acts with a sense of purpose with a more mechanical explanation, more like "feedback." Nevertheless, much of the scientific community came around to accept the theory's main point that life on earth helps regulate the earth itself. In effect, both scientists and theologians were beginning to use common language, even though not altogether intending the same meanings. James Parker Morton, formerly of New York's Cathedral of St. John the Divine, says that the "very nature of this hypothesis shows that we are at a new moment when scientific and religious inquiry is directed to the same reality and discussed in common language."[19]

Body, Mind, Spirit, and Medicine

People passing by the vast ballroom of a Boston hotel were puzzled. At one moment, a distinguished doctor was holding forth on the latest research on placebos, neurobiology, and cardiology. A few minutes later, a thousand heads bowed in guided meditation. Then the audience applauded enthusiastically as a Pentecostal preacher gave riveting testimony of a healing he experienced as a youth.

This eclectic event, half conference, half camp meeting, was sponsored by Harvard Medical School—all part of an unprecedented effort to integrate the clashing worlds of medicine and spirituality. Since the mid-1990s, the school's Mind-Body Medical Institute has been bringing together doctors, nurses, and religious leaders to compare notes and share experiences on the intersection of spirituality and medicine.

Introducing each address with searching questions and tales of his own experiences was Dr. Herbert Benson. With his white hair and wire-rimmed glasses, Benson resembles the old country doctor. But this was the same forward-thinking physician who studied Transcendental Meditation practitioners during the 1960s and 1970s and pioneered the "relaxation response." Now Benson was reaching out beyond the world of alternative religion, getting the attention of rabbis, mainline Protestants, and Roman Catholics.[20]

○

In the new millennium, greater appreciation for the connection between spirituality and health will inspire and challenge the fields of medicine and religion.

Holistic health, once the darling of the New Age movement, and faith healing, formerly the province of Pentecostals and the Christian Science church, went mainstream in the 1980s and 1990s. Pollster George Gallup predicts that healing will be the major theme of the religious future. It's called "the faith factor," and if growing numbers of researchers are correct, having it makes you healthy.

Setting the standards for research was a major study in 1988. It involved a group praying for coronary patients, and a control group that did not receive prayer. Those being prayed for ended up with fewer cases of congestive heart failure during recovery, had to use less medication, and experienced fewer complications.[21]

Benson forecasts that the medical establishment will turn to healing techniques that draw on spirituality, religion, and other self-help traditions—in no small part because they're seen as cost effective. Since HMOs force medical providers to cut costs by reducing patient visits, preventive and nonmedical treatments will be favorably received. This bottom-line thinking, combined with the mounting studies on the beneficial health effects of faith and spirituality, will accelerate the acceptance of spiritual and psychological practices within the medical establishment. "In ten years when you go for a check-up, I predict that your doctor will not only ask about your medical history but also about your belief system," says psychiatrist Richard Friedman.

Consider the doctor-patient relationship at the medical offices of Dr. Dale Matthews of Georgetown University Medical School. Along with taking blood pressure and writing prescriptions, Matthews offers a method of treatment his colleagues may still find shocking. He prays with them. After examining the legs of one elderly patient, Matthews encourages the woman to join her church choir. "The best thing you can do for your health is to keep praising God every day," says Matthews, as he writes out the Bible citation of Colossians 3:17 on a prescription pad and hands it to the patient.

Doctors are sold on the physical benefits of faith. A 1996 survey of members of the American Academy of Family Physicians reports that a remarkable 99 percent think religious faith helps patients respond to treatment. The study, conducted by Yankelovich Partners, found that most of these doctors thought spiritual techniques should be part of formal medical training, and 55 percent report they use these techniques as part of their current practice.[22] In fact, the spirituality-health connection is finding a place in medical education. The National Institute for HealthCare Research reports in 1997 that nearly one-third of American medical schools offered courses on spirituality and healing.

What kinds of spiritual practices benefit health and healing? Studies find prayer and congregation attendance have beneficial effects. But meditation, and meditative varieties of prayer, seem to have the greatest effect. Researchers say the "relaxation response" from repetitive words, chanting, and prayer helps in the treatment of heart disease, chronic pain, and infertility. And it doesn't seem to matter if the contemplative practice is a

Buddhist meditating, a Muslim reciting the Koran, or a Catholic saying the rosary. Since these different practices have similar effects on health, Benson notes, it may mean they all share the same underlying reality— something that might lead to greater unity and peace among religions.

At the same time, these findings may concern some religious leaders. If Buddhist meditation and Quaker prayer have the same effect on health, how important are the distinctive beliefs that undergird these practices? Those interested in health could come to value prayer or meditation for their physical effects more than their spiritual significance. Dr. Matthews draws a distinction between "intrinsic" and "extrinsic" faith and their effect on health. Those whose faith is part of their identity (intrinsic) do experience positive health benefits. Others who might use spirituality as a way to achieve status or health (extrinsic) are less likely to benefit, and may actually experience negative health effects.

If spirituality and religious belief influence body and mind, can it work the other way around? What role does the brain play in shaping and even generating spiritual experiences? Brain research has discovered that religious and mystical experiences are colored by how the brain functions. Researchers at the University of California at San Diego's brain and perception laboratory studied patients suffering from an unusual form of epilepsy and concluded that parts of the brain's temporal lobe region may influence how intensely a person responds to religious beliefs. People suffering from temporal lobe seizures have long reported that their attacks were accompanied by intense mystical experiences, and that they were often preoccupied by religious thoughts between seizures. "We like to suggest that there may be neural circuits in the temporal lobe that may be part of the machinery of the brain that is involved in mystical experiences and God," says researcher V. S. Ramachandran. Researchers stressed that these findings do not negate the validity of God, but merely suggest that humans may be "hard-wired" for mysticism and divine communication.[23]

Connections between body and spirit have also drawn the attention of the fitness industry. By the mid-1990s, gyms and spas were marketing spirituality to their customers. Writing in the women's magazine *Allure,* Martha Barnette reports that "spirituality-speak" has become a regular part of the program at gyms and spas, "providing a kind of one-stop shopping, where the faithful go to feed their spiritual hunger." It is hard to know where the beauty and fitness ends and the spirituality begins when programs of "aromafitness" are offered and facials are promoted as helping customers come into "alignment with their finest selves." Barnette concludes that this may all just be "the same old self-indulgence with the shiny new language of spirituality. We suspect they spend a lot less time navel gazing than they do studying their cellulite in the mirror, and that the spiritual enlightenment they claim from exercising is actually just a good old rush of endorphins."[24]

Similar questions are asked about religious visions and near-death experiences. If personal faith promotes human wellness, it is not a huge next step to conclude that we are genetically constituted for mystical experience. Or as Benson writes, "Our genetic blueprint has made believing in an Infinite Absolute part of our nature. By the process of natural selection, mutating genes deemed faith important enough to the survival of our forefathers and mothers that we were endowed with the same tendencies. . . . Evolution favors religion, causing our brains to generate the impulses we need to carry on—faith, hope, and love becoming part of the neuromatrix with which we approach living."

Another area of future controversy between religion and brain research will concern the increasing use of mind-altering drugs to alleviate psychological ailments, especially character and personality problems. Drugs such as Prozac and newer anti-depressants differ from earlier medications in that they not only relieve serious depression but also seem to work on personality traits, such as self-esteem and anger, and promote a general sense of well-being. These, of course, are states of mind long considered the province of religion and spirituality. Spiritual groups with a strong therapeutic dimension are more likely to be in conflict with the psychopharmacological revolution, viewing it as unwelcome competition. Witness the Church of Scientology's anti-Prozac campaign. Religions that emphasize a transcendent God are less concerned because they have invested less in fostering psychological growth and adjustment.

An analysis of how Buddhist practitioners are affected by the use anti-depressants found that most meditators using Prozac did not think it conflicted with their religious practice. Most of those interviewed said Prozac and similar drugs do not deal with the "dark night of the soul" or other existential predicaments that spur people onto a spiritual path. A Zen monk adds, "Taking medication is kind of like sitting in a chair rather than sitting cross-legged on the mat. Whether there's something wrong with people's legs or the neurotransmitters in their brains, we need to adjust the practice so they can experience it."[25]

Research on substance abusers has questioned the wisdom of viewing excessive drug and alcohol use in purely medical terms, and using new drugs to block the feelings of pleasure created by other drugs. Steven Hyman of the Brain, Mind, and Behavior Initiative at Harvard University found that these attempts are not very successful because they don't give anything back to the addict. They lack the "spiritual therapy" component of organizations like Alcoholics Anonymous. Andrew and Thomas Delbanco write that self-help groups that draw on spirituality provide addicts with a "compensatory pleasure." This may come from spiritual experience, or simply taking responsibility for their actions in a "productive love that goes outward, seeking no reward, to other people and, through them, to God."[26]

POSTSCRIPT

AMERICAN SPIRITUALITY—
MYSTICAL AND PRACTICAL

STEVE AND JULIE, the "church shoppers" we met at the beginning of our book, face a bewildering number of spiritual teachings, religious denominations, and competing congregations in their faith journey. Like most busy families in the 1990s, they have neither the time nor desire to become professional seekers, trying on every spirituality. This young family did find a church to join and seem likely to grow in their Christian faith in the new millennium. Others, like Miriam, the baby boomer who drifted from Judaism to mystical Christianity to the free-wheeling commune of an Indian guru, seem destined to wander the spiritual path forever, trying to recreate her chemically induced *satori* of the 1960s.

Despite their differences, Miriam, Steve, and Julie all found their spiritual interests through social networks of family, friends, and co-workers. As spirituality becomes separated from religious institutions, friends and relatives will swap spiritual teachings and techniques as freely as they trade tips on child-rearing and favorite recipes.

For those belonging to religious congregations, and for seekers who go it alone, the range of spiritual options will be one of the disorienting facts of life in the new millennium. Products and services peddled in the religious marketplace may change, but the gap between religious institutions and personal spirituality will shape the American search for faith. As we will see in Part Two, rising religious choice will not necessarily weaken spiritual commitment. Indeed, religious individualism can help inspire vibrant new faith communities.

49

Observers of American religion have long noted how the individual believer is elevated and revered in our nation's faith. In 1831, the United States of America was still in its adolescence when the French visitor and social philosopher, Alexis de Tocqueville, noted the importance of private spirituality in American religion. "The American at times steals an hour from himself, and laying aside for a while the petty passions which agitate his life, and the ephemeral interests which engross it, strays at once into an ideal world, where all is great, eternal and pure," Tocqueville wrote. "Religion is not less useful to each citizen than to the whole state."[1]

At the turn of the next century, William James, the American psychologist and philosopher, was one of the first to document the blending of psychology and spirituality into a practical, personal, and private religion. Calling it "religion of healthy-mindedness," James observed how the "New Thought" schools of American spirituality promote "systematic exercise in passive relaxation, concentration, and meditation, and have even invoked something like hypnotic practice."[2]

Closer to our own time, American sociologist Robert Bellah has documented how the philosophy of "utilitarian individualism" underlies most aspects of American life, including religion. "Utility replaces duty; self-expression unseats authority," he writes. "'Being good' becomes 'feeling good.'"[3]

In the new millennium, this individualized approach to religion will become more widespread as Americans seek inspiration from personal spiritual experience, rather than from doctrine handed-down through creeds or religious hierarchies. We have already seen how two young Buddhist initiates, Brother Mark and Sister Jennifer, as well as William, the member of an Assemblies of God congregation, lay claim to such experiential forms of faith. Pentecostal Christianity and meditative traditions like Buddhism will carry experiential spirituality in the opening decades of the next century.

Because these faiths and spiritualities are based on individual experience, they are easily "mixed and matched" by spiritual shoppers. But so are more traditional teachings. Americans take traditional practices and beliefs out of their religious context and put them on spiritual shopping lists—whether they are Gregorian chants, Native American vision quests, angels, or the mystical Jewish practices of Kabbalah.

Meanwhile, the tendency to apply spiritual principles to secular activity will challenge the separation of the sacred and social spheres of American life. While the attempt to find "spirit" in everything can degenerate into a diffuse and meaningless spirituality, it could also bring a new sense of wholeness to everyday life.

For many people, spirituality is about unity and reconciliation—whether it is expressed by New Age interconnectedness with Mother Earth or the monotheistic view that all people are children of God. Other spiritual movements arise along the boundaries of one's gender, sexuality, and racial or ethnic heritage. The men's and women's movements are the most tangible examples of "segmented spirituality." As they moderate their course and assimilate into religious organizations, these movements will no longer be mere catalysts for spiritual separatism. The future of these spiritualities will depend on how well they are integrated into the everyday life of religious congregations.

We have already seen how Americans are drawn to practical religion—to spiritual practices that not only connect them with the sacred, but fix things, from problems on the job to persistent arthritis. As spirituality is further detached from traditional religion, it will be viewed as a means of solving problems. In the new millennium, many Americans will be more concerned with therapy than theology.

In the world of business, spirituality will be seen as a means of increasing productivity and employee satisfaction. There will be a blurring of boundaries between the religious marketplace and other segments of the business community—whether in book publishing, Hollywood, high-tech, or health clubs.

Likewise, spirituality will be increasingly viewed as something that is medically and psychologically beneficial, even something that can be manipulated by market-driven medical practitioners seeking lower costs and higher profits. Venturing further into the future, new discoveries in biology, brain research, and pharmaceuticals point to a whole new market of products and technologies to trigger and intensify mystical experience and spiritual well-being.

For seekers and believers, spiritual growth will be a balancing act between discipline and grace. For many it will be a journey that broadens into a concern for others through fellowship and greater community involvement. It is to these institutional and social dimensions of the religious future that we now turn.

PART TWO

SEARCHING FOR COMMUNITY

4

CONGREGATIONS AND CONSUMERS

Marketing to Seekers

There's plenty of parking at California Christian Center, a sprawling mega-church serving the fast-growing bedroom communities of the Central Valley. Its massive modern sanctuary rises from parking lots of Biblical proportion, just off the busy freeway that connects valley residents to the Home Depot, K-Mart, and other megastores a few off-ramps down the highway.

Both the parking lots and the sanctuary are packed for Sunday services, but there's something happening here every day of the week. For many of its 3,800 members, this is not just a church where they come for Sunday worship. It's where they recreate, educate, socialize, and spend much of their lives. Its fully accredited high school has 350 students, with another 600 attending its elementary and intermediate school, plus 150 more in its day-care center. Its high school is state-of-the-art, with computer labs, libraries, art studios, a band room, two softball fields, one baseball diamond, and a football stadium where its Christian athletes compete with teams from neighboring secular schools. Its athletic director serves both the school and the church. Adult members use the same facilities for their own sports activities.

Like many megachurches, California Christian Center doesn't play up its affiliation with its Pentecostal denomination. Instead, it stresses that it's "Bible-based" and "family oriented." In some ways, the megachurch is a little denomination unto itself. It has spawned a dozen smaller churches and schools, who view its large complex as a kind of Pentecostal cathedral for special events and celebrations. One of the spin-off congregations, Valley Christian Church, is nearly as large as the mother church, and just opened a new 2,500-seat sanctuary.

Steve and Julie, the young "church shoppers" we introduced in Chapter One, were very impressed the first Sunday they walked into the old Valley Christian chapel.

"Everybody was nice and friendly," Julie recalled. "Even though I wasn't Pentecostal, I felt at peace when we walked in. It felt like the place where I should be."

Steve, who never went to church as a child, was a bit put off at first by the lively style of worship, but soon felt comfortable. "We liked the music and the fact that they had a big band with contemporary music," Steve said. "It was familiar. They'd have concerts with Christian bands you'd hear on the radio. And they had lots of good programs for kids."

After about three months, however, Steve and Julie became dissatisfied. "It was so big that it was hard to meet the same people on Sunday," Steve said. "You couldn't get planted. It was too impersonal. You felt lost in the shuffle." They eventually settled on a smaller Pentecostal church that was not part of the California Christian network.

Jim, a leading lay member at California Christian Center, said his megachurch has found a way to overcome the impersonal feeling that drove Steve and Julie away. "The secret to large churches like this is not that they're large; it's all the small groups we have within the church so people don't get lost," he explained. "There are lots of ways for people to identify with the church. We have a singles' group with 200 to 300 people. We have a seniors' group. There are groups for people with drug and alcohol problems. They meet at different times throughout the week, then we all come together on Sunday."

o

Despite its conservative evangelical doctrine, California Christian Center has a consumer approach to Christianity, a market-based ministry. It is user-friendly. It provides all the life services its members need—a singles' ministry to meet your mate, a school and day-care center for your kids, a softball team for the whole family, a seniors' group for your parents, not to mention a place to park your car. **In the new millennium, more and more American congregations will take this market-based approach to find new members and keep the ones they have. Megachurches embody the consumerism, eclecticism, and the conservatism shaping the religious future. They are the evangelical answer to Home Depot.**

There have been large congregations throughout American religious history, but size was often dictated more by circumstance than design. In the early 1970s, "superchurches" emerged that intentionally sought to draw the multitudes into their pews by featuring high-profile preachers and Sunday school campaigns. The megachurches emerged a decade later, targeting larger crowds through more sophisticated forms of marketing. Willow Creek Community Church in suburban Chicago pioneered the development of this market-based approach to outreach and worship. Megachurches may have 10,000 members, or no more than a few hundred. What they have in common is that they are fast-growing and use contemporary services to attract spiritual seekers and unchurched Americans. Megachurch leaders unashamedly admit the influence of business and management theory. One leader cites management guru Peter Drucker's formula as his inspiration: "What is our business? Who is our customer? What does the customer consider value?"

Megachurches are adorned with few ecclesiastical trappings. Crucifixes and stained glass windows are rare, and the building itself may be rented. Function is more important than form as they attempt to appear unintimidating and culturally relevant to seekers. Visitors are greeted with contemporary music, often performed by professional bands, rather than traditional hymns accompanied by an organ. Writer Charles Trueheart notes that music is a symbolic issue for megachurch pastors. "Whether a church uses contemporary music or not defines what kind of people it wants. When it uses contemporary music, it's saying it wants unchurched people—particularly those of childbearing and child-rearing age."[1]

These congregations are marked by flexibility. Services may have no fixed order, and they can be held in the afternoons or on Saturday. The sermons are more a source of teaching than preaching. They focus on practical matters, such as family concerns and personal growth, not doctrine, sometimes mixing psychotherapeutic concepts with biblical teaching. They often emphasize religious experience. They seek to feel God's love, not understand church theology—a theme that plays well with the decreasing importance of denominational doctrine among baby boomers. Many megachurches have been influenced by the charismatic and Pentecostal movements. Their large size and many functions make them less dependent on denominational support and affiliation. Prominent megachurches such as Willow Creek have formed their own quasi-denominational network of churches. There is an emphasis on forming relationships, often expressed in the kinds of small groups found at California Christian Center.

Megachurches allow newcomers to become involved at their own pace. Visitors are not buttonholed for special attention. The tight communal embrace of traditional small-town churches, which stresses the formation of primary, long-term relationships and loyal participation, gives way to the suburban megachurch's looser-fitting, impersonal structure. They let members decide how much they want to be involved. Members may join a twelve-step program and then a small Bible study group before actually attending a worship service. For example, the 20,000-member Second Baptist Church of Houston, Texas, provides a menu of singles' groups, day-care centers, elementary and secondary schools, and even a health club. Most American congregations are not large enough to implement many of these innovations. But many smaller churches, especially those that are evangelical in orientation, view megachurches as centers of faith in their communities and often attend programs to learn church-growth strategies.

Megachurches reflect the conservative shift in American religion. Most of the largest are evangelical. One survey of mainline Presbyterian churches found that thirty-four of the thirty-nine largest Presbyterian churches were evangelical.[2]

Megachurches have inspired mainline and liturgical churches to add contemporary services to their programs to attract people who would not attend traditional services, and to reemphasize programs for children and adolescents. Yet the attempt by mainline denominations to open model megachurches has met with less success than more independent, home-grown efforts.

After watching their membership decline for a quarter of a century, some mainline Protestant churches are following the lead of their fundamentalist brethren and using computerized demographic studies of their neighborhoods and other sophisticated marketing techniques to fill their pews. In San Francisco, church-growth consultants Richard Southern and Robert Norton won contracts in the 1990s with some of the most theologically liberal mainline congregations in the nation. "Mainline churches don't have to die," said Southern, who left a financial marketing business in Los Angeles to start his church-consulting firm. "Anyone can learn these marketing and outreach techniques. You don't have to change your theology or your political stance." Southern's firm provides a detailed demographic study of a church's neighborhood and suggests ways the church can attract new members—including baby boomers worrying about the religious education of their children or their own midlife crises. Most of the changes that Southern's firm suggests involve "an essential paradigm shift in the way church is done," a shift that puts the needs of potential "customers" before the needs of the institutional church. "Who says church has to be at 11:00 A.M. Sunday?" asked Southern. "Baby boomers think of churches like they think of supermarkets. They want options, choices, convenience. Imagine if Safeway was only open one hour a week, had only one product, and didn't explain it in English."

In addition to finding out how many of the church's neighbors believe in God or embrace "traditional American family values," the study breaks down the local population into such "lifestyle segments" as "struggling multiethnic" or "new-money professional." If a congregation realizes that it has a lot of "rising potential professionals" in the parish, Southern said, it may want to offer free workshops on stress reduction or begin some kind of child-care program for overworked, two-income couples. Other changes might be simply providing free parking, using popular music in worship services, or making sure that visitors are "welcomed but not singled out."

In the free-wheeling economy of the 1990s, churches began marketing and advertising themselves with as much sophistication as corporations launching new products or politicians selling themselves to voters. Percept Group, Inc., a church-marketing firm based in Costa Mesa, California, provides congregations with three-ring binders full of maps, charts, and detailed social, racial, economic, religious, and psychological profiles of their target communities. Survey data tell church planners whether the people in their neighborhoods prefer an "emotionally uplifting" worship style or one that is "intellectually challenging." Public opinion polls tell pastors whether the people in their neighborhood are more concerned with personal and spiritual problems, family problems, or community problems, and what type of media campaign is most likely to reach them.

C. Peter Wagner, a professor of church growth at Fuller Theological Seminary in Pasadena, agrees that mainline churches are putting more emphasis on marketing and church growth. "During the 1970s, the mainline denominations were developing theological justifications for their declining membership. They were attempting to show that this was just a purging of deadwood and were very indifferent about it," said Wagner, who has taught church growth at Fuller since 1975. "In the '80s, once the decline had gone on for 20 or 25 years, they began to get alarmed." Wagner disagrees with Southern's idea that liberal churches can attract a significant number of new members without changing their liberal theology. Citing church growth studies, Wagner said that it has been shown that churches with "a strict conviction that Jesus Christ is the only way are the churches with more growth potential."[3]

Mainline marketing may be working. Denominational statistics from the mid- to late 1990s show a possible flattening of membership declines in mainline churches. Although by no means a reversal of the steep membership losses experienced in the 1960s and 1970s, this evidence may point toward renewed religious commitment in some mainline congregations.

In many ways, Catholic parishes are America's original megachurches. Like their Protestant counterparts, Catholic parishes are often large, multipurpose structures offering a diversity of activities, such as Masses for specific age and ethnic groups and various social and fraternal organizations. The average parish is still eight times larger than the average Protestant congregation. Catholic journalist Tim Unsworth writes that "non-Catholics are attracted to the Roman church by the colorful liturgy, the large, varied community and lung-filling music, while many of their Protestant cradle churches have turned into clubs that are anti-growth. The large, incense-filled Catholic churches offer a certain anonymity that allows both shoppers and seekers to feel comfortable."[4]

Recent research on Catholic parishes in revived urban centers shows how they are changing to meet the demands of religious consumers. Parish memberships were once restricted to geographic neighborhoods, but the new urban parishes are based on choice, drawing members from across a metropolitan area. These parishes have built up strong preaching and music programs to attract newcomers. They offer numerous programs during the weekdays, such as lecture programs and small group discussions to draw those working or living nearby.[5] Other American Catholic churches directly borrow features of the Protestant megachurches. Youth leaders use marketing techniques to attract and welcome unchurched and disaffected young people to special Masses. For example, the ministry of St. Timothy's Church in Mesa, Arizona, parallels those of large, growing Protestant megachurches in the Sunbelt. The parish has grown from 1,500 to 4,500 families in a decade, attracting many through its quality music and 100 active groups—ranging from prayer groups to seminars on unemployment. The parish also has a strong evangelism program that reaches people through advertisements, radio spots, and other marketing techniques. As other megachurches established satellite ministries throughout the country, St. Timothy's founded a liturgical youth ministry program, Life Teen, that now boasts about 300 chapters across the nation. St. Timothy's demonstrates that models of megachurch ministry need not always forsake denominational identity, as the parish emphasizes Catholic teachings and loyalty to the pope.[6]

Meanwhile, many African Americans are returning to traditional black churches, and bringing change with them. As with other baby boomers, these seekers want to provide a faith for their children and find a meaningful support system for themselves. African-American megachurches are growing fast and, like their white counterparts, stress personal spiritual experience. They offer charismatic practices and worship, even in denominations not known for their charismatic focus, such as the African Methodist Episcopal Church. Social concern and political involvement have been hallmarks of the black church, but writer Beverly Lawrence notes that these returnees have introduced a new emphasis on self-help and networking to use the skills of new members to help the church community. These churches also mirror the surrounding culture, adopting Afrocentric worship and customs rather than bringing in a rock band.[7]

In the Conservative branch of Judaism, "magnet" synagogues have been established and marketed to singles, seniors, and other specific target populations. These synagogues feature "user-friendly" worship and liturgy, which draw on both traditional and contemporary sources. Jewish Community Centers, once largely based around secular endeavors such as adult education and recreation, are adding religious programs to their menus. Like Christian seeker services, they provide "nonthreatening entry points" for disaffiliated Jews to move into Jewish life.[8]

Whether Catholic, Protestant, or Jewish, seeker-sensitive congregations tailor their message and practice to the sensibilities of the surrounding culture. The emphasis on choice and being "user-friendly" responds to the consumerism and individualism of the wider society. Megachurches feel familiar to baby boomers who studied in large schools, attended huge rock concerts, and shop in sprawling suburban malls. Some observers say it may be more accurate to speak of the megachurches as "regional churches." Greater geographical and social mobility of Americans forces congregations to focus beyond their immediate neighborhood.[9]

In the new millennium, Americans will develop new kinds of congregations. Churches targeting the smaller generation that followed the baby boomers, Generation X or the "baby busters," are different from the churches of their older siblings and parents. In a way, Generation Xers are just like baby boomers—only more so. The social forces of consumerism and pluralism shaping the lives of baby boomers are even stronger for baby busters. According to recent research, baby busters exhibit an even greater degree of alienation from religious institutions.[10]

In the 1990s, veteran evangelist Billy Graham used the hottest Christian rock bands to fill his Christian crusades with members of Generation X and the next demographic group, the "Millenials," those people born after 1982. Back in the 1950s, when Graham's evangelical machine first got moving, rock and roll was condemned as "the devil's music." Today Graham has no problem attracting teenagers with popular bands like dc talk and Jars of Clay, which fill stadiums with potential young converts. "It's Christian rock in the sense that the lyrics are Christian, and we try to see that the people get copies of the lyrics so they can follow the music. And the lyrics are really Gospel," Graham said in an interview. "We have to think in terms of generations changing—this is called the Generation X by some. Many people are wondering, How can the church appeal to them? How can the church deal with them? They had the same problems we had forty years ago. The problems haven't changed in the hearts of young people; it's just the materialism and the sex and the television and the amusements that have changed, not the individual person. He still suffers from loneliness, he may still suffer from frustration. Most young people today are searching for something. They don't quite know what it is. They want to find something they can hold on to and believe in."[11]

Some Christian leaders have found that Generation Xers focus more on relationships and intimacy in ministry, whereas baby boomers emphasize high-quality performance. Small groups are emphasized in baby-buster ministry. Generation X churches allow young people to engage in social service, through voluntarism and discussion groups. Evangelism is seen as a gradual process rather than a sudden conversion. Baby-buster ministries also emphasize lay leaders, rather than hierarchy or "superstar" leadership. Generation Xers are more likely to see their pastor more as a coach.[12]

Meanwhile, church attendance by returned baby boomers appears to be decreasing. A survey by the Barna Research Group found that for 1996 only three in ten baby boomers had recently attended church. In the years 1991 through 1995, more than four in ten had attended services in a given week. In 1991, half of all boomers had attended church in the past seven days.[13]

Neither baby boomers nor Generation Xers put great importance on denominational loyalty. The idea of attending church to maintain tradition has fallen out of favor. In their research on mainline Presbyterian baby boomers, three sociologists found that younger church members had little attachment to Presbyterian doctrine or identity and showed little commitment to the church.[14]

Sociologist Wade Clark Roof says many baby boomers identify less with theology, more with special church groups devoted to environmentalism, abortion issues, or charismatic Christianity. Church members may have more in common with like-minded believers in other denominations than with those sitting in the next pew. This interplay encourages people to switch from one church or denomination to another. Today, it's not unusual for someone to attend a Quaker meeting while belonging to a small Episcopal church group, or for a Roman Catholic to frequent a Buddhist meditation center. Roof calls it "mixing and matching."[15]

In researching three seeker churches—Calvary Chapel, Hope Chapel, and Vineyard Christian Fellowship—sociologist Donald E. Miller found that many of the values from the 1960s, such as informality and a stress on experience over doctrine, are still present among baby-boomer members. Miller is among many church watchers who see mainline Protestant churches moving to the sidelines. He sees Vineyard, Calvary, and Hope as the new wave of American Protestantism. Miller calls their young, enthusiastic members "post-modern primitives."

"They acknowledge and utilize many aspects of postmodern culture, yet they find in the biblical tradition—in particular, the 'primitive Christianity' of the first century—an underpinning for a radical spirituality that undermines the cynicism and fragmentation of many postmodern theorists," he writes.

According to Miller, these "new paradigm" churches share many characteristics. They were started after the mid-1960s, and most of their members were born after 1945. Seminary training of clergy is optional, and lay leadership is highly valued. They have extensive small-group ministries, and tolerance of different personal styles is prized. Worship is Pentecostal, and Bible-centered teaching predominates over topical sermonizing. Worship takes bodily, rather than merely cognitive, form. "What struck me was that these people were not singing *about* God, they were singing *to* God," Miller writes. "Something seemed to be reaching back to them—or stirring deep within their individual psyches."[16]

Why Strict Churches Grow

For Thomas, a young accountant from Pittsburgh, Christianity is serious business, a life-changing commitment. Tom was not looking for an easy church when he became a member of his fast-growing evangelical congregation. Members practiced a strict form of Christian discipleship known as "shepherding." Each shepherd took a flock of twelve young disciples and marched them down the road to righteousness. Tom's eyes sparkled when he spoke of his shepherd, whom he called "a living example of following Jesus."

"If all the gospel of Jesus Christ is going to do is change my Sunday schedule, then I'm not interested," he said. "I want something that is going to change my finances, my sex life, the way I work, the way I keep my house, and the way I fix my yard."

In the late 1970s and early 1980s, the shepherding movement was one of the quiet controversies within the American evangelical movement. Strident, secretive, and authoritarian, its 100,000 to 250,000 members were organized into a pyramid-shaped church government pointing toward five preachers based in Mobile, Alabama. Spread through secret cells, they planted new churches across the country and infiltrated existing Baptist, Pentecostal, and other evangelical congregations. They became so controversial that even TV evangelist Pat Robertson, the former presidential candidate and founder of the powerful Christian Broadcasting Network, spoke out against the movement, calling it "an unnatural and unscriptural domination of one man by another."

Some of the movement's leaders confessed to authoritarian excesses, others died, and the shepherding movement dropped off the radar screen by the late 1980s. Many of its members, however, went on to become active in the Promise Keepers, the Christian men's movement that received national attention when it filled the National Mall in Washington, D.C. in October 1997 with hundreds of thousands of shouting, praying, repenting Christian men.

Promise Keepers founder Bill McCartney has acknowledged being "discipled" by a shepherding movement leader in the 1970s. Speaking before the sea of Christian men stretching from the Capitol to the Washington Mall, McCartney declared, "Nobody can go home without the same plan. Every man connected to a church, every church connected to each other. We propose that every man returns home and submits to the authority of a local shepherd. You have to say to your pastor, 'How high, how far, how much?'"

This resurgence of religious commitment goes far beyond the evangelical movement. It can be seen in the increasing use of "spiritual directors" and the rising appeal of strict disciplines and practices in the Roman Catholic, Orthodox, and mainline Protestant churches.

Take the case of Simeon, a twenty-seven-year-old teacher with a long beard, glasses, and an intense expression. Simeon lives in a book-lined apartment in lower Manhattan and is active in an Orthodox church in Brooklyn. Like 40 percent of the members of his parish, he is a convert to Eastern Orthodoxy. He was raised as a lukewarm Catholic, but longed for a faith that burned with prayer and passion.

"All the energy I had invested in the church was not of service to anyone," he said. "I was at a point where I could not identify anything that was religious in what I did or how I lived."

In his Orthodox parish, Simeon felt a liturgy that "organically linked private prayer with public prayer. Before when I didn't pray, I would feel guilty. But now when I forget to pray, I am aware of neglecting my soul." Orthodox disciplines of regular fasting, formal prayers, and confession provide the sense that "you're not doing it alone. The people from my own community are doing it, and our devotions become a part of me." In Orthodoxy he found others who valued the practice of common rituals. He found a "place where I could invest my energy and it wouldn't be wasted."

o

In the new millennium, churches that demand the most from their members will be the ones most likely to grow. Although there is nothing new about the intense religious devotion of Thomas and Simeon, there are new ways of understanding this phenomenon in a contemporary American context. And what could be more American than looking at all this through the lens of capitalism and the free market?

As religious groups adopt a consumer approach to ministry, some scholars see market-based dimensions to religious change and growth. This approach suggests that religion is not significantly different from other spheres of human activity. Religion can be understood by rational-choice theory, the idea that people weigh the anticipated costs against the expected benefits of joining a congregation. This theory came into national prominence with the book *The Churching of America* by Rodney Stark and Roger Finke, as well as through the work of economist Laurence Inannaccone. Such theorists argue that the American religion scene is a free market, with providers flourishing or declining depending on how much they expect from their members. Those with rigorous religious practices and strict membership requirements discourage "free riders," people who take advantage of religious benefits such as wedding and funeral services without making a commitment to the congregation. At the same time, they provide rewards, such as generating a sense of belonging and community, not to mention eternal salvation.[17]

These revisionist concepts have produced some criticism among scholars. They point out that many relatively nonstrict megachurches are growing faster than smaller hard-line fundamentalist bodies. Other religious professionals who see their mission in more spiritual terms are uncomfortable viewing their work through an economic framework. "Finke and Stark's world contains no God or religion or spirituality, no issue of truth or beauty or goodness, not faith or hope or love, no justice or mercy; only winning and losing in the churching game matters," writes church historian Martin Marty.[18] But even critics agree that much of American religious life functions as a marketplace driven by competition and choice.[19]

These market-based theories can help explain the growth of conservative evangelical churches and the decline of liberal mainline Protestant congregations. Seeker churches often do not appear strict, as they preach few doctrines and seem to make few demands upon consumers. Yet these congregations offer members several avenues for spiritual growth, including Bible studies and prayer meetings that foster the integration of new members into small groups. Eventually, they are expected to make a strong commitment to the church, and receive the benefits of belonging to a tight evangelical community. As mainline Presbyterians relaxed their traditional observance of the Sabbath and other time-consuming practices, members were deprived of the benefits of belonging to such a religion—the distinctive sense of identity and communal belonging. This sets in motion a continuing pattern of decline. In the same way, religions that establish or reestablish strict practices, such as the evangelical Assemblies of God, have registered sharp growth.

Besides faster growth rates, congregations with a strong identity tend to generate higher levels of giving. In the 1996 book *Money Matters,* researchers found that churches such as the Assemblies of God pressure members to show their devotion to God and church by pledging generously. Mainline churches make fewer demands upon members, which often translates into a more lax approach in supporting a congregation's ministries.[20]

Stark believes that not only will the evangelicals and other religious conservatives come to dominate the religious stage but that some mainline bodies will also shift toward a more conservative position to "become new players in the religious growth market."[21] In November of 1997, for example, the National Conference of Catholic Bishops began considering a proposal that would once again require meatless Fridays for Roman Catholics.

Strict demands on Roman Catholics have long been placed on members of Opus Dei, a tightly organized lay group that has greatly increased its worldwide influence and American presence under the pontificate of John Paul II. Founded in Spain in 1928, Opus Dei requires an unusual amount of devotion and obedience among its lay members, some of whom agree to live a life of celibacy and devote themselves to proselytizing friends and colleagues. Many live a Spartan life of self-sacrifice, including engaging in "mortifications of the flesh" such as self-flagellation. Even those members who marry, or intend to marry, agree to submit to the authority of Opus Dei priests.[22]

These new demands on members are also being seen in some African-American churches and American synagogues. At the 10,000-member Bethel African Methodist Episcopal Church in Baltimore, church leaders took a page from the Nation of Islam and started "Mighty Men of God," a ministry wherein young men are required to follow a strict code of personal behavior. A Conservative Jewish synagogue in Washington, D.C., has attracted young urban professionals emphasizing lay leadership. But at the same time, the synagogue is quite traditional, stressing a "no-nonsense" approach to observance of Jewish law. The rabbi said of the congregants, "The fact that our service is more demanding does not scare them away; on the contrary, that is what they want. Their attitude is, 'If I am going to do this, I might as well really do it.'"[23]

Traditional Congregations and Worship Wars

Sacred soundings from an ancient tongue echo through the sweet incense and marble saints of the Roman Catholic sanctuary as Tara kneels down in prayer: *"Pater noster, qui es in caelis; sanctificetur nomem tuun; adveniat regnum tuun; fiat voluntas tua sicut in caelo et in terra."*

No, this is not Rome, circa 1955, but New York, circa 1995. And this is not a church filled only with aging worshippers or elderly traditionalists resisting the modern liturgical changes of the Second Vatican Council. It is filled by people like Tara, a thirty-year-old dancer from Massachusetts, the child of Unitarian and Congregational parents who rarely took their family to church.

As a young girl, Tara would often visit friends' churches and composed her own prayers and rituals before going to sleep at night. During her college years, however, she became a "basic heathen, dating and partying a lot, using drugs and drinking."

After moving to New York to pursue her dance career, Tara got interested in feminist spirituality, and read books on astrology, the New Age, and alternative religions. Tibetan Buddhism soon caught her attention. "I was always drawn to the purest expression of things, even in dance. I always wanted to find the source of things. Tibetan Buddhism had that purity. The faith was handed down from one generation to the next." She was drawn enough to the faith that she moved into a Tibetan Buddhist center with her boyfriend.

Later, when they married and went to Italy, she was surprised by an "extremely powerful" attraction to the Catholic churches and shrines she visited. Tara started praying the rosary and reading Catholic authors such as Thomas Merton and G. K. Chesterton. "I was beginning to feel more comfortable in Christianity," she says. "It was not as foreign as Buddhism. As hard as I tried, it was hard to escape the familiarity of Christianity."

Back in New York, Tara tried to find a church home for her new faith. She attended several Catholic parishes, but she found herself dissatisfied with the modern music and user-friendly liturgies. Then she came across a Latin Mass recently permitted by her diocese. She finally felt at home and eventually was baptized at the parish. "The music, the art, the liturgy, everything comes together in the Latin Mass," she said. "Something sacred is taking place."

○

As the new millennium unfolds, many young and middle-aged Christians and Jews are returning to traditional congregations and time-tested rituals, proving that the "spiritual supermarket" does not necessarily lead to wild religious experimentation. In the future, divisions may sharpen between congregations favoring more traditional forms of ministry and those promoting contemporary worship.

In a religious marketplace based on choice and eclecticism, one congregation can borrow from traditional sources—Gregorian chants and contemplative prayer—as easily as another can draw from psychotherapy and rock music. The underlying concept of "seeker" congregations is that churches should meet the wider consumer culture on its own ground. Ideas and practices—however strongly they may be tied to one's denominational tradition—may be abandoned if they stand in the way of drawing new members.

Traditionalists counter that members new and old must conform their identities and lifestyles to established practices and teachings even if they disturb modern sensibilities. Innovations in worship, they say, result in the "dumbing down" of believers, producing theologically illiterate congregations.

Lutheran theologian Carl Braaten sums up the traditionalist view: "In America the consumer is always right, and if the consumers want 'Christianity Lite,' then get rid of the vintage traditions. Replace the excess baggage of tradition with the garbage of today's pop culture. We're told we've got to quit being hide-bound to traditional ways of being church. We need to be more user-friendly, to make people feel that the transition from life in the secular world to life in the church is smooth and comfortable. The new pagans cannot understand the meaning of things like pulpits and altars and baptismal fonts or stained glass windows that speak of mysteries not of this world, and whose symbols tell of the strange world of the Bible and its story of salvation."[24]

Signs of doctrinal conflict are evident across the spectrum of American Christianity. In early 1996, evangelicals, mostly from Reformed and Lutheran churches, formed the Alliance of Confessing Evangelicals, a group that sought to return to the theology and confessions of the Protestant Reformation. The new group issued a declaration condemning the "pragmatism and consumerism" of the church growth movement and the contemporary evangelical "dependence upon such modern idols as politics, sociology, marketing, and psychology."

In the Lutheran church, conservatives charge that efforts to replace traditional hymns with contemporary songs from non-Lutheran sources challenges the substance as well as the expression of the faith. Lutheran worship is not only based on its liturgy but also on classical hymns from the past four centuries that teach and elucidate doctrines and themes from the Reformation.

As Tara's story suggests, tomorrow's worship wars will not simply be a battle between young believers in booming megachurches and elderly parishioners holding on to time-worn liturgies. In Part One, we documented how many young and middle-age Jewish and Christian seekers are returning to traditional sources of faith in their personal spirituality. This is also happening in traditional churches and synagogues. There has been an influx of once-secular Jews to Orthodox Judaism; many young professional converts are trading their independent lifestyles for the observant life of the traditional Jewish communities. Conservative and Reform Judaism have re-introduced traditional rituals and practices into their services and observances.

Eastern Orthodoxy and Roman Catholicism have each drawn in new waves of converts in search of traditional faith and practices. In Catholicism this interest can be seen in the growing number of parishes serving the pre-Vatican II Latin Mass, often drawing young people like Tara by its mystery and transcendence. Catholic religious orders for women that stress traditional teachings and wearing full habits have been shown to draw twice as many recruits than more liberal, mainstream orders. New life has been injected into the once-ethnic confines of Eastern Orthodoxy by converts won over by its rich liturgy and spirituality. In some cases, congregations—from independent charismatic to Episcopalian—have converted to Eastern Orthodoxy en masse.

Mainline Protestant denominations, such as the Presbyterian Church (U.S.A.) and the United Methodist Church, have adopted liturgies and observances more in keeping with historic Christianity, such as holding frequent communion services and following the historic church calendar. The nondenominational Center for Evangelical and Catholic Theology, established in 1991 by Lutherans at St. Olaf College, Northfield, Minnesota, has spearheaded attempts to reconcile Roman Catholic and Eastern Orthodox theology and practices with Protestant belief.

There is also a "convergence" movement among evangelicals blending traditional and sacramental Christianity with more contemporary strains of the faith. New denominations such as the Charismatic Episcopal

Church and the Evangelical Episcopal Church have a unique mixture of contemporary evangelical and traditional Anglican elements. The Evangelical Episcopal Church, which quickly grew after its founding in 1995, allows for both contemporary and liturgical services. Between 1992 and 1996, the Charismatic Episcopal Church grew to include about 200 parishes, with two or three churches joining every month. Many of the pastors are Pentecostals who have adopted liturgical practices such as reciting creeds, celebrating weekly communion, and wearing ornate clerical vestments. A typical service may have a procession of robed clerics dispensing a cloud of incense accompanied by a contemporary Christian "praise band." At one moment worshipers make the sign of the cross, at another, they speak in tongues.[25]

There are other examples of this return to the historical sources of one's faith. They can include a Quaker recovering the simplicity of George Fox's founding religious vision, or a Presbyterian rediscovering Calvinist theology. A small but growing movement of African-American Pentecostals is moving from free-form worship to adopt liturgical worship practices. The movement does not signal solely a turn to ancient Catholic tradition among blacks; proponents of the "high-church" movement see their priestly garments as linking them with their African past.

This turn to tradition is often explained as an attempt to find spiritual roots and an anchor of authority in a rapidly changing world. Market-driven, seeker-based innovations may introduce the unaffiliated to congregational life, but they don't always provide the benefits of traditional religions—rituals and wisdom tested by generations of experience. A growing number of evangelicals and charismatics involved in seeker-sensitive and contemporary worship are moving to more tradition-based faiths. Megachurches may have revolving doors, with many seekers arriving and born-again "traditionalists" leaving several years later.

In the new millennium, the paths of tradition and consumerism will converge. Choice and selectivity will play a part in even the most ardent traditionalists' faith. Sociologist Peter Berger argues that the modern person chooses to follow a traditional religion as one option among a whole range of lifestyle choices. Such believers selectively retrieve elements from their tradition that meet social needs and provide personal benefits. For instance, the Latin Mass and Gregorian chant are a specific tradition representing only one period in the history of Catholicism, but they are retrieved because they provide a measure of mystery and transcendence for modern Americans. Since traditional religions operate within today's religious marketplace, they too are thrust into competition for adherents. They must present their faith's teachings in a language and manner that is understandable and attractive, stressing elements of the tradition that are the most relevant to consumers unschooled in Christian basics.

Although it may not please worship warriors in either camp, current trends suggest that congregations will adopt a "both-and" rather than an "either-or" stance when it comes to seeker services and traditional worship. Most congregations will not limit themselves exclusively to seekers or traditionalists. They will attempt to keep a grasp on their identities amidst the flux of the religious free market, without losing touch with the seekers to whom they are called to minister. Catholic "megaparishes," Jewish magnet synagogues for niche markets, the Charismatic Episcopal Church, and myriad other hybrids may be tomorrow's models for this meeting of traditional religion and consumer spirituality.

Grounding Spirituality in Congregations

It was an eight-day spiritual vacation run by Roman Catholic nuns and Roman Catholic priests, convened at a Roman Catholic convent in California. Fifty-two participants, most of them Roman Catholic, signed up for the mostly silent "holistic retreat." At times, however, it was hard to find the Catholicism at this Roman Catholic event. Retreatants spent their days in sessions of Zen meditation, body work, guided imagery, dream workshops, yoga, prayer, and worship. There was time for swimming, jogging, and walking along the oak-lined trails that traverse these forty acres of land owned by a Roman Catholic religious order.

"Our retreats are not exclusively Catholic, like they used to be," said Father Harry, a Roman Catholic priest who studied for six years under a Zen master in Japan. "We still have preached retreats, but the accent now is not so much on dogma but on experience. It used to be highly mental—but now we use imagination, body movement, chanting."

East meets West in the convent's basement, which houses a traditional Japanese Zendo, a meditation room where a painting of Buddha shares the same wall with a large cross. There's a small Zen rock garden in one corner, a large open Bible in the other.

Retreatants are assigned a personal spiritual director—a priest, nun, or lay person—with whom they meet every other day for counseling and guidance.

"This week has given me the opportunity to heal some past hurts and wounds and reflect on my life," said Laureen, a sixty-five-year-old woman who raised a family of thirteen children and now lives alone with her husband. "For many years, my vocation was to raise a large family. Now it's taking another direction."

Dolores, a forty-seven-year-old housewife, was at the retreat to take a break from her busy life taking care of two teenage sons. "This gives me the time and space for discovering who I am," she said. "There's so much useless stimulation in the outside world. I need to have some quiet and privacy—some time when I don't have to cook or drive anyone anywhere. It's important for your mental health and well-being to remove yourself from your ordinary circumstances. I find I can listen to God better that way."

o

In the new millennium, even traditional institutions like Roman Catholic convents will bend to the dictates of consumerism and the plethora of spiritualities in the wider culture. At the same time, the most esoteric of spiritualities will find institutional expression.

Gnosticism, paganism, and "green" spirituality have all established organizations in which followers can meet, compare notes, and draw sustenance from fellow practitioners. Proponents of diffuse New Age teachings find the structures and discipline of community life valuable in helping to pass on the faith to future generations. But the wide appeal of a particular tradition's spiritual teachings does not guarantee it will flourish in an institutional form.

For instance, as discussed earlier, Buddhism as a personal spirituality may flourish at the expense of the growth and stability of Buddhism as an organized religion. People may learn how to meditate at their local Zen Center but not join the organization or pass this religious practice on to their children. Jan Nattier writes that Buddhism must move from being a private "religious preference" to being grounded in the "everyday practice of families and larger social networks to find a stable future."[26]

Many mainstream congregations will struggle with the new marketplace of religion. Clashes between spirituality and religious faith are nothing new, but the growth of noninstitutional spirituality shows that congregations are failing to help people come to a knowledge of God— or it could mean that people are searching for cosmic affirmation rather than personal salvation. "We are merely searching for assurances that the way of life we are already living is pretty much OK," writes author Craig Dystra. "We are not seeking anything like the radical care for others and obedience to God that marks authentic religious community."[27]

There is a complex interplay between congregations and the spiritual marketplace. It's unlikely that the Southern Baptist Convention will allow veneration of Elvis anytime soon, but individual Baptist believers will still pray at the altar of "The King." Though the Roman Catholic hierarchy not will overturn its condemnations of Gnosticism, those esoteric teachings will continue to seep into Catholic church programs and retreat workshops.

New spiritual currents find their way into a variety of religious institutions, thereby demonstrating the eclectic nature of American religion. There is a growth of inner spirituality—from mystical Judaism to contemplative meditation—in religious groups that previously showed little interest in such practices. Yet spiritualities that appear very exotic when encountered in a bookstore become domesticated when filtered into congregational life. Congregations tailor the messages and practices of other spiritualities to fit their own vision and sensibility. To do otherwise and import spiritual teachings and techniques directly from other traditions—be it Buddhist meditation, Sufi dancing, or goddess spirituality—may in the long run be more baffling than beneficial to congregants.

This process of incorporating spiritualities from outside one's tradition is evident in the growing number of Catholic groups using the enneagram, a technique that identifies personality types to foster spiritual and personal growth. The enneagram was originally designed by Oscar Ichazo as a mystical system that he says was not very Catholic at all. Catholics deemphasize the system's emphasis on sexuality and humanity's potential for divinity.

United Church of Christ (UCC) congregations have been in the forefront of introducing spirituality techniques and disciplines to mainline Protestantism. These innovations include the use of "spiritual directors," advisers who guide congregation members in spiritual growth—a practice that has long been associated with Catholic monasteries, not white-steepled Congregational churches. The UCC and other mainline churches have also adopted the practice of "journaling," or keeping spiritual diaries, from the human potential movement. UCC literature attempts to link such practices to its Puritan spiritual heritage, noting that Puritan divines and ordinary members regularly chronicled their spiritual development in diaries.

Spiritual direction may not be so traditional when it blends with the self-help movement and psychotherapeutic concepts and practices. This overlap between spiritual direction and psychotherapy has led to a debate about the boundaries and differences between these two fields. Confusion may arise, for example, when spiritual mentoring becomes a business relationship between client and therapist. Topics that come up in sessions of spiritual direction include divorce, death of family members, addiction, loss of faith, religious conversion, or confusion about the meaning and direction of life. "It can be very similar to what a therapist does, but we are always focusing on the movement of God in your life," said Pam

Sullivan, the founder of La Casa de la Luz, a personal growth center in Northern California that trains spiritual directors.

Many spiritual directors have begun to charge fixed fees for their services. Traditionally, those seeking spiritual direction might make a contribution to the church. But today, many clergy and lay people are offering their services outside the institutional church and expect to be paid for it. Some long-time spiritual directors are distressed by this trend. "It's not that kind of relationship," said the Reverend Alan Jones, dean of Grace Cathedral in San Francisco and the author of a book on spiritual direction.[28] "Why does every American transaction have to revolve around money? Much of what is called 'spiritual direction' today is overpsychologized and very trendy." Jones said the blending of psychology and religion ignores essential differences between the realms of the psyche and the spirit. "Psychotherapy is about ego-forming and ego-coping. Spiritual direction is about ego-surrendering," he said. "Psychotherapy can help you fix your leg, but it doesn't tell you where to walk."[29]

Another traditional spiritual practice finding new applications is keeping the Sabbath. The traditional observance of the Sabbath in Jewish and Christian traditions was driven by the weight of law and custom. The interest in the Sabbath today is driven more by the modern concern to convey a sense of spirituality and well-being for the overworked. Today, there is a growing movement toward stricter Sabbath observance among mainline Protestants through revived organizations such as the Lord's Day Alliance. Dorothy Bass writes that Sabbath observance helps set limits on materialism and other activities that deplete the earth's resources. Bass adds that the pattern of rest created by the Sabbath seeks to convince believers of all kinds that their fulfillment comes through a spiritual life rather than one based on material acquisition and frenetic activity.[30]

Borrowing spiritual practices from other faiths can unearth neglected elements in one's own tradition. When Catholic nuns started offering massage therapy and the anointing with oil to patients, they undoubtedly borrowed much of these practices from holistic health. Yet these sisters' new ministry of caring for the body as well as the soul also gave them a new way of expressing the Catholic teaching of the sacredness of the bodily and physical world.[31]

Among all the different spiritual teachings and techniques in religious congregations, healing is likely to be one of the most important ones in the future. John Koenig writes that there will be a new convergence between belief and contemporary medicine, bringing congregations into closer interaction with medical professionals. Koenig adds that congregations are likely to become involved in promoting healthy behavior, particularly as their members age. The new presence of "parish nurses" in thousands of congregations also points to this trend. The emphasis on healing and health will be especially evident in small groups and special healing services. Such services involve intercessory prayer and various kinds of touching or anointing, often including, in the Christian context, an emphasis on the Eucharist, or among charismatics, the gifts of the spirit.[32]

These forecasts can be applied to other faiths. Events sponsored by Harvard Medical School have explored the relationship between spirituality and health among Muslim, Jewish, Hindu, Christian, Buddhist, and other religious traditions. At a 1995 conference in Boston, Harvey Cox of Harvard Divinity School saw strong connections between Pentecostal teachings on the healing energy of the Holy Spirit and traditional Chinese healing methods. Congregations and individual believers who dig deep into their respective traditions find striking commonalities with the spiritual sources of other faiths. A synagogue seeking to make connections with the interest in inner-spirituality will find much common ground between its traditions of Jewish mysticism and the Kabbalah and Buddhist or New Age teachings.

In the new millennium, this growing religious pluralism will bring organized and unorganized spiritual groups into closer proximity, inspiring even more borrowing and eclecticism. Yet the growth of religious pluralism could paradoxically encourage a re-connection with one's particular tradition. Congregations and faith traditions may seek to recapture their own identity when the "competition" forces them to realize they cannot be all things to all seekers. In other words, why should seekers attend a United Methodist congregation for its use of Buddhist meditation practices when they can find the real thing at the new Zen center across town?

Many congregations will find it hard to embrace seemingly contradictory religious beliefs. How far can congregations go without losing the religious identity that drew their members in the first place? There is little evidence that congregations built upon the "mixing and matching" of spiritualities can experience stable growth. Religion historian Robert Ellwood writes that the dynamics of religious history "strongly mitigate against this sort of syncretism." "Historically we find that when current religion fails to meet current needs, the upshot is inevitably new revelation and new intensive religious movements, most often within an existing faith, not contrived syncretism on a large scale."[33]

5

CONGREGATIONS ON THE CUTTING EDGE

Small Group Revival

Phillip and six other young adults meet in the basement of a New Jersey church for their weekly Bible study session. They are supposed to be discussing the Gospel According to St. Matthew this evening, but the conversation soon veers toward more personal subjects, like family difficulties, work problems, and Phillip's hearing disability.

"Why am I deaf? What does God have against me?" asks Phillip, the anger and frustration rising in his voice.

Gus, a relative newcomer to the group, turns to him. "I don't know, Phillip," he says. "I have no idea why you're deaf, but you can't blame God."

It may not have been the answer Phil was looking for that night, but at least his small group offered a place to ask those tough, personal questions—something that could not be voiced upstairs on Sunday in the reverent setting of the church sanctuary.

Across the country, in the California coastal community of Santa Cruz, Daniel and six other men meet at his house every Monday night, but not to watch Monday Night Football. They light a candle, burn some sage, read poems they have written. "It's not as hokey as it sounds," he says. "We try to bring in some kind of ritual element to open the door to the sacred, and get into things bigger than our own personal problems."

They work jobs as diverse as cabinet maker, school counselor, and stereo salesman. They range in age from thirty-three to eighty. They take turns leading the group. Since they began meeting, two men have left, and two have joined them. Two have battled cancer, and two have gone through divorce.

In addition to providing a sense of the sacred, Daniel says, their group offers an alternative to expensive sessions with a private psychotherapist. "That's not to say it has been easy keeping it going. We have to push ourselves to get beyond surface talk."

Laurie and her small group gather every Wednesday night in a quiet room at the First Congregational Church north of San Francisco. They arrange the chairs in a circle. They light a candle. Laurie opens a thick blue book and begins reading from Lesson 78. "Let miracles replace all grievances," she says.

Her gathering is among thousands of small groups that regularly meet at churches and private homes to discuss *A Course in Miracles,* a three-volume metaphysical text that combines Biblical references, spiritualism, and self-help psychotherapy.

Its author, the late Helen Schucman, a Columbia University psychologist, began writing the text down in 1965, claiming that a mysterious voice was dictating its message to her. Over the last twenty years, the book has been popularized by New Age inspirational writers such as Jerry Jampolsky, Roger Walsh, Frances Vaughan, and Marianne Williamson.

Laurie says the course and her weekly "Miracles" group has become a central part of her life. "As soon as I get up in the morning, I try to read a lesson so that I'll retain it consciously," she said. "I've noticed myself being more conscious and having fewer knee-jerk reactions."

Debra, a Catholic and feminist theologian in Washington, D.C., gathers every other Sunday evening with a small group of women. Each meeting begins with a potluck dinner, and features a home-grown liturgy of prayers, songs, discussion, and the sharing of bread and wine. "Whoever hosts the meeting creates the liturgy," she says. "We have a real cross-section— married Catholic women, lesbians, women religious."

Alienated by the Roman Catholic Church's refusal to ordain women, Debra and her circle of friends have taken church into their own hands. "We are Catholic women with more degrees than most of the bishops have," says Debra, who holds master's degrees in divinity and sacred theology from a leading Catholic seminary. "Liturgical structures on Sunday morning are not working. People are turning to groups where they can speak their own spirituality out loud and be supported in that."

Small groups are especially popular for those belonging to evangelical megachurches and large, hierarchical organizations like the Roman Catholic Church, partly as a way around the impersonal feeling in many large parishes and congregations.

"Stuff can happen in a living room that can't happen in the cathedral," said the Reverend Miles Riley, a Catholic priest and communications

consultant who works with bishops and church leaders across the country and around the world. Riley says the U.S. Catholic Church is lagging
behind Latin America and many Third World nations in the development
of small "Christian base communities."

"Everywhere else in the world, the church is organized in small Christian communities," he said. "Their model [is] the twelve apostles gathering
around the Lord, a group small enough to be in the same boat—because
we all *are* in the same boat."[1]

---------- o ----------

**The emergence of the small group movement will be more than a
passing trend because these gatherings are at the fulcrum of forces
affecting religion and society in the United States.**

Small groups address very large social issues—the search for intimacy
and community, the decentralization of church leadership, and the rising
role of women and the laity in religious life. They provide safe havens to
groups interested in spiritual growth, healing, self-help, and psychotherapy.

Gallup reports that four American adults in ten meet in small religious
groups.[2] In another study, sociologist Robert Wuthnow found that small
groups often focus on support and discussion of "secular" issues such as
addictions, relationships, and parenting, even though they often meet in
churches, synagogues, and other religious facilities. Not surprisingly, a
large percentage of these groups also revolve around Bible study, prayer,
and Sunday school.[3]

Many Catholic small groups are much more than Bible study or prayer
groups; they are taking on parish functions such as celebrating baptisms,
communion, and confirmations. Within the New Age movement, "ceremonial circles" have emerged in which the emphasis on community and
group spirituality is seen as an alternative to the guru-disciple relationships in many new religious movements. Among American Hindus, small
groups have emerged in private homes. These groups often involve worship, discussions on a wide range of subjects, and fellowship. Sociologist
Prima Kurien found that these groups meet needs in the American Hindu
community that are not addressed in temple ceremonies. Indian parents
fear that their children are losing the faith as they assimilate. At the same
time, many adults and older immigrants have more leisure time for religious and cultural activities.[4]

Cell-group churches—congregations that are made up of small groups
with few or no larger gatherings of members—are also growing.
Although these churches have been hailed as the wave of the future, they
appear to work best in urban areas and in already-growing churches. In
studying cell churches around the world, researcher Mikel Neumann

found that they appeal to people with high levels of education and socio-economic standing. Adopting a cell structure "turbocharges" growth that is already taking place in a congregation by eliminating direct dependence on a charismatic pastor and transferring it to dynamic gatherings of believers.[5]

Another reason these small congregations will grow in the future has as much to do with city planning as group dynamics. Increasing calls for tighter zoning laws in suburban and urban communities, often discouraging congregations from building and expanding their churches, will also encourage the growth of cell congregations in the new millennium.

Small groups are in the vanguard of American religion because they disperse leadership throughout the congregation, rather than contain it within the office of pastor, priest, or rabbi. Small groups help people find community in a society where ties of neighborhood, family, and church are frayed. Wuthnow's study shows that small groups restore the link between spirituality and community, correcting the tendency for modern spirituality to become so internalized that it has little connection with other people or the outside world.

At the same time, the kind of community life that small groups generate differs from forms of belonging found in traditional religious congregations. A fine balance between individuality and community is sought among small-group participants, encouraging a process of give and take whereby one can openly express disagreement. This "spiritual individualism" is not encouraged in most traditional congregational settings, where the laity sits quietly and listens to the clergy's sermon. The range of choices provided by congregations using small groups provides another way for consumerism and individualism to coexist with community and intimacy. Participants pick a group that best meets their needs, and can quickly move on to another group if they become bored or dissatisfied.

Gallup found that small groups do not necessarily compete with regular religious services and congregations, and may actually complement them. For example, a higher than average participation in small prayer groups was found among church members and recent church attenders.[6] Perhaps the main difference between small-group religion and traditional congregations is that small groups, by their very nature, are based more on experience and relationships than on doctrine and theology. Participants share their spiritual struggles and attempts to relate religious teachings to their personal lives. But small groups can be based around conservative beliefs as much as liberal and noninstitutional spirituality. In fact, Wuthnow finds conservative beliefs reinforced to a greater extent than liberal ones in small groups.

Though there is often an effort to bring small groups in line with denominational tradition, small groups make their own imprint on institutional religion. Wuthnow writes that small groups tend to orient their members "toward thinking of spirituality less in terms of ecclesiastical tradition, less in terms of theological knowledge, and more in terms of practical experience. Small groups may encourage members to regard biblical wisdom as truth only if it helps them in daily life. Groups generate a do-it-yourself religion, a God who makes life easier, a programmed form of spirituality that robs the sacred of its awe-inspiring mystery and depth."[7]

How congregations relate to the dynamism of small groups will be a central question in the new millennium. Although religious leaders look to small groups to revitalize their institutions, they often find it difficult to control them once they get off the ground.

Those meeting outside of church facilities, such as the Catholic feminists who gather in Debra's home in Washington, D.C., need not answer to the institutional church. But what about the small group that meets with Laurie at the First Congregational Church? Should Christian churches allow groups to discuss *A Course in Miracles*, which purports to be a new revelation from God? Should they ban nonofficial teachings in small groups, or use them as a way to bring nominal Christians into the fold? Small groups connected to larger congregations have more social influence in their communities than independent ones, such as self-help groups.

In the 1990s, the explosion of self-help "recovery" groups meeting in church basements got the attention of pastors across the nation, many of whom were shocked to discover that there were more people meeting in their church basement on weekday nights than in their sanctuary on Sunday morning.

Consider the scene at a suburban Lutheran church in the San Francisco Bay Area. Six nights a week, this church provides space for six different "twelve-step" recovery groups—from a Sex and Love Addicts Anonymous meeting Tuesday evening to an Alcoholics Anonymous gathering Friday night. Although only eighty Lutheran parishioners attend services on a typical Sunday, some 200 people in various recovery groups fill the Lutheran parish hall during the week. "It's happening in most of the churches in our county," the pastor explained. "It freaks out our members. They're asking, 'What are we doing wrong?'"

Not surprisingly, church leaders are visiting their own basements and parish halls to see what they can learn from the practical, down-to-earth spirituality of the fast-growing twelve-step movement. Twelve-step spirituality is based on a technique devised in 1935 by an Ohio surgeon and a former New York stockbroker, two alcoholics who had spiritual awakenings in the midst of drunkenness and despair. Sometimes called "the secret church," Alcoholics Anonymous (AA) has steadily grown into a North American fellowship of more than a million men and women who admit they are powerless over alcohol and agree to put their trust in a "power greater than ourselves." AA members work to overcome addiction and rekindle a sense of the sacred through support groups and the twelve steps, which include taking "a fearless inventory" of themselves, making amends to those they have harmed, and improving their "conscious contact with God." In recent years, about 200 other groups—from Incest Survivors Anonymous to Cocaine Anonymous—have adopted the AA model of regular meetings as a way to free their members of compulsive behavior. Nationally, estimates of the number of Americans in the entire recovery movement range from two million to twenty million, depending on who does the counting and how the movement is defined.

The Reverend Richard Rohr, a Franciscan priest and founder of the Center for Action and Contemplation in Albuquerque, New Mexico, says the movement is a lesson for church leaders. "In the institutional church, we are preoccupied with denominational differences, belief systems, and doctrinal statements. But the spirituality of the twelve steps comes out of people's actual experience," he said. "I believe the twelve steps will go down in history as the significant authentic American contribution to the history of spirituality."

Mary, a former Roman Catholic nun who now runs a counseling center for people in recovery, agrees. Several years ago, at age forty-two, she found herself hitting bottom as "an unemployed alcoholic nun with two master's degrees."

"You can know a lot about religion and not much about spirituality," she said. "It was AA that showed me why spiritual practices are important. I put religious clothes on to cover up how I felt. I was trained to be a spiritual director, but it's only now that I really feel like one. If Jesus came today, I think he'd be more comfortable in a twelve-step meeting than in most churches."

Sylvia, program coordinator of a San Francisco outreach program, is doing similar work in the Jewish community. Despite a commitment to nonsectarianism, many AA groups have a distinct Christian flavor. Sylvia helps Jews see that there is no conflict between Judaism and the twelve steps. "People in recovery are searching for meaning," she said. "Despite our material wealth, we still have this inner need. We have a God-shaped hole in our soul, and we try to fill it with drugs, alcohol, or other things."

"Mainline churches have been slow to respond," said Frank Riessman, director of the National Self-Help Clearinghouse in New York. "The self-help movement has taken over the role of building up families and communities. They have become the new neighborhood."

Not everyone is applauding this new neighborhood. James Hillman, a leading psychologist and social critic, sees the explosion as part of a troubling trend—the "psychologizing of America."

"You used to belong to a real community, go to ward meetings, and fight over political issues, over neighborhood issues," he said. "Now our emotional loyalties are tied to other fat people, or other alcoholics. It's selfish. It's drawn a tremendous energy away from other causes, away from politics and ecology. They have drawn citizens into thinking of themselves as patients, rather than citizens."[8]

To which Riessman replies: "You can cry about them, but the old institutions are not there, and you won't get them back. A new kind of community is being built."

Power to the People in the Pews

Times have certainly changed for Father Jack, an aging Roman Catholic priest with a big-city parish.

"In the old days, the pope wrote a letter to the bishops, the bishops wrote a letter to the priests, and the parish got the word in church," he recalls. "There was a lot of safety in that, a lot of security. We had this certainty about our faith. After all, we were the only ones who had the one true church."

Raised in Portland, Oregon, by Irish-American parents, Jack decided to become a priest when he was eight years old. Both his parents died before he reached adulthood, and he always remembered something his mother told him before she died. "Jack," she told him, "I'd do nothing in the world to make you become a priest, but if you became a priest, I'd be the happiest mother in the world."

Sitting in the rectory of St. Paul's parish, the gray-haired priest said he had no idea of the changes that were to come when he took his final vows after World War II. At that time, the pastor ran the parish, no questions asked, and the people in the pews passively obeyed—or at least they pretended to obey. "When I was ordained in 1948, I saw the priesthood very differently than I do today. We dispensed things—the sacraments—to the people. It was clear-cut, very definite. And I assumed I'd be doing that for the rest of my life."

What changed Jack's life, and the lives of millions of American Catholics, were the sweeping church reforms of the Second Vatican Council, held in Rome between 1962 and 1965. Vatican II redefined the church as "the people of God," and the people in the pews began to assert themselves as parish leaders and decision makers. Jack, still a young priest during the council, was all for the changes. "We had some pastors back then who were real tyrants," he recalled. "There was no collegiality, no sharing, no participation in decision making. They were masters of all they surveyed."

Today, echoes of Vatican II are still heard at St. Paul's, a middle-class parish with 2,200 members. There are a parish council and numerous committees to help run programs and make decisions. Around 160 lay ministers have been trained to help distribute Communion, prepare young people for the responsibilities of marriage, explain the meaning of baptism to young parents, and help grieving families.

"Before, the priests did all that," Jack said. "My basic message today is that all of the people in the parish are called to some basic ministry. Part of my job is to find their abilities and talents."

o

While the Roman Catholic Church may be the clearest example, the rising power of the people of the pews has been felt across the American religious landscape. **This decentralization of power away from clergy and into the hands of laypeople will have an impact both inside and outside congregations well into the new millennium.**

As we noted earlier in this chapter, the growth of small groups is closely associated with the rise of the laity. This trend also dovetails with the increasing consumer mentality in American ministry. Offering multifaceted services through large congregations requires the delegation of authority from pastor to parishioners.

Congregational consultant Alan Nelson sees this shift as part of a broader revolution in postindustrial culture. Computers and information technology utilize networks and relationships over autocratic leadership. Meanwhile, the entrance of women into church leadership softens management styles, stressing relationships and feelings over obedience and authority. Rising education levels in postwar generations also create a demand for greater participation and shared decision making. Ideas about clergy as authoritarian leader and CEO are fading away, Nelson says, replaced by "a kinder, gentler leader much more representative of a servant leader." Ironically, he notes, churches with clear models for "servant leadership" in their tradition and scripture often lag behind many secular organizations in adopting these new leadership styles.[9]

Congregation specialist Lyle Schaller forecasts that in the next two decades the ministry of the laity will be the norm rather than the exception.

He finds that a new breed of "house churches" are characterized by a high degree of lay involvement. All church functions in these congregations—teaching, worship, fellowship, and outreach—are conducted by laypeople. In more traditional congregations, Schaller sees a future in which paid staff run the church and lay volunteers are engaged in a wide range of ministries. This would bring a number of changes to church structures. The role of the clergy and program staff will shift from conducting and micromanaging ministry to "challenging, enlisting, training, placing, nurturing, and supporting volunteers who do the ministry."

For example, the old model of church leadership called for clergy to make most hospital visits, whereas the new model has nearly all hospital calls made by trained volunteers who build on their own life experience. This life-training model can apply to a whole range of ministries. Counseling of married couples would shift from being mainly the province of the pastor to trained volunteer couples. This couple may have contemplated divorce, found a way of rescuing their marriage, and so more effectively counsel a couple in similar straits. Sunday services would also be transformed. While the pastor led the liturgy under the old model, the laity-empowered church calls on a team of trained volunteers, assisted by paid staff members, to lead worship.[10]

In the new millennium, these changes will be more widespread than one might imagine. There is increasing interest in lay ministry not only in evangelical environments, but in mainline Protestant and Anglican churches with a "high" view of the ministry. Episcopal writers Richard Kew and Roger White find that until recently, the model of ministry has been to "allow the laity to pick up the odds and ends of ministry that the ordained do not want; in tomorrow's world, we court disaster if we continue this pattern rather than enabling lay men and women to be full participants in the whole ministry of the church."[11]

As we learned from Father Jack, the Second Vatican Council sparked an explosion of lay ministry in the Roman Catholic Church. Although the conservative ideas of Pope John Paul II have dampened some of that fervor, the continuing shortage of priests in the Catholic church gives Rome little choice but to give more power to the laity. It has also created a whole new order of ordained ministers in the Roman church—married male deacons who perform many functions once reserved for celibate priests.

Consider the vocation of Deacon Bill, an ordained Roman Catholic deacon in the Diocese of Oakland, California. Happily married and the father of six children, Bill has gotten used to the members of his 2,000-family suburban parish calling him "Father."

As one of dozens of deacons in the diocese, Bill can perform baptisms, witness marriages, deliver Sunday sermons, preside at funerals, and assist the parish priest in a range of liturgical duties. "At a baptism, I explain to people that I'm a deacon, I'm married, and we wear our stoles across our arms," said Bill, who is retired and volunteers around thirty hours a week to the church. "People accept it pretty well."

Across the bay in San Francisco, the archdiocese has embarked on an ambitious plan to train laypeople to serve the church. Launched in 1994, more than 1,000 Catholics have graduated from the archdiocese's School of Pastoral Leadership in its first two years of operation. Father David Pettingill, the program's director, said this type of Catholic education encompasses the daily experience of people's lives, not just learning the catechism of the Catholic church. "People realize how very much a part of church they are when they hear the church described in its new way since the Second Vatican Council," he said. "Eyes have been opened to the fact that the church has something wonderful to proclaim and the style of proclamation need not be tied down to a previous century. It's not something you memorize and read out of a book at people. It is something that you first experience and then describe."[12]

Despite Pope John Paul's refusal to consider the ordination of women, the increasing presence of married deacons and lay men and women in liturgical roles is changing American Catholic ideas about ministry. "In time the laity may not even care to observe the distinction between the new Christ-bearers and ordained priests, despite the Vatican's 'infallible' teaching that the former are forever excluded from the ranks of the latter," writes Catholic historian R. Scott Appleby.[13]

As Catholic parishes grow larger and more diverse, many are seeking an equally diverse leadership team, not just a small group of celibate male priests. For instance, the Pax Cristi Catholic Community in Minneapolis, a pioneer in lay preaching, calls for its preaching team to be gender balanced.[14]

This move toward greater involvement of the laity can also be seen in Judaism, especially in renewal movements that stress more egalitarian leadership. "Many people feel the synagogues they grew up in were spiritually deadening," said Rabbi Michael Lerner, a former antiwar activist and editor of *Tikkun* magazine. "There was too much materialism, too much focus on money and power, too much sexism, too much homophobia, and too much of a requirement for blind allegiance to Israel."

Lerner, who attracted national media attention when first lady Hillary Rodham Clinton borrowed one of Lerner's slogans, "the politics of meaning," started a synagogue in San Francisco in 1996, trying to blend social activism and spiritual growth. "People are legitimately estranged from their Judaism," he said. "I want to create a synagogue where whatever is said is spiritually real and alive."[15]

American Buddhist groups have also sought a renewal that empowers the laity. The translation of Buddhism from the East to West has introduced lay leaders where there were once only priests and monks in leadership. In the 1980s and 1990s, a series of scandals over authoritarian leadership and sexual improprieties at the San Francisco Zen Center in California, the Naropa Institute in Colorado, and other well-known Buddhist centers prompted a reexamination of guru-disciple models imported from Asia. Some centers began electing leaders, or instituting other democratic reforms. "We are trying very hard to find an American Buddhism, without throwing away the Buddhism we already have," one leader explained.

Empowerment of the laity is also a major factor behind the phenomenal growth of the Church of Jesus Christ of Latter-day Saints. In the five decades since World War II, Mormon membership has doubled every fifteen years, thanks to a tireless force of 50,000 young missionaries proselytizing at home and abroad.

Back in 1980, when there were 4.6 million Mormons in the world, Professor Rodney Stark predicted that there would be 265 million of them by the year 2080. His colleagues laughed at him. Eighteen years later, the Mormons are approaching the ten million mark and moving ahead of his projections. "The big thing to remember is what happens with exponential growth," said Stark, a non-Mormon sociologist of religion at the University of Washington. "You double a thousand, and it's only 2,000. But once the numbers get big, they start to get gigantic. The same thing happened with the early Christian church."

Those inside the Mormon church say a major reason for the dedication of Latter-day Saints and their rapid growth is that the church has no paid clergy. Mormon missionaries—or their parents—actually pay the expenses of their two years of proselytizing. In addition to regular tithing, all active Mormons volunteer countless hours to run their church and help other Mormons in need, creating a strong sense of community and a feeling that they *are* the church.

"Mormonism is not just a belief system," said Jan Shipps, a professor of history and religious studies at the University of Indianapolis and a leading non-Mormon authority on the Latter-day Saints. "It provides an entire structure for life."[16]

Some observers believe that the lay revolution may carry some unintended consequences for congregational life. Historian Eugene McCarraher asserts that just as the pre-Vatican II Catholic church in the United States may have been influenced by the blue-collar class and clericalism, the new lay influence in parishes has introduced a managerial, corporate mind-set into American Catholicism. As American Catholics have become well educated and have gained employment in the upper levels of the American workplace, laypeople have brought their professional expertise into parish council meetings and other ministries. McCarraher asks whether modern corporate values such as diversity, inclusiveness, and openness might foster what he calls a "Starbucks Catholicism," where a sense of tradition and history would be eclipsed by modern techniques.[17]

Across the American religious spectrum, the empowerment of the laity goes far beyond the walls of individual churches, temples, and other congregations. Laypeople now ascend to the highest positions in religious denominations, to leadership positions once reserved for people with "Rev." in front of their names. In the last three decades, when clergy and denominational leaders have issued statements and declarations on social and political matters, they have tended to minimize the role of the laity in formulating and thinking through such matters. Even when laity were given input into decision making on social issues, such as involving the economy, statements were still issued through the office of bishops or denominational executives, thus giving the impression that religious leaders had a special wisdom on both spiritual and worldly matters.

On both the local and national level, lay leaders are bringing American religion out of sanctuaries and into society. In the future, lay ministry will focus as much on what happens during the weekdays as during Saturday or Sunday worship. Unlike the clergy, laypeople have no other choice but to spend most of their time outside of congregations. Much of that time is spent in the workplace, where, as we saw in Part One, there are increasing efforts to integrate spirituality and the world of work. Whether congregations can equip their members to bring their faith to bear on their work and to view their occupations as a form of ministry is another question.

That is exactly what took place at Colchester Federated Church in Connecticut, where alongside the traditional cross at the altar are law books, computer parts, tax forms, and football helmets. Each week the congregation highlights a specific occupation or activity. A church committee interviews members about their work and helps the pastor compose prayers for them as they stand in their places at Sunday worship. This all came about after the congregation decided it was sending "contradictory messages" about taking their faith into the world. "Preaching, worship, and programs effectively communicated the biblical mandate to go out and do ministry," the pastor explained, "but the church only encouraged members to serve the institutional church." In 1993, the congregation reorganized around eight "ministries" that members could take part in: workplace, community, home and family, stewardship, gifts and leadership, mission and witness, education, and church life. The sixteen people who are the chair and vice chair of each ministry automatically join the congregation's board of deacons.[18]

Protestant evangelicals form "guilds" geared to specific professions, such as lawyers and doctors. The Strategic Careers Coalition of Colorado Springs helps professional Christians enter the marketplace and infuse it with Christian ideals. Although critics of the religious right view this as an attempt to infiltrate secular institutions, these "marketplace Christians" do not see their work as political but as an attempt to integrate their faith, values, and vocations.[19]

Encouraging and equipping the laity was traditionally thought of as a Protestant innovation, stemming from the teachings of Martin Luther and John Calvin about the religious vocation of all Christians as they work in the world. But other traditions are inspiring members to integrate their faith and work. For instance, Catholic parishes, both independently and through umbrella groups such as the National Center for Laity, have formed small groups to reflect on their occupations.

Women and the Changing Face of Ministry

Cheryl Kirk-Duggan sang her first church solo at age four in a black Methodist church in Louisiana. She was educated at a Presbyterian seminary in Texas, and earned her Ph.D. at a Baptist university.

Installed in 1997 as director of the Center for Women and Religion at the Graduate Theological Union in Berkeley, a consortium of nine Protestant and Roman Catholic seminaries, Kirk-Duggan leaned back and smiled when asked to give an impromptu sermon on women and the resurrection.

"Isn't it interesting," she said, "that if you look at all four Gospel accounts—Matthew, Mark, Luke, and John—men were not at the foot of the cross? They booked! They ran! Peter was chicken! But the women were there. And who was there at the tomb? They were women. Women were the ones to go tell the disciples to bring forth the message."

Kirk-Duggan, ordained in the Christian Methodist Episcopal Church, comes out of an African-American denomination that has ordained women for more than a century. Nevertheless, she said, many black churches don't want to see a woman behind the pulpit. And women can be as resistant as men to the idea.

Kirk-Duggan said many churchgoers, black and white, see the world spinning out of control, and want their churches to be "safe and unchanging."

"They'll say, 'Hey, I was baptized by a man. I was married by a man. My parents were baptized and married by a man. By God, I want a man up there in the pulpit!' People get so hung up on the maleness of Christ, or the maleness of his apostles. If you go that route, then all the priests in the church should be Jewish and in their thirties."

Kirk-Duggan likes to wonder what would happen if women, who comprise most of the people in the pews, realized the power they had to change the church. "I'd like to see what would happen if women in one of these churches that doesn't ordain women would simply not show up for services on Sunday, or stop paying their tithes," she said. "Just watch how quickly a new revelation would come down from above."

With or without a new revelation, Kirk-Duggan said, women are finding a place behind the pulpit, and changing the face of ministry. "There's a softening of the office of pastor," she said. "It's not the top-down hierarchical mode, the patriarchal way of saying, 'I am priest,' or 'I am minister.' Women are more community-based. They give more people voices."

o

It's hard to imagine a trend that will have more impact on the future of American religion than the rising numbers of women taking up leadership in churches, synagogues, and other congregations. Women will change both the style and the substance of religion, inspiring a faith that is less rigid and hierarchical.

Women are already flooding into ministry, and one of the best ways to map the religious future is to examine the nation's seminaries. At six of the nine seminaries of the Graduate Theological Union, for example, women now outnumber men, and they are closing in on the Southern Baptists and Roman Catholics—the last vestiges of patriarchal ministry. It is a trend mirrored in seminaries across the country.

At the Episcopal Church Divinity School of the Pacific, there are seventy women seminarians and only twenty-five male students. Women are also found in large numbers at the main Southern Baptist seminary in California, Golden Gate Baptist Theological Seminary, despite the fact that few Southern Baptist churches will call women as pastors. Nevertheless, in 1997, nearly a third of the 440 students on that Baptist campus were women.

In mainline Protestant churches, the proportion of women clergy is rapidly approaching that of men. Women are also gaining a place in the pastorates in evangelical churches, especially in Pentecostal and charis-matic congregations. Women may serve as co-pastors with their husbands in these churches, but whether conservative or liberal, religious institu-tions are giving women greater access to leadership positions. For those religious bodies prohibiting women from clerical leadership, especially the Roman Catholic Church, it is an issue that will not go away.

In 1995, Vatican's Sacred Congregation for the Doctrine of the Faith declared that the Catholic Church teaching that women cannot be ordained to the priesthood was "infallible" and closed to further discus-sion. Nevertheless, both the Catholic Theological Society of America and the College Theology Society, an organization of university theology and religious studies professors, have refused to go along with the Vatican edict, and continue to study and debate the issue.

Despite the Vatican position, rising numbers of women enroll in Catholic seminaries. At the Franciscan School of Theology in Berkeley, for example, 40 percent of the students were women in the spring semes-ter of 1997. One of them, Harriet, gave up a legal career to become a Catholic lay minister, or, she hopes, a priest. "I'm just going to let God take care of what's going to happen in the end," she said. "Who knows where we'll be in ten years?"

In Catholic parishes in the United States, women already outnumber men in most types of nonordained ministry. Though women are not empowered to perform sacraments such as consecrating the bread at Mass, they may assist in the communion service as eucharistic ministers, and serve as lectors, lead adult Bible study, and even run priestless parishes as "pastoral associates."

As the concept of ministry and religious vocation moves away from the exclusive province of ordained clergy, the influence of women in leader-ship will be felt everywhere. Though some evangelical megachurches may limit the pastorate to men, women in these congregations' small groups and other ministries have assumed leadership positions. There has also been a strong influx of women into the Reform, Conservative, and Recon-structionist rabbinate. Other religious traditions with exclusive male lead-ership in other countries have succumbed to egalitarian and feminist influences upon arriving in the United States. Female leadership and fem-inist ideas have revolutionized many American Buddhist communities, where women have reworked the liturgy and inspired a more democratic form of practice.[20]

Despite all these new leadership options for women, there's a downside to this trend. Many of the denominations that have welcomed women into leadership, such as the Episcopal and United Methodist churches, are the ones that are losing market share and social influence. This "good news/ bad news" scenario goes further. Although ordained women found it easier to get jobs in the 1990s, they are not necessarily moving into full-time pastorates. Many men are leaving temporary positions, part-time jobs, and other positions like hospital chaplains, and there is a disproportionate increase of women replacing them.[21] Though these positions may meet the needs of some women clergy, such as those with young children, they may also "ghettoize" women into marginal positions. The influx of women into the pastorate may also hasten the graying of the clergy, since many women are entering the ministry at later stages of life. Meanwhile, the shrinking number of positions in declining mainline churches creates stronger competition and a possible backlash against women clergy.

"You hear people talking about the 'good old days' at seminary," said Paula Nesbitt, a sociologist of religion at Iliff School of Theology in Denver, "about how they used to get the 'best and the brightest.' That argument only holds if you ignore all the women."

Nesbitt, author of *The Feminization of the Clergy in America,* said the status of the clergy was already in decline when large numbers of women began entering the field. The greater number of women seminarians, she said, has only continued that trend. "There has been a common understanding that when women enter an occupation, its prestige and its salaries go down," she said. "We started to see those changes back in the 1960s."

Not everyone sees the tendency for women clergy to move into nonconventional positions, rather than traditional pastorates, as a sign of discrimination, as women hitting the "glass ceiling." Other research shows that women often choose positions such as community ministries and hospital and prison chaplaincies, not because of discrimination, but because they want more personal interaction in their ministry. This different style of ministry shows how female clergy will change church life. Women clergy have been found to have ministries based strongly on relationships. Their preaching and style of leadership stresses the sharing of personal information and puts less distance between clergy and laity. Women clergy will accelerate the move from strictly hierarchical forms of leadership to team leadership models.

Other research suggests that church environments shape ministry style as much as the gender of clergy. A survey of 4,000 pastors conducted by Hartford Seminary found that among conservative congregations such as the Assemblies of God, clergy were more apt to take an authority-based style regardless of whether a man or woman was at the helm. Among liberals, male and female Unitarian clergy were most likely to share power with members of their congregation.[22]

Some see the growing proportion of women in the clergy as furthering
the "feminization" of organized religion. Since surveys consistently show
women to be much more active in organized religion than men, *Newsweek*
religion writer Kenneth Woodward argues that the growing proportion of
women in leadership may further discourage participation among men and
deprive them of role models and masculine spiritual symbols. Woodward
sees a future where woman ministers using female imagery for God preach
every Sunday to congregations of mainly women.[23] Even in evangelical and
Catholic churches where men retain leadership positions, there is increasing concern that masculinity and religious practice are seen to be in conflict. This is one reason why religious men's movements like Promise
Keepers and the Million Man March have gotten so much attention. Some
of those opposing the ordination of women argue that maintaining a male
presence in the clergy is the best way to provide a balance to the pre-
dominantly feminine influence found in most congregations. Proponents
of the growing movement toward lay involvement, team ministry, and
decentralization of congregational life counter that when leadership is dis-
persed throughout the congregation, members are provided with a variety of male and female role models.

Eugene McCarraher questions whether authoritarianism and abuse of
power is solely the province of male clergy. Noting the growing influence
of women in Catholic parishes, the historian asserts that the "vertical
authority of male priests will be supplanted by the horizontal authority
of female laity as women come to effectively run the church in the twenty-
first century." He adds that the concerns women bring to parishes, such
as diversity and nondirective leadership, do not automatically translate
into greater democracy in parishes and congregations. He cautions that
"horizontal modes of authority have their own forms of authoritarianism, ones that operate through interpersonal relationships rather than top-
down dictation."[24]

Controversies around inclusive language are also sparked by women
clergy and feminist theology. Although feminist theology is not monolithic, the issue of inclusive language carries wide appeal among women
religious leaders and will be the most controversial feminist innovation in
congregational life. The conflict over revising traditional texts and hymns
to remove "sexist" language will be just as intense as the war between
proponents of traditional and contemporary worship.

Feminist liturgies have reformulated the Christian Trinity from "Father,
Son, and Holy Spirit" to "Creator, Redeemer, and Sustainer." Maternal
symbols for God are juxtaposed alongside masculine imagery. In the Jewish tradition, the feminist use of inclusive language focuses more on the

immanence of the divine, rather than the transcendence of God, referring to God as the "wellspring of life," rather than "king" or "judge." Inclusive language advocates say these revisions are not substituting female for male imagery of God, but adding the voice of women's spirituality to worship and theology—a voice long silenced in traditional churches. Those opposed to inclusive language argue that the tradition's use of male imagery serves a distinctive purpose—stressing the transcendence of God—and that changing historic symbols and formulas changes the theology.

Attempts to introduce inclusive language in liturgies and hymnals have met with mixed results. A United Methodist hymnal that deleted traditional male representations of God and attempted to be inclusive of women and racial minorities sparked controversy when it was released in the late 1980s. Yet a survey conducted by Don Saliers of Candler School of Theology of 112 congregations in 1993 found greater acceptance of the hymnal among the laity. A large majority of the congregations were positive and even enthusiastic about the hymnal.[25] On the other hand, a study of women clergy in generally liberal New England Congregational churches of the United Church of Christ found that while the laity gradually came to accept and appreciate their woman pastors, they had more problems accepting inclusive language. Sixty-three percent of respondents believed that inclusive language in hymns, prayers, sermons, and scripture is not important, while 83 percent did not like female metaphors for God. These findings show how the issue of inclusive language may seriously divide clergy and laity in the new millennium.

Researcher Allison Stokes writes that "Clergywomen understand, as many in congregations often do not, that much is at stake in the use of language that is inclusive. The connection between the role of women representing the Divine and the words we use in speaking of the Divine is inextricable."[26] The Catholic Church makes similar claims, stressing the importance of the priest being male in representing Christ at the Mass, a position that many American Catholics oppose, judging by their significant level of support for women's ordination. Many American laypeople, regardless of their stance on inclusive language, are not convinced that the clergy, through their gender at least, uniquely reflect or represent God.

Margaret Miles, dean of the Graduate Theological Union, first came to San Francisco Theological Seminary back in the 1950s as a "good little minister's wife." She typed her husband's papers, ignored her own intellectual development, and joined a group of seminary wives called "The Parsonettes."

"There were no women in the ministerial programs," said Miles, who returned to the Bay Area forty years later—after a divorce and eighteen years as a professor at Harvard Divinity School. "It feels like a very different world today. One thing drawing women to ministry is they are socialized to be caring and nurturing toward other people. So it's a natural. Many women are also drawn here by deeply felt political commitments to revise social institutions, like churches and synagogues, that have been entirely designed and administered by men, and to wonder what these institutions would look like if women had thought them through."

Miles was asked what kind of Easter sermon she'd deliver if the topic was women and religion. "I'd start by saying Christianity has a shameful past on this issue, as do other world religions, by marginalizing and oppressing women," she said. "At the same time, women in ministry is a rediscovery of one of the essential tenets of Christianity—Galatians 3:28: 'There is no male and female, for all of you are one in Christ Jesus.' Women are bringing new life to an ancient tradition that had come to an impasse. That's a very hopeful thing."[27]

6

RELIGION IN THE POST-DENOMINATIONAL ERA

FutureFaith: Downsized and Decentralized

In an inner-city warehouse and former discotheque, Vineyard Christian Fellowship begins its Sunday morning worship with a six-piece rock band, complete with drums, keyboard, and electric guitar.

Two overhead projectors beam lyrics onto a wall. Four hundred congregants of varying ages and ethnicities sing out for the first forty-five minutes of the service, some swaying from side to side with arms held high. Others clap their hands, shouting "Praise Jesus!"

Nearly everyone in the service, including the preacher, is informally dressed. There's an unmistakable intimacy in the room. It feels real. "People are just being people here, not putting on a Christian overcoat," says Monica, a nurse attending this morning's worship.

After the music dies down, the congregation's associate pastor offers an informal, self-revealing sermon full of personal stories about his own life struggle. "Every single one of us is dealing with stuff," he says. "And He's going to expose it."

This service in San Francisco's trendy "South of Market" district in the fall of 1997 has its roots in the Southern California summer of 1974, when Kenn Gulliksen, a born-again Lutheran, gathered five people together in the living room of a private home. Vineyard Christian Fellowship grew out of the countercultural "Jesus Freak" movement in the 1960s and 1970s, and grew so fast that Gulliksen let it all go in 1982, troubled that his creation was turning into another religious denomination—which was exactly *not* the idea.

Gulliksen turned the burgeoning movement over to John Wimber, a Quaker-turned-Pentecostal who saw it grow to more than 400 congregations across the United States and another 200 around the world. In the early 1990s, some of the Vineyard congregations parted ways when the "holy laughter" Pentecostal revival, also known by some as the "Toronto Blessing," swept through the movement.

"Many people don't consider us a stable church," said Paul, one Vineyard pastor. "We're committed to trying new things, and that sometimes stretches the comfort zone."

John Wimber died in November 1997, and as the new millennium approached, Vineyard Christian Fellowship was once again at a crossroads. Debate still rages over how "denominational" the movement should become. "We are not policy driven," Paul said. "The government structure primarily exists to facilitate a relationship and connectedness between the local churches."

Another pastor put it this way: "Vineyard is growing up," he said. "And there's a fear that when it becomes a denomination, it dies."[1]

o

In the new millennium, religious denominations will lose influence to local congregations and new coalitions of believers like Vineyard Christian Fellowship. Two words describe the future of religious denominations—downsized and decentralized.

Most church watchers and religious leaders agree that the old mainline denominations—Methodists, Lutherans, Presbyterians, Episcopalians— are losing influence over people in the pews. They are certainly losing members. Since the early 1960s, the Episcopal Church has lost more than half its members, while groups like Vineyard Christian Fellowship have exploded. There is less agreement among church leaders over how mainline denominations should change, whether they can, or even should.

Numerous studies have shown the long decline of denominational loyalty. In 1958, only one person in twenty-five had left their childhood denomination. By 1984, one out of three had left or switched.[2] Denominational "switching" is common not only among the laity, it is growing among clergy as well. Congregations looking to attract "the unchurched" avoid denominational labels. Grace Baptist Church becomes "Grace Church."

In American Protestantism, the loosening of denominational ties creates a free-market environment in which an entire Presbyterian congregation goes Pentecostal, or an Episcopal parish turns Eastern Orthodox. This congregational switching can take surprising turns. In 1993, the pastor of a Vineyard congregation in San Jose, California, took his entire flock into the Antiochian Evangelical Orthodox Mission, trading in "praise bands" and prophesy for ornate vestments and icons of the Virgin Mary.[3] Examples of these wholesale denominational defections reach well into the hundreds, and church growth specialists say that the pace is quickening. Switching is easier because the clergy have grown more independent. In the past, pastors wanting to change denominations would quietly leave their flock. Now, defecting ministers may tell their parishioners, "This is really not where we belong," says Lyle Schaller, a specialist on congregational trends.

That is exactly what happened in May 1998 when a group of conservative evangelical pastors in the United Methodist Church in California threatened to leave the denomination and take their flocks with them.[4] On the surface, the defections were in response to increasing conflicts about gay rights in the denomination and disagreements over the nature and authority of scripture. Just as important, however, was conservative frustration over denominational politics and church government—over an entrenched liberal bureaucracy that, in the view of conservatives, only hindered evangelism and church growth. "We're tired of operating under an outdated, two-hundred-year-old system. It's top-down. We build up a church, then they put in a pastor who doesn't match up with the congregation, and it kills the church," one of the evangelicals complained. "In the twenty-first century, the way you do church is different. We have to change like the car companies changed in the 1980s—be fast and flexible. We want to grow churches."

In today's religious scene, a conservative Episcopal priest has more in common with a neighboring Eastern Orthodox priest than with his fellow Episcopalian clergy with a liberal bent. New divisions within denominations and growing cooperation between like-minded religionists of different traditions will make such switching common in the future.

Denominational ties are so weak that some have begun advertising for congregations. Consider a recent ad in *Christianity Today* magazine for the Evangelical Episcopal Church International, a newly formed conservative denomination. It offered interested readers "ministry opportunities" in the positions of bishop, priest, pastor, and deacon. It advertised the denomination's "contemporary liturgical worship," along with opportunities for "apostolic succession." Reverend Michael Owen, presiding bishop of the denomination, which had grown to over 200 parishes since its founding in 1995, said advertising for denominations may have been "unusual until recently, but there's a need for many leaving mainline churches to know there are alternatives."[5]

Since the early twentieth century, associations of congregations and parishes were organized under a corporate model that sought to bring order and efficiency to the sometimes unruly world of religious life. For half of the twentieth century, this corporate model worked well; it enabled congregations to extend their presence to a national level through electing trusted leaders, publishing periodicals and educational curricula, and organizing ecumenical and social relief programs. During the 1960s, the trust between leaders and their constituencies broke down, especially within mainline denominations, as respected leaders were replaced by impersonal bureaucracies.

Special interest groups emerged in these growing bureaucracies, often around social concerns involving race, gender, and left-of-center politics. National staffers had little connection with their mainly middle-class constituencies, many of whom saw their church straying from its spiritual mission. Meanwhile, there were important changes in patterns of church giving. Causes favored by local congregations gradually received a greater share of money than national programs.[6]

Starting in the 1980s, denominations finally began responding by localizing, downsizing, and decentralizing. Many of the mainline denominations moved their corporate headquarters from New York City to smaller cities in the South and Midwest. These moves were based on the sentiment that church leaderships needed to get in touch—at least symbolically—with memberships outside of the New York–Washington axis. Congregations, rather than denominations, are now seen as the primary mission organization of American religious bodies. Rather than seeing themselves as the center of religious life, denominations have begun to channel more resources to congregations.

The sweeping national social statements and political activism that drew so much criticism and controversy in the past two decades have been scaled back and the work of congregations and community associations targeting local issues has been emphasized. Denominations have—often reluctantly—begun to allow "parachurch" groups to provide services for their members and congregations. Parachurch or para-denominational groups are organizations that stand outside of congregational and denominational life, such as the evangelical relief organization World Vision. They are specialized agencies that do one thing well, rather than all-purpose religious organizations.

Sociologist Nancy Ammerman sees new networks of liberal and moderate Southern Baptists as models of this "postmodern denomination." They avoid structures that mirror those of the wider Southern Baptist Convention. Rather, they work through coalitions—subcontracting, networking, and taking advantage of new computer technology. Describing the moderate Alliance of Baptists, Ammerman writes: "It looks for people that need a voice and have needs that are going unmet. It has a tiny national staff and meets in an annual convocation for education and worship. There is no thought of becoming a 'full-service' denomination. Rather, it is a specialized organization with an identifiable niche, capable of forging alliances for the purpose of pursuing specific short-term goals." Although the alliance publishes alternative literature and has started a seminary, these initiatives have not come under control of the organization, and are offered to those in other liberal and moderate Baptist bodies.[7]

Perhaps the greatest strides toward decentralization have been made by evangelical and, particularly, Pentecostal churches, which have historically invested far less than mainline bodies in creating denominational bureaucracies. For instance, the International Pentecostal Holiness Church, one of the largest Pentecostal groups, transformed itself in the mid-1990s from a traditional and strongly hierarchical body to one emphasizing the enabling and empowerment of congregations. The denomination's headquarters in Oklahoma City was renamed as the Pentecostal Holiness Resource Development Center. B. F. Underwood, the general superintendent of the denomination, said, "We decided that what had been the headquarters was not supposed to be there to dictate. It's there to provide support and resources to the local church." Congregations are now permitted a wider latitude in choosing which of the denomination's seventy-five ministries are suited to their needs.[8]

Another example is the fast-growing International Church of the Foursquare Gospel. Within this Pentecostal denomination is a movement of younger "seeker" congregations known as Hope Chapel. Other Foursquare congregations are diverse, ranging from the traditional Pentecostal First Foursquare Church in Fresno, California, to a racially mixed urban ministry in Chicago. Church president John Holland says, "We don't try to make a pastor 'Foursquare.' Rather, we encourage pastors to use their gifts and individual strengths to reach those in the community around them. You will not find a 'typical' Foursquare congregation." Pentecostal historian Vinson Synan notes that without bureaucratic baggage, the church allows local pastors to implement their own strategies for ministry as long as they remain within doctrinal bounds. Even the Foursquare training of ministers is often tailored more to individual needs.[9]

Other new forms of church government are coming to the surface of American religion. Megachurches are setting up satellite congregations throughout the nation, in a phenomenon Russell Chandler calls "parameter churches." Steve and Julie, the California church shoppers in

Chapter Four, joined one of these congregations. Suburban megachurches have also set up "chapels" in the inner-city. Eventually these churches become semi-autonomous congregations, part of a new church network.[10]

Despite all these changes, it may be too soon to forecast the demise of the current denominational system. Sociologist Robert Bellah points out that despite all the mainline declines, in the early 1990s the "Heartland" Protestants—Methodists, Lutherans, American Baptists, Disciples, and Reformed—still made up 24 percent of the American population. When you include the more "culturally elite" Protestants—Congregationalists, Presbyterians, Episcopalians, and Unitarians—the total rises to 33 percent of the American people. That is still about twice as many members as the combined numbers of the Southern Baptists, Pentecostals, and other white evangelical Protestants. Roman Catholics, meanwhile, remain the largest American religious group by far, claiming a quarter of the U.S. population.[11]

John Mulder of the Presbyterian Church's Louisville Seminary, concedes that there has been cutting back of national staff among Presbyterians and other mainline Protestants, and a funding shift from national causes to local congregations. But even if congregational giving continues to move to the local level, "denominations are sufficiently well-endowed so that they won't disappear," he says. This is because endowments—such as individual gifts earmarked for specific causes—and foundation giving have assumed greater importance in mainline denominations. In the Presbyterian Church, Mulder says, only 30 percent of funding comes from local congregations. A major source of money today is donations willed by deceased Presbyterians.

It is estimated that more than $10 trillion will be given away in the wills of older citizens as they die in the next few decades. Independent foundations created for such planned giving have been established for the Episcopal Church and the Presbyterian Church (U.S.A.) members. But since these foundations are independent, they may lead to further decentralization. Givers often distrust donating to national church leaderships and prefer foundations, where they can earmark gifts to specific causes. They are more likely to give to missions or charity than support programs to rebuild centralized bureaucracies.[12]

Not surprisingly, denominational officials are wary about all this downsizing and decentralizing, and not only for reasons of self-preservation. At the 1996 General Conference of the United Methodist Church, delegates pushed a variety of plans for downsizing and simplifying, proposing "new paradigms" to replace national church bureaucracies. Theologian William Willimon writes that many national church leaders feel threatened by the new mood. "Some women and ethnic-minority delegates feared that without the current complex of quotas, rules, and mandated structures they would lose the ground they had only recently gained."[13]

Denominations provide a collective voice and public expression for church positions on social and other issues. Critics of decentralization fear religious groups will lose any chance of influencing American society if local expressions of faith overshadow a unified national voice.

Decentralization will also change the way clergy and lay leaders are trained. Though it is still uncertain how seminaries will navigate post-denominational currents, a widespread concern has emerged that today's seminaries are out of touch with the changing needs of people in the congregations. John Fitzmeyer, associate dean of Vanderbilt Divinity School, says that seminaries are facing problems from all sides. On one hand, denominations expect leaders to meet "pre-ordered" standards. On the other hand, schools have had to lower their expectations of students, since they are often ignorant about doctrine and come to seminary as "seekers or questers." At the same time, the faculty has become more specialized in their disciplines, showing "no common theological calling."[14]

Seminaries have begun to change, sometimes by following the lead of corporate America or other organizations in the nonprofit sector. They have entered into new partnerships with other schools. Three Philadelphia seminaries—Eastern, Westminster, and Lutheran Theological Seminary—formed an alliance to teach urban pastors of African-American churches. Seminaries have also forged new relationships with congregations—even those independent and self-contained megachurches. A federation of evangelical seminaries grants credit for leadership education programs conducted by Willow Creek Church, the pioneer megachurch. In fact, megachurch pastors have been in the forefront of challenging the traditional separation of seminary and congregation. If the purpose of seminaries is to train people to work in congregations, they argue, why not close the gap and incorporate these schools into the parish? These kinds of questions will take on more urgency in the new millennium as denominations lose much of their centralized power and congregations and informal networks gain greater influence.

Another trend is the founding of new "niche" seminaries focusing on specific concerns, such as particular ethnic populations or geographic localities. The Logos Evangelical Seminary in Pasadena, California, targets its ministry training programs to the world's Chinese people. A decade ago, Charlotte, North Carolina, had no seminary; today there are four. An example of the home-grown quality of these schools is Southern Evangelical Seminary in Charlotte, a niche school that emphasizes apologetics (defense of the faith) and began on the campus of a large church.[15]

Renewal Groups: Following the Spirit

Walking into the spirit-filled auditorium, the scene looks like another Protestant revival meeting. There are outstretched arms, upbeat music, and that lively Pentecostal feeling. But when the first wave of sweet-smelling incense sweeps across the arena, heralding a solemn procession of white-robed priests, it turns into a Roman Catholic Mass.

This blend of priesthood and Pentecostalism—high church meets holy spirit—fuels one of the fastest-growing movements in the Roman church, the Catholic charismatic renewal. It combines traditional Catholicism with Pentecostalism's emotional conversion experiences, ecstatic worship and joyful liturgies, and occasional outbreaks of faith healing and speaking in tongues.

"It looks Pentecostal, with praying in tongues and raised hands," said one Catholic charismatic priest. "But we believe everything the Catholic Church teaches and promotes. We're Catholic."

Allowing charismatic worship is one way the nation's Roman Catholic bishops have tried to stem the tide of Latinos leaving their church for evangelical and Pentecostal congregations. Sometimes, they leave anyway.

Consider the story of Rosa, a Mexican-American immigrant who became active in the early Catholic charismatic movement. In just a few years, her parish prayer group got so large that it rented a nearby storefront. Hundreds of immigrants from Mexico and Central America packed their storefront service. Before long, however, the worship and teaching of her Spanish-language services got the attention of the local bishop. Though Rosa is Catholic, her husband is an ordained minister in the Assemblies of God, born in El Salvador to Protestant missionary parents.

"People accuse the Catholic charismatic movement of being Protestant because we clap our hands," says Rosa. "We just want to center ourselves in Jesus Christ and be open to everyone."

Unable to control the storefront ministry, officials with the local archdiocese soon severed all ties with the group. "Their tenor became more ecumenical and more Protestant," one official explained. "We had to ask whether we could continue to promote a group that was not really Catholic anymore.

"When people hear what they think is the call of the spirit outside the confines of the church, this is what happens," he added. "One of the dangers of the charismatic renewal is the danger of developing your own brand of authority."

o

New kinds of religious organizations and movements emphasizing personal spiritual experience will arise in the new millennium, offering services once provided by traditional religious congregations and denominations.

"Para-denominations," renewal movements, and special interest groups operate on the periphery of religious denominations and have emerged as a major presence in the American religious landscape. Lutherans, Methodists, or Roman Catholics who develop a consuming interest in experiential worship, certain church teachings, or a particular social issue naturally gravitate to these groups, whether they are charismatic prayer meetings, anti-abortion organizations, or gay and lesbian support groups.

Para-denominations, which include groups like Campus Crusade for Christ, Habitat for Humanity, and Promise Keepers, are sometimes seen as competing with denominations, often generating more allegiance and financial support than official religious bodies. For instance, Promise Keepers' expertise in men's issues kept several evangelical denominations from starting their own men's ministry at denominational headquarters. Of course, these partnerships between para-denominations and old-style denominations spark tension. Denominational leaders may suspect their teachings and identity are diluted through outside influences, as we saw in the story of Rosa and her parish prayer group that went Pentecostal.

Other kinds of spiritual renewal call for more sacramental and "catholic" forms of worship, such as those favoring a return to the traditional Catholic Mass, or the Taizé movement, an international ecumenical Christian order that has attracted a large number of young adults to its services, which are marked by chanting and meditation. Feminist religious groups comprise another type of renewal movement. They often cross denominational boundaries, are based outside congregations, yet provide an outlet for spirituality, fellowship, and theological discussion. As with other renewal movements, these groups operate inside and outside organized religion. Debra, the Washington, D.C., feminist who hosts a small group in her home, has turned away from the Roman Catholic Church. At the same time, feminist theology has found an accepted place in other sectors of institutional religion, especially within mainline Protestant seminaries.

One movement that will strongly influence American Judaism in the new millennium is Jewish renewal. This renewal movement began around the *havurah*—intimate prayer and study fellowships formed as an alternative or supplement to mainstream synagogues, often mixing traditional ceremonies with home-grown worship. Today Jewish renewal includes a wide range of groups promoting spirituality, healing, ecology, social action, and a recovery of Jewish mysticism.

Some observers even see traces of the Jewish renewal spreading to Orthodox Judaism, such as in new Orthodox women prayer groups or among newly observant Jews with backgrounds in yoga, meditation, and spiritual healing practices. Rodger Kamenetz, who has written on the movement, predicts that the Jewish renewal "will come to be seen as a research and development laboratory for the entire community," inspiring innovations in liturgy, spirituality, and feminist theology. Jonathan Sarna of Brandeis University, a critic of some aspects of the renewal, says that when historians examine the influence of the renewal on American Judaism, "they will see shades of difference, rather than a revolution." By the time Jewish renewal hits the mainstream, he says, "it will be greatly toned down so it doesn't scare off the more traditionalist elements in the ranks."[16]

Renewal groups display a number of common features. By their very nature, they practice and proclaim a more intense form of spirituality. They often include people whom sociologist Max Weber called "religious virtuosos." These individuals have a certain knack, a special receptivity toward things spiritual. This intensity in renewal movements can easily unite people from different backgrounds and traditions. They become unofficial ecumenical movements, bringing people together over a common spiritual experience—whether it is healing, Jewish mysticism, or ancient liturgies. As we will see in the upcoming section on ecumenism, flexibility in structure and an emphasis on common beliefs and experiences rather than the fine points of denominational doctrine make renewal groups harbingers of a new kind of religious unity.

These same movements can act as highly divisive forces in organized religion. When participants of renewal groups seek a closer relationship with a typical congregation, they may find little of the enthusiasm, spiritual vitality, and intimacy they found in renewal, and often wish to import this fervor into the institution. "Old-guard" members may be turned off by the spiritual intensity of these "true believers," or resent their sense of spiritual superiority. As we saw with Rosa and her local archdiocese, there can be a good deal of suspicion of these newcomers among religious officials, particularly if their beliefs and practices are perceived to be in conflict with accepted doctrine and practice. A tug of war breaks out between those "holding fast" to established ways and those "pressing forward" to new spiritual frontiers. These conflicts can lead to schisms in denominations and congregations, even within families or other personal relationships.[17]

Rosa's charismatic renewal group shows how these movements can fragment religious institutions. Hailed as creating a new ecumenical future in the late 1960s, the expectations surrounding the charismatic movement were more modest by the 1980s. Many charismatics in mainline Protestant churches left to form independent congregations and even their own denominations. They became frustrated by the lack of receptivity toward their experience and discouraged by liberal theological currents in their churches. Denominational leaders and clergy uncomfortable with charismatic practices such as speaking in tongues may have muttered "good riddance" upon watching the charismatics leave. This same parting of the ways is beginning to take shape in the relations between various denominations and other renewal movements, particularly feminist groups that have come to see mainstream churches and synagogues as irreversibly sexist and patriarchal. In the future, the decentralizing trend in many religions may give more space for renewal movements and other special interest groups to function. But the problem of charismatic spirituality clashing with institutional religion will continue even if larger structures are decentralized. A major challenge facing religious bodies will be how to capture the dynamism of religious renewal without letting these movements scare off less enthusiastic members.

Patricia Wittberg, a sociologist and Catholic nun, writes that Protestants and other religious groups have historically had difficulty creating a place for "spiritual virtuosity." Established Protestantism, she says, "has tended to expel virtuosi rather than accept a dual standard of virtuoso and mass religiosity within the same denomination." This is mainly due to the concern that permitting movements within denominations conflicts with the idea that all members are spiritually equal. These sentiments, however, ignore the fact that there are differences in religious interest among believers, whether from childhood upbringing, later life experiences, or even genetic predisposition. Wittberg writes that attempts to "deny the existence of religious virtuosity" causes a "watering down" of religion.

"Once this watering down has taken place within a church, its religious virtuosi no longer feel sufficiently challenged by their membership," she writes. "If a church fails to provide such an outlet for those who feel called to do more for their faith, it runs the risk that its most committed and fervent members will desert it for 'holier' churches. Recent studies have shown that this is precisely what is happening to the various mainline Protestant churches in this country."[18]

Catholicism, Eastern Orthodoxy, and much of Anglicanism have traditionally been able to keep renewal movements within the institution without encouraging widespread schism and fragmentation. Religious orders and the ancient tradition of monasticism provide havens for religious virtuosos who may be seen as contentious and divisive influences in other groups. Although St. Francis was often locked in conflict with the bishops and cardinals of his day, church leaders recognize, often through hindsight, that people like him bring new energy and innovations into the institution.

Nevertheless, there has been a dramatic drop in the ranks of the Catholic religious orders over the past thirty years, a fact that highlights the difficulty of maintaining the balance between renewal and mainte-nance in religious institutions. For instance, in 1965, there were 4,110 women entering religious communities and only 491 dispensations granted for nuns leaving the orders. By 1970, when Vatican II reforms were in full swing, there were 662 women becoming sisters and 2,456 dis-pensations granted. Sociologists found that this decline took place pri-marily among liberal and more moderate religious orders that modified their religious lives to accommodate the modern world, such as allowing greater personal freedom in lifestyle and dress. In fact, conservative women's orders stressing the wearing of the habit and adherence to tra-ditional practices are twice as likely to have recruited new members than liberal orders.[19]

These more traditional orders, like conservative religious groups in gen-eral, make stricter demands for belonging but generate greater benefits for members, such as a stronger sense of community and identity. Sister Witt-berg predicts that the religious communities that will flourish in the future will be those that emphasize such elements, as well as evangelization.[20]

At the same time, there need to be connections between renewal groups and mainstream religion. Renewal movements and religious orders are, by their very nature, countercultural. They embrace communal forms of intense religiosity. Contact with mainstream religious denominations can help renewal groups avoid the perennial problems and temptations of spir-itual sects—abuse of power and authority, and the tendency to form an elitist mind-set that isolates members from society and ordinary believers.

Ministering in a Multicultural America

Raul was just a toddler when his uncle was slain by paramilitary death squads and his family fled El Salvador for a new life in Los Angeles.

Ten years later, in the early 1990s, Raul was watching television in his family's modest home in Southern California when he saw a Spanish-language offer for a free video entitled, "Our Heavenly Father's Plan." He called the toll-free number.

Mormon missionaries personally delivered the tape, and Raul soon joined the Church of Jesus Christ of Latter-day Saints. Before long, he inspired his mother, raised as a Seventh-Day Adventist, and his father, a card room employee and a nominal Catholic, to do the same.

"As soon as the missionaries started giving us lessons, our house became more peaceful," said Raul's mother, Gloria. "I really felt the Holy Spirit in the house."

Today, Raul and his family spend lots of time at the new $10 million Mormon church center in the riot-torn heart of south-central Los Angeles. The sprawling center is filled with Spanish-speaking church members from Mexico, Guatemala, Honduras, El Salvador, and other Latin American nations.

Across town, in a more well-to-do section of Los Angeles, another group of Mormons are gathering at Wilshire Chapel. This stately sanctuary with beamed ceilings, wrought-iron chandeliers, and shimmering stained glass was once the center of white Mormon power in California. Visit this Hollywood chapel now, and you're likely to find it bustling with Korean Mormon choirs, Latino worshipers, and African-American missionaries for the Latter-day Saints.

Once considered the American archetype of white, middle-class religion, the U.S. Mormon Church is fast becoming a rainbow communion of multiethnic believers. And Southern California—with its worldwide mix of displaced people looking for new roots, new life, and new community—is ground zero of the new Mormon America.

Mormons call their local congregations "wards," and their list of California congregations includes Spanish wards, Korean wards, Armenian wards, Vietnamese wards, Chinese wards, Samoan wards, Tongan wards, Laotian wards, Cambodian wards, Japanese wards, and Filipino wards. There are also rising numbers of African-American Mormons in English-speaking wards in Oakland, Los Angeles, and other cities.

Despite Mormonism's image of being a white church of the suburban West, fewer than half of the church's new members in California are Caucasian. In the greater Los Angeles area, only a third of Mormon converts in the 1990s have been white.

That's an amazing turnaround for a church that once equated spiritual evolution with becoming "a white and delightsome people" and that did not allow black men to serve as priests until 1978.

Mormonism's racist past dates back to controversies surrounding slavery and abolitionism on the American frontier. Mormon Church leader Brigham Young, who led the Latter-day Saints from Illinois to Utah, preached that blacks were cursed with the "mark of Cain."

By 1978, when the late Mormon president and prophet Spencer Kimball proclaimed a new revelation and reversed the no-blacks rule, the old racial restrictions were wreaking havoc at home and abroad. There were boycotts of Utah and the football program at Mormon-run Brigham Young University, along with growing dissent by many rank-and-file Mormons. Meanwhile, no one was sure who could become a Mormon priest in church growth centers like racially mixed Brazil, where the Mormons were about to open their first South American temple.

In the Mormon church, all adult male members in good standing may hold priestly power, performing baptisms and consecrating the bread and water during Sunday communion service. Keeping blacks from the priesthood effectively kept them out of the church. Whether Kimball's racial revelation was divinely inspired or politically expedient, its long-term effect was to send the church on a growth spiral in Africa, Latin America, and the Caribbean. At the same time, it helped transform Mormon California into a multicultural church.

Robert, a black Mormon missionary in Los Angeles, was born into a Roman Catholic family in Haiti but converted to Mormonism as a teenager in Miami. Now age twenty, he says he is not bothered by the fact that his new church did not allow blacks to serve as priests or missionaries until 1978. "What made the difference for me is I came to know the church was true," he said. "When I read the Book of Mormon, I feel closer to Christ."

Nevertheless, Robert says the church's racist reputation is often a problem when he tries to spread the Mormon gospel in black neighborhoods in Los Angeles. "It's an issue," he said, "but I'm black myself, and that says a lot."

○

Ministering to the different races and ethnic groups of multicultural America will be a central concern for religious institutions in the new millennium.

This concern reaches far beyond finding new strategies for evangelism and outreach. Multiculturalism touches on matters of religious identity and sparks divisive debates over "inclusiveness" in religious communities. Ethnic separatism and solidarity in congregations are still strong forces in some segments of American religion. Some studies suggest that even when the second or third generation of immigrants are assimilated, they still want to worship with people of similar backgrounds. Case studies of African Americans, Latinos, and Korean Americans show that whereas these Americans may speak English and are more culturally assimilated than their parents and grandparents, they still prefer a congregation geared to their ethnic group.[21]

Although the diversity debate rages throughout American society, it is of particular concern to Christians, whose tradition calls on them to minister to all people. Mainline Protestant denominations actively foster multiculturalism. They have often done so through a "top-down" approach, reserving leadership positions for minority groups. In fact, minority representation in United Methodist Church government is much higher than among its overall membership.[22] Denominations such as the Evangelical Lutheran Church in America and the United Church of Christ have also established affirmative action programs to bring people of all races into policy-making positions. These Lutherans enacted a quota program to increase minority membership to 10 percent by 1998—the denomination's tenth anniversary. Yet from 1988 to 1997 the Lutheran's minority membership moved from just under 2 percent to slightly more than 2 percent. Between 1988 and 1995, African-American membership declined by 6,000 and Hispanic membership in Spanish-speaking congregations went down by 2,000.[23]

Another North American example is the United Church of Canada. It has tried to attract new immigrants by including non-Western forms of worship, displaying black portrayals of Christ, and appointing minorities to leadership posts. Yet most of the new immigrants who have joined the United Church have formed their own congregations rather than join existing ones. The denomination wants to bring ethnic congregations into closer contact with the rest of the church, but it is not easy, since new immigrant churches are often more conservative than other congregations.

Mormon church leaders have had similar problems mainstreaming ethnic congregations. In 1996, California officials with the Church of Jesus Christ of Latter-day Saints announced they were abolishing more than 200 foreign language wards, explaining that those segregated units were not fostering a "oneness of spirit," and that it was time for immigrant Mormons to worship in English. "There was fierce opposition by some groups to the plan," one Mormon leader explained. "One entire group went and joined the Methodist church." Faced with a budding ethnic revolt, Mormon leaders backed down and decided to take a slower approach to assimilating minority members.

Evangelicals have consistently done a better job at attracting and assimilating minorities. Hartford Seminary sociologist Carl Dudley found in his research that congregations that are the most vocal about diversity often have less success achieving it. "Churches that unite people across cultural boundaries can name the deeper religious source of their unity," he writes.[24]

Canadian sociologist Reginald Bibby found that 14 percent of evangelical church members are from new ethnic groups compared to about 2 percent of United Church of Canada members. Evangelicals attract such newcomers, Bibby found, because of their spiritual emphasis. "It's extremely difficult for religious groups to reach out beyond their historic base," he said. Referring to mainline churches in Canada and the United States, Bibby said attempts to set quotas in leadership positions or to link diversity with sexual orientation and controversial social issues "might be noble, but they are also incredibly naive. There's a real danger that there's going to be erosion and alienation among the churches' traditional base. The result may be that these churches will not recruit new members and not keep their old ones." Bibby keeps his advice short and simple for congregations seeking to reach out to diverse communities: "There should be cultural sensitivity with a reemphasis on spirituality."[25]

This "unintentional multiculturalism" is also found in the Buddhist group Soka Gakkai, which has drawn large numbers of African Americans to its spiritual teachings and practice of chanting for desired goals and enlightenment. In explaining this appeal, one black member of the group says, "The organization itself does not try to attract black folks or Spanish folks or any special kind of folks. It's just that it's based on humanism, and because of its humanism, it attracts everybody. . . . If other Buddhist organizations go out and try to attract black people, then I think they've failed already." One women adds, "Why does Soka Gakkai attract people of color? I think race is still the most polarizing issue in this society. People hear 'race' [and] they jump on both sides of the issues right away; but we don't focus on the problems, because we're always offering solutions. I think it's appealing to people of color because it gives them a sense of hope."[26]

Spirituality and a strong religious identity, however, are not magic bullets in attracting diversity. Religious groups must work hard to keep diverse memberships, often through restructuring services and trying new ways of doing things. Sociologist Caleb Rosado writes that the key to maintaining multicultural ministry is "unity in diversity." Strong leadership is required, as well as a willingness among clergy to share power. Rosado concludes that the concept of "one family" should be emphasized at every opportunity.[27]

Sociologist Nancy Ammerman predicts that responding to new patterns of immigration and economic change will be among the most difficult challenges facing American congregations in the future. Ammerman found that most congregations undergoing population shifts and economic change try to hold onto their old identity, and fall into decline. In many of the congregations Ammerman studied, the sharing of meals was an important builder of community. Adaptation to changing neighborhoods can mean different things to different congregations, ranging from serving different food at meals of fellowship to changing the kinds of hymns sung, the length of sermons, and the religious symbols on display. Conservative and liberal congregations have similar problems adapting to diversity. Ammerman also discovered that, despite all the affirmative action enacted at church headquarters, denominational programs have had little impact at the local level.[28]

Christians are not the only ones dealing with multiculturalism in America. Islam, one of the nation's fastest growing faiths, has an incredibly diverse following in the United States, and a new generation of Islamic Americans struggles to separate the true meaning of Islam from the Old World traditions their parents brought with them from Iran, Pakistan, Indonesia, or the Middle East. At the same time, hundreds of thousands of African-American converts to Islam are becoming more orthodox in their Muslim practice, including many who are joining temples once monopolized by recent Islamic immigrants. "We're looking for an American Islamic practice," said a leader of the Islamic Center of Southern California, the thirty-two-year-old son of an American mother and a Turkish father.

Another young Islamic American, Faris, was born in Baghdad and still an infant when his family moved to the United States in 1964. His Muslim consciousness was forged in Southern California, where he attended a white, upper-middle-class high school, and like so many other Muslim students, faced harassment by classmates during the Iran hostage crisis in the 1970s and later events of Middle Eastern turmoil. Today, Faris works as a computer engineer in Northern California's Silicon Valley, where he juggles his life and his faith—going to movies, following San Francisco Giants baseball, and finding ways to fulfill the Five Pillars of Islam, which include praying five times a day and fasting during the daylight hours of the month of Ramadan.

Each day at work, Faris and several Muslim colleagues at his semiconductor plant gather for afternoon prayers in the firm's parking garage. That prayer time is fine, in fact, often better than at local mosques for Friday prayers, where Faris does not always feel so comfortable.

Many mosques remain somewhat cliquish centers for Pakistanis, Arabs, Pacific Islanders, black American converts, or other Muslim ethnic groups. "A lot of mosques are, unfortunately, divided into cultural camps," he said. "Maybe our mission as first-generation Muslim Americans is to break down these stigmas and cultural barriers, to become a whole community."[29]

Technology and Virtual Religion

It's a cold, rainy weekend, so Arthur opts not to venture outside to attend the church of his choice. Why bother, he thinks, when storm clouds threaten and the spiritual search is but a "click" away?

Calling up his Web browser, he types the word "religion." Several clicks of the mouse later, he's staring at the home page of "Angels on the Web." Soothing harp music drifts from the little speakers behind his screen as he considers his options.

Art maneuvers his cursor around the big advertisement for licensed products from NBC's *Touched by an Angel* television show. Live talk in the "Angel Chat Room" seems more interesting. Once inside, he eavesdrops on a conversation between "LUVANGELZ" and "ANGELSINLIGHT." After a few minutes, he becomes bored with the subject at hand, "Where is angel heaven?" He leaves the angel groupies floating in cyberspace.

Clicking back to the religion directory, he wonders whether the Roman Catholic Church has something more interesting to say about angels. Looking at the Vatican Home Page, tastefully designed so the screen looks like aging yellow parchment, he calls up "The Holy Father" and gets a picture of Pope John Paul II. All of the pope's apostolic exhortations, encyclicals, and other writings are right there at his fingertips in English, French, German, Italian, Latin, Polish, Portuguese, or Spanish. He surfs past a few daily bulletins from the Vatican Press Office and settles into the Vatican archives.

Art calls up the *Catechism of the Catholic Church* and searches for the word "angel." But there's a glitch in the system, and his screen fills with previews of the "Artwork of the Angels Exhibition," one hundred pieces from the Vatican museum that will tour the United States in 1998. They're such wonderful paintings that he completely forgets he has been trying to consult the Roman Catholic catechism.

Wondering what the non-Christians are offering today, he clicks back to the directory and calls up the Islam Home Page. It's not quite as classy as the Vatican site, but he takes a peek at the Koran before moving on to the Buddhists. He is mysteriously drawn to the Nichiren Shoshu Cyber-tour of the Taisekji Temple at the foot of Mt. Fuji. He looks at a map of the site and clicks on different spots, walking through the Sanmon Gate, past the five-story pagoda, and into the grand reception hall.

Looking out the window, the sun is breaking through the clouds. Art signs off, wondering whether he can still make the 11 A.M. Sunday service at the First Presbyterian Church.

o

Computers are changing many areas of religious life—from management of finances to denominational publishing. But their most significant effect in the new millennium will be the way computers and other communication technologies forge direct links between individual believers and religious groups, thus creating bonds based on common concerns, bypassing denominational control, and transcending geography.

Although Internet connections will never replace real congregations, these computer networks can complement them and create entirely new communities of faith. Prayer, instruction, and fellowship are all found in the cathedrals of cyberspace. One survey of prayer and religious teaching forums on the Internet found that while many participants missed the personal contact of meeting in actual groups, they valued the sense of control they had in determining how much time to devote to spiritual practice. Those afraid of public speaking and participation in religious groups found new strength in on-line forums.[30]

For most people, the Internet may merely serve as an introduction to an off-line spiritual community. Many congregations and denominations now have home pages on the World Wide Web to provide inquirers with information about their beliefs and activities. As a wide range of religious teachings and texts are freely circulated via computer, individual seekers have more opportunities to examine prospective congregations and traditions. This can foster greater interchange, discussion, and understanding between people of different faiths. In San Francisco, for example, Grace Cathedral, the seat of the Episcopal Diocese of California, has done pioneering work through "GraceCom" by organizing live interfaith conferences and other events over the Internet.

In 1996, Cardinal Roger Mahony of Los Angeles urged that Web sites going by the name "Catholic" be required to uphold official church teachings.[31] But it is exceedingly difficult to crack down on unapproved computer forums or Web sites. Religious bodies that maintain tight control over their teachings and discourage free exchange between members and leaders will have difficulty navigating in the computer age. An "unofficial" group of believers from a certain denomination can just as easily establish a Web site or discussion forum on church doctrine as can headquarters, thus further blurring the lines between leadership and laity in the new millennium.

In 1994, the Church of Scientology went on-line with an electronic bulletin board, intending to introduce people to the faith by citing basic teachings and listing Scientology centers around the world. Soon, however, the bulletin board was filled up with the views of critics of Scientology. Dissenters and critics started their own bulletin board, which posted variations of Scientology ideas and attracted believers who were seeking "alternate mind-clearing technologies or religions" but were not especially interested in joining Scientology and paying for officially approved courses.[32]

In addition to offering an introduction to new communities and providing a forum for alternate views, the Internet can create a sense of fellowship and provide access for believers far from centers of their faiths. For instance, Jews who live in the rural South, far from the rest of organized American Jewry, can easily plug into networks of co-religionists from around the country and forge new links with organizations in Israel. A Mormon in Maine can find fellowship and support from teaching centers and other Mormon organizations in Salt Lake City through Internet access. Computers also give new religious movements, including controversial ones like Heaven's Gate, the Southern California "suicide cult," a powerful device to recruit new members.

In the future, computers will be common tools for spiritual study. Sacred texts from around the world are already available on user-friendly CD-ROMs and over the Internet, giving anyone with access to a computer the opportunity for in-depth study. There are dozens of Bible software programs on the market. Often these programs utilize images as teaching tools, thus allowing users to get a better feel for Biblical scenes and settings. The growing capacity for computers to carry visual images and the integration of computer technology with television and video will encourage visual forms of communication.

Communications scholar Stephen O'Leary finds that online religious groups are reviving the use of "iconography, image, music, and sound" in religious ceremony. "Surely computer rituals will be devised that exploit the new technologies to maximum symbolic effect. It does not seem too far-fetched to think of cyber-communications as coming to play a major role in the spiritual sustenance of postmodern humans." O'Leary adds that this transition from written text to image and other sense-based media will have a profound effect on religious life.[33] Congregations that base their ministries on text, such as preaching and scripture reading, may have difficulty reaching generations brought up on computer images and graphics.

Satellite technology, like computers, will decentralize religious life and create new bonds between believers of different traditions. Though teleconferencing and satellite TV have long been used by some church groups, the application of this technology is now focusing on "distance learning." For instance, the evangelical Church Satellite Network designates more than one hundred churches as training centers where clergy and leadership teams from surrounding congregations come together once a month for instruction by Christian leaders. Technology provides congregations with inexpensive access to well-known speakers and gives participants the opportunity to interact with presenters.[34] The fundamentalist Bob Jones University beams courses to 250 Christian schools across the United States, offering advanced programs that schools might otherwise be unable to afford.

Some religious leaders resist satellite programs, fearing the weakening of denominational ties when those from different religious bodies gather at satellite sites and interact with popular teachers. Unofficial movements within denominations can also create their own satellite networks, adding to the decentralizing and potentially divisive effects of high technology. For instance, a satellite and computer network known as the International Catholic University sought in 1995 to override the "liberal" Catholic colleges and create an "orthodox" Catholic educational system. This system, started by Catholic TV broadcaster Mother Angelica, links professors and students through electronic meetings and mini-courses on traditional Catholic spirituality and theology. Mother Angelica, an outspoken and strongly conservative nun, has reached 50 million households.

On the other hand, satellites can bring denominational leaders closer to people in the pews, as participants and presenters electronically mingle at local learning centers. For instance, when Bishop H. George Anderson was elected head of the Evangelical Lutheran Church in America, he inaugurated a program of satellite conferences with the laity to discuss theological and social issues that have divided his denomination.

Other forms of electronic media, such as television and radio, have long been used by religious groups, and provide another illustration of how technology can inspire religious pluralism and decentralization. The broadcasting of religious services during the 1950s and 1960s evolved into a new breed of independent and entrepreneurial "televangelists" by the 1970s. Charismatic and evangelical broadcasters preached a simple message that was fine-tuned to the masses, and used entertainment to attract viewers. Later, the monopoly of televangelists in American culture gave way to other religious expressions. The scandals of the late 1980s around televangelists Jimmy Swaggart and Jim Bakker helped create alternatives like the National Interfaith Cable Coalition in 1988, which has grown to represent over sixty-five religious groups. The coalition has its own channel called Odyssey, which features multifaith programming, including a religious game show testing viewers on their spiritual knowledge. The lower costs of cable television have also created a niche for minority religions. Hare Krishna TV, broadcast out of a temple in Houston, Texas, mixes popular culture, such as a punk band playing a speed-metal version of the Hare Rama mantra, with practical instruction in alternative medicine and vegetarian cooking.[35]

The future of religious broadcasting among the evangelicals and charismatics will be diverse and niche-oriented. Just as in congregational life, there has been a noticeable trend toward entertainment in television ministries. Talk shows, dramatic presentations, even cooking and aerobics programs are common fare as Christian broadcasters seek to reach a broader audience. An example of such innovation is the Pittsburgh-based daily drama, *His Place*. The show is a cross between the *700 Club* and *Cheers,* as fictional Christians and non-Christians meet in a diner and discuss religion and social issues. The growing number of cable channels and the use of digital technology combining computers, telephones, and television will accelerate the diversification of religious media in the future.[36]

Christian Unity from the Bottom Up

Crowded into pews once warmed by George Washington and Betsy Ross, hundreds of Episcopal Church bishops packed Philadelphia's historic Christ Church in the summer of 1997. They sat beneath church bells financed by Benjamin Franklin's lottery. Two hundred years after the American revolution, the purple-shirted members of the House of Bishops faced a revolution of their own.

Confronting them at their church convention were the litany of issues that has divided the nation's mainline Protestant and Anglican denominations into warring camps. High on the agenda was a historic ecumenical proposal that cut to the very heart of what it means to be an Episcopalian.

For church traditionalists, the changes sweeping through the Episcopal Church were all part of a decades-long capitulation to the sexual revolution, the gay rights crusade, the feminist movement, and other harbingers of cultural decline. Now the House of Bishops was about to approve a proposal calling for "full communion" with the nation's largest Lutheran denomination. Members of the traditionalist Episcopal Synod of America were drawing a line in the sand. They would not stand by while their House of Bishops compromised their holy office in some desperate move to unite with another declining denomination. "For 2,000 years, we've had the sacraments handed down from bishops to priests. It's that apostolic order that distinguishes us," said one active member in the traditionalist movement, a housewife who devotes countless hours to the cause. "The church hierarchy is liberal, but the members are not. Our people just leave the church with broken hearts."

Those supporting the ecumenical plan said the bishops were merely legislating what had already happened in Episcopal parishes across the country. Old-fashioned distinctions between "Episcopal" and "Lutheran" were meaningless to most Americans. And besides, the traditionalists were harking back to a perfect church that never existed. "If you really understand our tradition, you see that right from the beginning our church was confused, innovative, and divided," said the Reverend Alan Jones, dean of Grace Cathedral in San Francisco. "There was never a pure church."

As it turned out, Episcopal Church leaders approved their historic agreement with the Evangelical Lutheran Church in America, only to have the proposal narrowly rejected at the Lutheran church convention later that summer. Although the Lutherans rejected closer ties with the Episcopal Church, they did authorize a separate proposal calling for "full communion" with three mainline denominations—the United Church of Christ, the Reformed Church in America, and the Presbyterian Church (U.S.A.).

Liberal Episcopalians say they have no choice but to join forces with other denominations. They have been losing members and money for thirty years and are finding it harder and harder to support big national programs from their New York headquarters.

All this denominational maneuvering is part of a major realignment of American Christianity in the post-denominational era. Churches with common views on the ordination of women and abortion rights are coming together in coalitions that blur traditional boundaries among Protestants, Anglicans, and Roman Catholics.

"Churches are cooperating around social issues," said one Lutheran pastor. "Dividing lines are drawn over the role of women, gay rights, and abortion, not around denominational ties."

———— o ————

All the ecumenical debate in the summer of 1997 illustrates yet another decentralizing trend in American religion. **In the new millennium, local congregations and special interest ministries will replace national church bureaucracies as the major force in fostering Christian unity.**

Gone are the days of religious denominations merging like Fortune 500 corporations. People in the pews greet top-down ecumenical plans with more indifference than enthusiasm. In the future, ecumenism and religious unity will grow from the grassroots, where it is more likely to capture the imagination of ordinary believers.

Social scientists see this as part of a broader "post-modern" shift. Whereas the modern mind-set wants to maintain structure and set boundaries, the post-modern view holds that organizations will be shaped more by inter-personal relationship than by rules and regulations. According to this view, ecumenical goals can be better achieved by widening relationships and dialogue between local groups, not by restructuring complex organizations to force "unity" from the top down.[37]

According to the Bible, Jesus prayed that his followers could "be as one." Historic Christian creeds state that there is "one holy, catholic, and apostolic church," and many take that to mean that all believers should unite under one church structure. Today's ecumenical leaders, however, propose a model of "reconciled diversity," which does not see Christian unity as uniformity in liturgy, structure, or even doctrine. This new appreciation for diversity is also found in revisionist Christian histories, which argue that uniformity—either in the early church or prior to the Reformation—has never been a Christian reality.[38]

Similar tensions run through Judaism, as seen in calls to overturn Jewish divisions and reunite as "one people." Conservatives call on all Jews to adopt orthodox practices and teachings, while liberal Jews move toward an ethical and cultural, rather than a primarily religious, Judaism. Jewish thinkers are starting to suggest that the growing diversity in Jewish life may not so much be a sign of weakening or fragmentation as much as one of vitality and innovation.[39]

As with denominational decentralization, the ecumenical movement is changing, whether or not national leaders are ready. Centralized organizations built to bring about ecumenical unity, like the National Council of Churches, have "reached a practical ceiling far short of their professed vision," according to theologian S. Mark Heim. Though the proportion of all Christians who belong to communions within the National Council of Churches continues to decline, the proportion outside that fold—Pentecostals, Roman Catholics, Southern Baptists, and independent evangelical churches—continues to grow. Heim sees a new ecumenism developing beyond the boundaries of the World and National Councils of Churches. It includes groups as different as the charismatic movement and Women-Church, Promise Keepers, and Witness for Peace. These are all Christians who have transcended historical divisions and nurtured "trans-denominational identity." Other examples of the new ecumenism include recent attempts at reconciliation between historically white and black Pentecostal churches. Another is an "Evangelical and Catholics Together" statement based around "traditional family values" and common ideas regarding the doctrine of salvation.[40]

Any discussion of grassroots campaigns for Christian cooperation would be incomplete without mention of evangelist Billy Graham. Preparations for his well-organized crusades for Christian converts begin a year before the event, and often result in the largest mobilization of local churches each host city has ever seen. In fall of 1997, for example, the Billy Graham Evangelistic Association organized California crusades in San Jose, San Francisco, and Oakland. Some 20,000 volunteers from hundreds of churches representing dozens of denominations took part in the preparations, thus fostering connections and relationships that will remain long after Graham moves on to his next crusade. All three Roman Catholic bishops in the Bay Area blessed the evangelist's efforts, and many Catholics took part in the planning. One key organizer of the San Francisco crusade was amazed at how local churches put denominational and political differences aside. "Catholics and Protestants are coming together," said one San Francisco organizer, himself an African-American evangelical. "Mr. Graham is the only person in the country who could bring together this diverse cross section."[41]

One of the keys to Graham's success has been his reliance on local congregations—something national ecumenical leaders should consider. Ecumenical proposals that will catch fire in the new millennium will be ones that do not seek to impose across-the-board uniformity, and ones that target specific issues—such as old-fashioned evangelism. More liberal Protestants may find common ground with Catholics on issues like immigrant rights, or opposition to the death penalty. In 1996, churches from across the spiritual spectrum came together to help rebuild Southern churches destroyed in a wave of arson attacks. On matters of liturgy and the sacraments, partnerships for Catholics will form more naturally with Eastern Orthodox or Anglican churches. These loose confederations can also be expressed in something as practical as the growing number of groups sharing building space and engaging in joint projects of charity or community development. These arrangements are often fueled more by considerations of economics and efficiency rather than ecumenical inspiration, but the effect is the same—bringing local churches together.

This unofficial ecumenical clustering, or what church historian Martin Marty has called "criss-cross ecumenism," is evident in the formation of the Association for Church Renewal, an umbrella organization for conservative renewal caucuses within denominations. This "criss-cross ecumenism" may also be a by-product of the various ecumenical proposals on the table in the summer of 1997. "Full communion" allows the sharing of communion, joint worship, and exchanges of pastors in the different churches. But unlike earlier plans that entailed a merging of ministries and unity from top to bottom, these proposals do not force top-down changes upon congregations. As one pastor writes, Reformed churches and

Lutheran congregations "can remain as separate as they now are if they choose."[42]

Changes in church relations, such as joint communion services and the sharing of pulpits, will only occur if local congregations initiate such arrangements. The defeated Lutheran-Episcopal agreement called for an eventual adoption of apostolic succession, whereby bishops see themselves in an unbroken chain of succession from the apostles' times. That was a change many Lutheran congregations opposed. This issue was not a problem in the Lutheran agreement with the Presbyterians and Congregationalists, who do not have bishops. A more traditional Lutheran parish may not tolerate a liberal United Church of Christ minister at its altar, and with this agreement does not have to. On the other hand, congregations that are part of the liturgical and confessional movement within the United Church of Christ would naturally gravitate toward "evangelical catholic" Lutherans.

Even though they use the term *full communion,* these new ecumenical relations will be selective and partial. They will flourish in the future because they are modest and decentralized, and will reflect the faultlines and fissures of post-denominational American religion. As one bishop said of the proposal for full communion between Lutherans and Episcopalians, "This proposal is not really changing anything. It's legislating the reality of what has already happened out there."

Interfaith Prayers: Peace Between Religions

Bright sunlight illuminates the magnificent stained-glass windows of the cool, cavernous cathedral as prayers, chants, and incantations are offered to a dozen deities, prayers that the world's religions would finally stop committing violence and oppression in the name of God.

Sikhs, Buddhists, Hindus, Mormons, Muslims, Christians, and Jews file past in an eclectic parade of miters, turbans, vestments, and saffron robes. Costumed children at this interfaith worship service bring flowers to the altar and commingle holy water from the Ganges, the Amazon, the Red Sea, the River Jordan, and other sacred streams.

Chosen to deliver the sermon is Faheem, a young man who brings tears to the congregation with tales of his experiences growing up as a Muslim in war-torn Afghanistan. Faheem, twenty-five, grew up amid scenes of horror, of weeping mothers with mutilated babies in their arms. "We, as people of faith," he says, "can transcend the boundaries that have divided us for so long."

This service at San Francisco's Grace Cathedral was just one expression of a small but growing movement that seeks to reconcile differences and promote understanding between the world's major religions. That effort gained momentum in 1993, when about 250 religious leaders from around the world met in Chicago to mark the 100th anniversary of the World Parliament of Religions and adopt "a new global ethic" that condemns poverty, environmental degradation, violence, sexism, and sexual immorality.

By the late 1990s, the movement had shifted to San Francisco and an interfaith initiative by Bishop William Swing of the Diocese of California. Swing traveled around the world in 1995, meeting with religious leaders from India to Rome to describe his dream of creating a place at the San Francisco Presidio, a decommissioned Army base, where the world's religions could come together for peaceful dialogue and conflict resolution.

In 1997, 200 delegates from historic religious traditions and new spiritual movements convened at Stanford University to write a charter for a new international interfaith organization, tentatively called the United Religions. Sitting down together at those discussions were Christian ecumenical leaders, black Muslims, American Jews, Australian aborigines, California pagans, South African Hindus, Thai Buddhists, British Baha'is, Catholic priests, Indian Sikhs, and other leading lights from across the spiritual spectrum.

Important details—such as how the United Religions will function and who will pay for it—were still to be worked out at a series of meetings leading up to June 26, 2000, when the interfaith organization is scheduled to be formally established.

"Religion almost always comes packaged in a 'winner-take-all' wrapping," says Swing. "Gentle Buddhists are hurling grenades in Sri Lanka. Hindus and Sikhs are murdering Muslims in Jammu-Kashmir. Muslims are killing Christians in the Sudan. Christians are killing Christians in Northern Ireland. Bethlehem is under the paralysis of religious hostilities."

Swing envisions the world's religions "coming together on a daily, permanent basis, in pursuit of global good." And what better place to do it, he asks, than at the Presidio, "where we could turn swords to ploughshares."

o

In the new millennium, growing religious pluralism will inspire fellowship, dialogue, and cooperation between Christians, Jews, Buddhists, Muslims, and other American faiths.

As with the ecumenical movement, however, interfaith relations that take place at rarified heights will have a hard time resonating with ordinary congregations and believers—especially conservative religious groups. Both the United Religions and the World Parliament of Religions are important initiatives in a religiously diverse world that keeps getting smaller. Nevertheless, real questions remain as to whether the cooperative energy behind these gatherings can filter down and inspire the rank and file of the world's religions.

Perhaps the most effective form of interfaith dialogue in the future will be the "home-grown" variety that focuses on tangible, local issues of common concern. This is happening in cities across the nation, where interfaith councils have been formed with broader memberships and are dealing with difficult issues like anti-Semitism, attacks on Muslim women wearing traditional Islamic garb, and neighborhood opposition to religious groups outside the Judeo-Christian mainstream. Whether in Bosnia or Los Angeles, interfaith strife breaks out at the local level, and that is where it must be addressed.

Interfaith cooperation has also developed around social issues like disarmament, poverty, and racism. More recently, conservative Christian and Jewish groups have formed alliances on their own issues, such as support for Israel and promoting traditional moral values derived from their common Judeo-Christian tradition. On the theological front, Jews and Christians are also entering a period of deeper dialogue, tackling historically divisive questions like the relation of Jesus to Jewish tradition. The recent development of a "two-covenant" understanding of the relation between Judaism and Christianity, whereby God is viewed as working in both religions, has brought Jews and Christians into closer relations to discuss their traditions and study scripture.[43] Mainline Protestant, evangelical, and Roman Catholic leaders have issued statements condemning past anti-Semitic attitudes and actions. Surveys show low levels of anti-Semitism among American Christians. The renewed call by Southern Baptists to convert Jews to Christianity at their convention in 1996 was a sign to some Jewish leaders of the obstacles that remain in interfaith relations with conservative Christians. Yet surveys continually indicate—even though the traditional mandate to evangelize Jews remains intact among evangelicals—that conservative Christians register highly positive attitudes toward Jews and Judaism.

Among Muslims, there are signs of growing cooperation with Christians and other religionists. Joint activism between Muslims and conservative Christians has taken shape over issues such as opposition to pornography, abortion, and euthanasia, and support for tuition tax credits and home schooling. Mainline Protestants, Jews, and Muslims have joined together to deal with poverty and immigration issues. Particularly noteworthy is the growing dialogue between Jews and Muslims addressing issues of common religious observance, such as dietary regulations, and the more delicate matter of politics in the Middle East.

Other recent arrivals to the United States are joining the interfaith scene as world religions find greater visibility and acceptance in American society. A study of American religious pluralism by Diana Eck of Harvard University found that the second-generation members of minority communities such as Muslims, Hindus, Buddhists, Sikhs, and Zoroastrians have moved from the outskirts of urban areas to city centers, as well as the suburbs. The urban inter-religious councils that were once largely Jewish and Christian are now multi-religious, even in largely Christian cities such as Tulsa, Oklahoma and Lincoln, Nebraska. The inter-religious nature of these councils can help mediate conflicts involving the new pluralism. For instance, the Interfaith Council of Metropolitan Washington, D.C., brought Jews and Muslims together in the wake of the Hebron massacre of 1994. Because of this new relationship of trust, the head of the Washington board of rabbis offered prayers on New Hampshire Avenue in front of the Muslim Community Center.[44] Another example of groundbreaking interfaith cooperation is the formation of a program uniting Christians, Jews, and Muslims in the Minneapolis and St. Paul area in volunteer work for disadvantaged children. The project links together human service groups from mainline and evangelical Protestant churches, the Masjin An-Nur Islamic Center, and the Jewish Community Relations Council, and has trained some 7,000 lay people.

Many American Buddhist, Hindu, and Muslim leaders see the roots of today's interfaith movement in the original World Parliament of Religions in Chicago in 1893, the first time those exotic faiths were given widespread, positive exposure in the American press. One hundred years later, members of these minority religions are finally entering the religious mainstream in the United States.

"We are no longer just dealing with European cultures," said one interfaith leader in Chicago, a Presbyterian minister who works with Baha'is, Buddhists, Hindus, Muslims, Jains, Jews, Sikhs, Zoroastrians, Native Americans, and a variety of Christian denominations. "People can't think in such narrow religious terms anymore. In the Chicago area, there are more Muslims than Jews, more Thai Buddhists than Episcopalians. There are 80,000 Hindus attending seventeen different temples in metropolitan Chicago. That's the kind of diversity we're talking about."[45]

POSTSCRIPT

EVANGELISM—NOT JUST FOR EVANGELICALS

SEASONED OBSERVERS OF American religion offer some deceptively simple advice when asked which churches and religious movements are growing the fastest. "You tell me," they reply. "Who's knocking on your door?"

There's no secret as to why evangelical churches are growing faster than mainline denominations. They try harder. They *evangelize*. Other factors may come into play—everything from demographics to economics to the movement of the Holy Spirit—but it is also true that evangelical and Pentecostal churches grow because they are out there actively seeking members. To use the metaphor of the religious marketplace, they advertise. This has little to do with theology. Churches that are outside the Christian evangelical family, such as the Mormons and Jehovah's Witnesses, are among the fastest growing in the world. Why? Because they are out there knocking on doors.

Of course, in today's high-tech world, there are lots of new ways to knock on doors. Since the 1950s, Pentecostal and evangelical preachers like Billy Graham, Oral Roberts, and Pat Robertson have entered your home whether you like it or not—provided that you own a television set. Frozen out of the mainstream network programming since the early days of radio, evangelicals were forced to improvise, innovate, and inaugurate their own independent communications networks by using the latest advances in broadcasting, satellite, and computer technology. This involves more than just getting their message onto the airwaves. Conservative evangelicals have also lead the way in the use of computers to organize direct-mail listings used for outreach, fundraising, and political lobbying—

something we will address in the coming pages. In the new millennium, religious groups that harness the merging and emerging technologies around television, telephones, and computers will be in the best position to get their message out to new generations of believers.

Evangelicals and Pentecostals do more than evangelize. They also tap into the persuasive power of entertainment. Steve, the "church shopper" with no religious upbringing, was initially drawn to the Pentecostal service by upbeat Christian pop music. The church band they heard when they walked through the door performed songs they had already heard on the radio. But the entertainment value in a Pentecostal service—the spiritual drama—only begins with the music. What could be more engaging than people claiming spontaneous healings, suddenly speaking in strange tongues, or being dramatically thrown to ground by unseen forces? That makes for an exciting Sunday service, especially when compared to the solemn dignity of the Lutherans, Presbyterians, and many other mainline Protestant churches.

This is not just entertainment. This is spiritual ecstasy, and it is another major reason for the explosive growth of Pentecostalism around the world. Whether these soul-shaking experiences and religious conversions are the true action of the Holy Spirit, hypnotic trance states, or some other psychological trick makes little difference. They *feel* real. They inspire people to change their lives and commit themselves to another power, whether it's a higher power outside themselves or an inner voice crying out from the depths of their soul. Pat Robertson, the hugely successful television evangelist, Christian businessman, and presidential candidate, built his empire by mixing entertainment and religious ecstasy. His *700 Club* broadcasts combine the created intimacy of the *Tonight Show* with the miraculous drama of Pentecostal revival—a blend of Hollywood and "Hallelujah!"

This combination of factors—evangelism, entertainment, and ecstasy—have fueled the dramatic rise of twentieth century Pentecostalism. In 1965, when church historian Vinson Synan did his first research on the roots of the Pentecostal movement, there were an estimated 50 million Pentecostal Christians in the world. In 1997, when Synan came out with a new edition of his study, there were said to be 217 million Pentecostals around the globe. Synan traces modern Pentecostalism back to John Wesley, the eighteenth-century founder of Methodism. Wesley, a priest in the Church of England and an American missionary, rebelled against the rigid Calvinism of seventeenth-century England. Wesley seized on two powerful forces that continue to shape the religious future—personal spiritual experience and the empowerment of the laity. "If the Calvinists taught that only the elect could be saved, the Methodists taught that salvation could be found by anyone," Synan writes. "If Calvinists could never be sure they were among the elect, Methodists could know from a crisis experience of conversion that they were saved. From the beginning, Methodist theology placed great emphasis on this conscious religious experience."[1]

Over the last two centuries, something very telling has happened to the mainstream Methodist Church, and the Anglican communion from which John Wesley arose. After dramatic growth in the nineteenth century, the United Methodist Church began to stagnate and then decline in the last half of the twentieth century. The same thing happened to the Episcopal Church, the Anglican communion in the United States. Both churches gained social influence and economic clout but ultimately became tired and complacent. Conservatives blame the rise of theological liberalism, and clergy who began to question the literal truth of the Bible and to preach a "social gospel" that was more concerned with economic injustice than personal sin and salvation. Whatever the reasons, the share of the spiritual marketplace held by mainline Episcopal and Methodist churches plummeted in the final half of the twentieth century, the same period when membership lists for Pentecostal denominations like the mostly-white Assemblies of God and the mostly black Church of God in Christ skyrocketed.

In the near future, it is hard to see a reversal of this trend. In the next section of the book, we will look at the approach of the new millennium. Religious groups that have traditionally played up the millennial vision of the Second Coming of Christ—such as Pentecostals, Mormons, and the Jehovah's Witnesses—are the ones that are already growing the fastest.

Nevertheless, as the Methodists and Episcopalians have demonstrated, and as the Bible preaches, he who is first may soon be last. Sociologists of religion talk about the natural cycle of religious change, of the inevitable decline of established religious bodies and the constant rise of reenergized sects, revivals, and renewal movements. Pentecostalism and the conservative evangelical movement have entered the American mainstream. Also moving from the margins to mainstream will be upstart religious groups in the Catholic Church, renewal movements in the Episcopal Church, along with immigrant religions and non-Christian groups. Evangelistic style will not be limited to evangelicals, as a wide range of congregations will employ evangelistic fervor and the emphasis on personal spirituality.

Countless developments could alter the religious future, but women are perhaps the most likely ones to hold the spiritual wild card. Women have been the bedrock of religious congregations for a long time, and their sudden emergence as the leaders of congregations, seminaries, and religious denominations will transform both the styles and substance of religion in America. More nurturing and nonhierarchical styles of leadership are already changing the daily life of congregations across the country and the denominational spectrum.

Likewise, religious leaders who are able to overcome the persistent racial segregation that infects our religious congregations may hold a key to the religious future. Many people are trying, from the conservative evangelical leaders of the Promise Keepers to the affirmative action activists in the liberal United Methodist Church, but most Sunday worship in the United States remains deeply segregated.

All congregations in the new millennium—large or small, black or white—will be shaped by the social forces of the American future, particularly by consumerism, decentralization, and pluralism. To grow, or merely to survive, they must consider the mood of spiritual shoppers in the religious marketplace. This does not necessarily dictate a bland uniformity and a franchise mentality. The religious free market encourages diversity, making room for a whole range of congregations, traditions, and beliefs. The marketplace in the long run favors congregations that have a strong identity. The importance of denominational doctrine *is* eclipsed by an emphasis on spiritual experience, but our overview of congregations with growing memberships suggests that their members eventually make the connection between experience and belief. The popularity of traditional movements, from Orthodox Judaism to the Latin Mass, show how spiritual seekers eventually reengage doctrine and theology, even if they are often first drawn to groups by the spiritual experiences or friendly feelings they provide.

This brings us back to our young friends, Steve and Julie. After a few years in their small Pentecostal congregation, they and their two children began another round of church shopping. What prompted their search was a heavy emphasis on a spiritual revival sweeping through the Pentecostal churches out of Pensacola, Florida. That revival began on Father's Day 1995 at the Brownsville Assemblies of God Church, and soon had the church overflowing with teenagers and others responding to fiery sermons about sin and repentance. By the spring of 1997, an estimated 1.6 million worshipers have flocked to Pensacola, and the revival has consumed many other Assemblies of God churches across the nation. But it was all too much for Steve and Julie. "They got too caught up in falling down and speaking in tongues and all that," Julie said. "I don't think that's the most important thing anymore."

Steve and Julie now belong to a Southern Baptist church, a reconnec-
tion with Julie's religious heritage. "Now I see that the *feeling* in church
isn't the most important thing," she said. "Now we are in a Bible-believing
church where they preach the word the way it should be preached, and
where you can grow in the Lord."

For Julie and Steve, growing in the Lord has meant looking at how they
think about the rest of world, how their religious beliefs relate to their
political views, how their Christian faith changes the way they treat the
less fortunate people around them. It is to that dimension of the American religious experience that we now turn.

PART THREE

SEARCHING FOR COMMON CULTURE

7

THE POLITICS OF FAITH

Reaching Out

Every weekday morning, Richard walks past the shopping carts, sleeping rolls, and disheveled bodies of the homeless as he heads from his subway stop to his office. "They force me to confront some of my own issues," he says, "like how to reach out to people in a way that isn't condescending, or how not to be overwhelmed by all the privilege I have compared to them."

Nearby, in an affluent suburb, Cora has come to realize that she spends much of her life "consciously avoiding people who are suffering."

"Last Sunday," she recalls, "I was at the shopping center. There was a street woman with a sign saying 'Work for Food.' I just couldn't help noticing how everyone was ignoring her."

Richard and Cora were among a thousand spiritual seekers and religious believers—most of them white and middle-class—who had just completed an experiment linking spirituality and social action. For ten weeks, they decided to stop ignoring all of the human suffering around them.

Once a week, they gathered inside the stately Scottish Rite Temple in Oakland, California, to ponder personal suffering and planetary despair and decide what, if anything, they should do about it.

Ram Dass, the popular author and spiritual mentor, was master of ceremonies of a participatory course they completed called "Reaching Out," a giant support group to encourage community service. Some 1,000 people spent $100 each to participate in the course, which provided referrals to community agencies seeking volunteers. Participants also engaged in small group meetings, along with weekly homework assignments of "inner work" and journal writing. Each week, under the gaze of television lights and cameras recording the proceedings for a public television series, Ram Dass ventured into the audience with microphone in one hand, prayer beads in the other, like a consciousness-raising "Oprah" searching for stories about the spiritual side of volunteerism.

"Hi, my name's Dana, and I work with AIDS patients," said a thin man, voice cracking. "One man I work with was going deaf. I was talking to him on the phone about it last week, and he was taking it in stride—almost joking. This week he was completely deaf. What I see is that it was not just his loss, but my loss, too. I can no longer relay my compassion to him with my voice, over the phone. It's hard to tell whose suffering is whose."

Ram Dass stood with his arms at his sides, fingered his beads and took a loud, deep breath. "You know," he replied, "this kind of work is far more than 'doing good.' When it's done with a good heart, it's unclear, at the end of the helping act, who is the helper and who is the helpee."

Reaching Out was designed both to inspire participants to community service and to provoke discussion of the spiritual implications of the work. To most people, however, Ram Dass is still best remembered for something that happened more than thirty years ago, back in the 1960s, when he and Professor Timothy Leary were removed from the faculty at Harvard University for promoting enlightenment via psychedelic drugs. Ram Dass, then known as Richard Alpert, went to India in 1967 in search of drug-free nirvana and became the disciple of a guru named Neem Karoli Baba. He returned to become one of the West's leading proselytizers of meditation and Eastern mysticism. Since the 1980s, through such organizations as the Seva Foundation, Ram Dass has been promoting a spiritual path known as "karma yoga," Hinduism's version of "do unto others . . ."

Reaching Out, with a budget of nearly $1 million and dozens of supporting staff members, was Ram Dass's most ambitious act of good karma.

"I go around the country lecturing, calling it 'Compassion in Action,' and people come out in droves to hear it," Ram Dass said in an interview. "Why do they come? Is it just guilt? Or is it some feeling that our hearts are not working right? What we've tried to do in this course has been a redefinition of an individual's identity so they no longer see themselves as separate from it all, but part of it all."

Richard, the subway commuter, used the course to decide what he could do about all the homeless in his midst. "My goal was to find a response between ignoring them and inviting them home with me," he said, "something that was both compassionate and doable."

What Richard came up with were two Saturday sojourns for which he, his wife, and their six-year-old son Billy made up a hundred bag lunches and passed them out around his weekday subway stop. For about $40, they were able to provide a peanut butter and jelly sandwich, two hard-boiled eggs, and carrot sticks to one hundred street people, who washed it down with coffee hauled around the city in Billy's little red wagon.

"Billy was a great inspiration," his dad said. "He had no difficulty walking up to people and saying, 'Do you want lunch?'"

○

Congregations, denominations, and individual believers do not exist in isolation from the rest of the world. Throughout American religious history, spiritual fervor and devotion has flowed from religious congregations into the wider arenas of education, work, family, and politics. Though American religious life indeed *is* becoming more privatized, and spirituality *is* often seen as just another offering in the growing service and information industry, there is a counterbalancing trend in American religion. Many people are making new connections between personal faith and public life.

In the new millennium, religious groups and individuals will become more self-conscious and forceful about extending their influence in society, thus forging new links between spirituality and social action.

There are many factors behind these latest efforts to link American religion and social life. Surveys show that many Americans, particularly baby boomers and busters, feel disenchanted by the workings of government and politics. Many are opting for local, voluntary forms of social action—programs often channeled through religious congregations and other community groups. There is also a shared sense by people across the political spectrum that social problems are more serious today, and that a moral and cultural renewal is needed now more than ever. In this concluding part of our book, we will show that all the pluralism, individualism, and consumerism in American religion need not have to prevent believers and faith groups from helping those less fortunate and from working for social change, even if their diagnosis of the problems and the solutions they offer are very different.

Ten years before he founded the Moral Majority, the Reverend Jerry Falwell spoke for many conservative Protestants when he said churches should tend to spiritual matters and not get involved in politics. Few churches would make that claim today. Sociologist José Casanova asserts that religion is being "de-privatized" throughout the world, including in the United States. The emergence of the religious right and the U.S. Catholic bishops' social activism has signaled this renewed role for believers in the public arena.[1] Groups long considered apolitical, such as the Buddhists, pagans, and spiritualists, have all shown rising involvement in social and political issues.

Even those opposed to overt political activity cite studies showing the social benefits of religious faith—from reducing crime to improving family life. Patrick Fagan of the conservative Heritage Foundation writes that whereas the social sciences have often viewed religious belief and practice in a dismissive manner, recent research shows that religion is both "an individual and social good." In a review of these studies, Fagan finds that 81 percent of them showed the positive benefit of religious practice, 15 percent showed neutral effects, and only 4 percent showed harm. He concludes that religious belief and practice keep families together and reduce social problems like substance abuse, out-of-wedlock births, and crime.[2]

Sociologist Nancy Ammerman sees religious congregations as great "generators of social capital," providing members not only with moral values but the leadership skills necessary to run a democratic society. Consider the role the church played for African Americans during slavery and segregation. No other institution was able to develop civic skills for African Americans like the black church. Churches created the social space for blacks to pass down their music, preaching, and stories, helping them to learn skills in communication, planning, and decision making, all of which would be crucial in later integration efforts.[3]

Religious Right Presses Forward

Pat Robertson and Jerry Falwell may be the household names of the religious right, but its rising star is James Dobson. His Focus on the Family organization operates from a forty-seven-acre campus in Colorado Springs, a sprawling city in the Rocky Mountain foothills famous for its view of Pike's Peak and its reputation as the new millennium's Mecca for conservative evangelicals.

Dobson, a conservative Christian psychologist and radio talk-show host, has been spreading his views on abortion, marriage, and child rearing for more than two decades. His program is broadcast from 2,500 radio stations across North America and 3,000 other outlets around the world. There is no denying the political clout of Focus on the Family, which boasts an annual budget of $114 million and some 1,300 employees, and of another Dobson-affiliated group, the Family Research Council.

Most who call in to Focus on the Family file prayer requests or order merchandise from Dobson's extensive catalogue of books, magazines, video tapes, and audio cassettes on how to save marriages, stay off drugs, avoid fornication, and find Jesus. The sophisticated telephone marketing system handles nearly 4,000 calls and 11,000 letters a day.

During the 1996 presidential primary, all of the Republican candidates visited his oak-lined offices in Colorado Springs or met with Dobson in Washington, D.C. Although Dobson declined to endorse anyone in the primary, he warned them all that their party faced electoral defeat if it failed to embrace the Christian right's crusade to outlaw abortion and to encourage organized prayer in public schools. "I'm very frustrated with the Republican Party and its efforts to move away from moral issues, and to only talk about taxes," he told a gathering of religion writers from major U.S. newspapers.

In 1995, Dobson assured a meeting of the Religion Newswriters Association in Colorado Springs that he would not join conservative evangelicals looking to form a third party. "I do not favor a Christian political party or theocracy," he said. "I won't lead it or motivate it."[4] Three years later, in February 1998, it looked as though Dobson was changing his tune. Speaking to conservative leaders in Arizona, he warned that if the Republican Congress continued to "betray" conservative evangelical voters, he would abandon the Republican Party and "do everything I can to take as many people with me as possible."

In a speech before the Council for National Policy, Dobson revealed that he did not even vote for Republican presidential nominee Bob Dole in 1996, but cast his ballot for a third party candidate, Howard Phillips, a conservative Christian who ran on the United States Taxpayer's Party ticket. Warning that the Republican Party had disillusioned conservative evangelical voters who helped them gain control of Congress in the 1990s, Dobson said the GOP has "laid the foundation for a revolution."[5]

---

o

Despite its long-standing dispute with secular Republicans, the religious right will remain an influential force in American politics, especially in local campaigns.

Since the rise of Jerry Falwell and the Moral Majority in the late 1970s, critics have predicted the imminent demise of the religious right. After Ronald Reagan left office and Pat Robertson lost his 1988 bid for the Republican presidential nomination, many thought the movement would lose its momentum. But the religious right only localized its activism and diversified its base, attracting a wider spectrum of evangelicals and charismatics under the Christian Coalition, which emerged from Robertson's foray into national politics. When Bill Clinton was elected president in 1992, there were similar forecasts that the baby-boomer generation would eclipse conservative religious politics. In 1994, that speculation was confounded when the Christian Coalition, under Ralph Reed, helped elect a conservative Republican majority in Congress. This time, Reed broadened the religious right agenda to include social and economic issues, such as crime and tax reform, and sought out Catholics, blacks, and Hispanic Christians. There was also an effort to reach out to religiously Orthodox and politically conservative Jews. In the reelection of President Bill Clinton in 1996, it once again looked as though the national influence of the religious right was on the wane, although Republicans retained power in Congress.

Like a conservative chameleon, the religious right continues to reinvent itself. Just how this broad-based movement will change in the future is hard to predict. Surveys indicate that many Americans identify with the religious right, but at the same time they are uncertain of its agenda and how it would be implemented. It is estimated that 27 percent of the total U.S. electorate is in "close" or "very close" agreement with the views of the religious right.[6] Another survey by the Pew Research Center found that public support for churches expressing political opinions runs highest among white evangelical Protestants.[7] At the same time, polls find that many evangelicals who identify with the religious right are unsure what the movement stands for. Nevertheless, American evangelicals have undergone a process of politicization under the religious right's influence that will provide a devoted pool of activists for future campaigns.

What has become known as the "religious right" has three components. Most influential today is the Christian Coalition, which has broadened its agenda beyond the "culture war" issues of abortion and school prayer. A second current in the movement wants to refocus on moral concerns such as abortion and euthanasia, and press the Republican Party to give them more prominence in its platform. A smaller faction of religious right activists want to form their own party because of what they saw as the unresponsiveness of Bob Dole Republicans to "traditional family" issues. These latter two groups could coalesce if the Republican Party backs away from contested moral issues, particularly abortion.

Until now, the activism of the religious right has not been a positive agenda of social change, but a defensive political campaign against what the movement sees as rising secularism in the broader culture. Legalized abortion ignited "pro-life" activism. Gay activism inspired new religious right opposition. This defensive posture has only grown in recent years, with the movement opposing court rulings on physician-assisted suicide and homosexual marriage. Although the Christian Coalition's drive to include Catholics and minorities and broaden its agenda was a proactive move, it has met with mixed success. Many blacks and low-income Americans have a hard time supporting a movement that wants to cut welfare and outlaw affirmative action.

Although oppositional politics remain a central factor in religious right activism, there are other forces seeking to bring fundamentalist ideology into prominence in the country. This current is especially evident in attempts to revive a "Christian" or "Bible-based" America. Some of the most extreme advocates of this approach follow the writings of R. J. Rushdoony, the controversial leader of the Christian Reconstructionist movement. Christian Reconstructionists seek to impose a strict Biblical law on modern society as a prerequisite for the Second Coming of Christ. In his writings, Rushdoony criticizes "the heresy of democracy" and claims that the Old Testament requires the death penalty for kidnaping, bestiality, homosexuality, witchcraft, and the "rape of a betrothed virgin." In recent years, however, most of the leadership of the religious right have not emphasized the "Christian America" themes but have tried to bring the movement into the mainstream.

Today, a much less strident notion of "Judeo-Christian values" or "traditional values" drives the religious right. The growing involvement of conservative Muslims, Orthodox Jews, and other conservative non-Christians has moved the religious right away from Christian nationalist themes. The religious right that will gain a greater following in the future will be more accepting of religious and ethnic pluralism and fighting the local fight.

That is already happening. In local elections across the United States, devoted candidates of the religious Christian right are flying far below the radar screen of the national media. They're running as "stealth candidates," undercover evangelicals committed to fighting abortion and gay rights on party platforms and to promoting prayer and tax support for religious schools on public school boards.

Conservative evangelicals across the theological spectrum, such as fundamentalists and Pentecostals, are putting aside doctrinal differences and launching a grass-roots crusade to transform what they regard as an immoral, secular society. "This is a God-inspired movement, and there's nothing the liberals can do to stop it," said one local organizer. "We need a return to wholesomeness in this country," adds another.

This quiet shift to local politics is based on the "San Diego model," a 1990 campaign strategy that ran a secret slate of about ninety candidates for school boards, city councils, even irrigation districts. Sixty of those candidates were elected, many of them by playing down their religious agenda, shunning established "candidate night" forums, and focusing their campaigns on registering members of fundamentalist and Pentecostal churches.

"They hid their agenda and took advantage of voter apathy and the anti-incumbency mood," said Kathy Frasca, a founder of the Mainstream Voter Project in San Diego, a watchdog group organized in response to the new campaign. "They have taken over most of the Republican Central Committees in California."

Sara Diamond, author of the book *Spiritual Warfare: The Politics of the Christian Right,* said conservative evangelicals have realized how relatively easy it is to get control of the Republican Party machinery or public agencies such as local school boards.

"Pat Robertson—a TV evangelist slammed by the national media—was doomed to failure and ridicule," she said. "It's better to run a lot of low-level people for dog catcher and city council."[8]

Religious Left "Born Again"

With little more than the story of David and Goliath to inspire them, some fifty religious liberals gathered in the auditorium of an inner-city Roman Catholic parish to plan their response to the political juggernaut of the religious right.

Over coffee and cookies, they reminisced about the good old days, talking about how they longed for the time when American religious leaders were identified with causes like social justice, civil rights, union organizing, and the peace movement—not anti-abortion battles, school prayer campaigns, and attacks on gay rights. At times, the Sunday afternoon session seemed more like a support group for frustrated liberals than the beginnings of a grass-roots movement.

"'Liberal' has become a dirty word," said the rabbi moderating the session. "We've become remarkably complacent. Our efforts have been somewhere between pathetic and apathetic. We've got to get back in there and organize our churches and synagogues."

Much of the debate at the meeting was over whether religious liberals should work with the religious right or "play hardball" against it. Suggestions offered at the forum—sponsored by Americans United for Separation of Church and State, the American Civil Liberties Union, and the American Jewish Congress—ranged from finding "common ground" with the religious right to "calling talk shows to counter right-wing rhetoric."

Clergy at the event complained that attempts to organize their churches politically are often thwarted by their congregants' desire for individual spiritual growth, or the assumption that politics should not be preached from pulpits. "Social justice is as important as worship," said one Catholic priest. "That is as religious as the prayers we offer in church."

Another clergyman, the pastor of a United Methodist Church, said members of the religious right "want to establish a government according to the God they understand."

Jill Hanauer, executive director of the Washington, D.C.–based Interfaith Alliance, a national network of religious liberals, said the main problem local liberals face is that "moderate people of faith are uncomfortable getting involved in politics."

"So much of our movement is just a reaction to what the radical right has been doing for the past fifteen years," she said. "Many of our people are uncomfortable because our reaction often seems negative." Nevertheless, Hanauer said liberal and moderate religious organizations have begun organizing in local communities where conservative Christians have tried to take over the school board or other local agencies. "This has been bubbling up for three to four years," she said. "People are looking for a national group to latch onto."

She concedes that the religious left is outspent and out-organized by the religious right. Her Interfaith Alliance was taking in about $2 million a year, compared to $20 million for the Christian Coalition. "It's not that their faith is stronger, but they have a fundamentalist position that tells them to defeat all pro-choice candidates," she said. "You don't have that in the mainline denominations."

They also do not have Pat Robertson, a charismatic national television figure and former presidential candidate, to rally the troops. Robertson's failed 1988 campaign for the GOP presidential nomination mobilized hundreds of thousands of conservative evangelicals. His *700 Club* television show draws a national TV audience tuned into his Christian Broadcasting Network. "It's much easier to mobilize the grass roots when you have charismatic personalities dominating a movement," Hanauer said. "Politically, they are much more focused in their perception of the bad guys."

o

Religious liberals and leftists will also seek closer ties to local congregations and other religious traditions in the future, but they will remain a relatively small presence in the public square.

The religious left will be a minority voice because it represents a smaller constituency and is less organized than the religious right. Just as evangelical and fundamentalist churches have outgrown liberal mainline churches, conservative activism draws upon a larger and more responsive constituency than the religious left. During the 1980s and 1990s, there were several attempts to counteract the religious right, but taken together they drew far fewer activists than the membership in the Christian Coalition alone. Because of their oppositional nature, the growth of these organizations, such as the Interfaith Alliance and Call to Renewal, may well be tied to the fortunes of the religious right. Rather than simply responding to the "threat" of the religious right, the religious left needs a positive agenda that can rally the rank and file of mainline religion.

Since the 1950s, mainline Protestant and Catholic leaders have been in the forefront of liberal issues, from civil rights in the 1950s, opposing the Vietnam War in the 1960s, nuclear weapons build-ups in the 1970s, to Central American military policy in the 1980s. For example, the U.S. Catholic bishop's pastoral letters on nuclear arms and the economy during the 1980s drew intense media interest and conservative opposition. These statements, along with frequent declarations from mainline Protestant groups like the United Methodist Church, gave the impression that these denominations were vital forces of liberal social activism, especially since they often had offices in Washington to lobby Congress.

During the height of this political activity in the 1980s, there were frequent allegations that the political positions taken by denominational leaders, activists, and clergy were out of step with the people in the pews. Conservative organizations emerged, such as the Institute on Religion and Democracy, which sought to challenge the liberal activism of mainline denominations on foreign and domestic policy. Even issues on which one would expect the unanimity of the left and right—such as how to respond to a series of arson attacks against black churches in the South—turned into pitched political battles. In 1996, the Institute on Religion and Democracy charged that the National Council of Churches (NCC) had exaggerated the extent of black church arson, had little evidence of a racist conspiracy, and had taken money donated to rebuild churches and used it to promote a "radical political agenda." That allegation got a pointed denial from the Reverend Joan Campbell, the general secretary of the church council: "Our critics say this is nothing but a hoax and it's just the NCC stirring up trouble," she said to a meeting of ecumenical leaders in Chicago. "I am proud of the NCC's long and noble history in promoting racial justice."

Though the campaign to rebuild burned churches was a major success for the NCC, which raised millions of dollars in a matter of months, the long-term political future of such activism is uncertain. Efforts to decentralize mainline denominations and relegate more power to congregations will undercut organized religious left activism. The end of the Cold War and a less active U.S. military presence in Central America inspired less religious left activity in the 1990s. The change could be seen in the toned-down activism of U.S. Catholic leadership. Although the liberal voice of

Catholic bishops can still be heard in their critique of welfare reform and immigration policy, they are not delivering the kind of high-profile social statements found in their earlier pastoral letters.[9] As we will discuss in the next chapter on emerging social issues, the religious left has favored state involvement in the economy and welfare at a time when this position is falling out of favor. It will have to adapt to such changing realities without losing its concern for justice and its role as a critical watchdog of the forces of power and social influence.

Many leaders are beginning to see that the religious left must have closer connections to local congregations, and it must avoid polarizing, across-the-board agendas on the left or the right. Coalitions of religious left activists are broadening their boundaries to include those who may have difficulties with liberal concerns such as legalized abortion or gay rights, and are targeting other issues. For example, Latino Pentecostal churches opposed to tighter immigration restrictions have linked up with liberal churches and Catholic groups.

Religious left activism in the future will accent its religious nature. The groups that have galvanized people to activism, such as the Catholic Pax Christi or Evangelicals for Social Action, have a stronger religious identity than groups involved in previous efforts. Call to Renewal, for example, uses evangelical doctrine to address issues such as environmentalism, peacemaking, and poverty.

Liberal and leftist voices can still be heard among a small but vocal cadre of activist Catholic bishops and black Protestant leaders such as the Reverend Jesse Jackson. They are focused largely on local programs to empower the poor, health care issues, and ecological concerns. Labor union activism among clergy and laity has seen a significant comeback after a long period of inactivity in the 1980s.

Not only Christians are involved in the religious left. Jews involved in social action are returning to their religious roots, rediscovering the community and ethical resources the Jewish tradition provides. Since the civil rights movement, many Jews seeking social change had turned to secular movements or worked as individuals with Quakers, Unitarians, or the ecumenical movement. Much of the new Jewish activism has developed under the banner of the Jewish renewal movement, which links the rituals and teachings of Judaism with liberal and radical social concerns. The Jewish magazine *Tikkun* is a major voice in this movement. Around the country, many Jews find that involvement in a community of faith can be a source of moral and social support for political activism. In San Francisco, members of Jewish congregations appeared at budget hearings protesting social service cuts. In Minneapolis, the Jewish Metropolitan

Organizing Project worked on state legislation to redress inequalities in public service between cities and the suburbs.[10]

American Buddhists are also becoming more politically active for liberal and leftist causes. The Winter 1998 edition of *Turning Wheel,* the journal of the Buddhist Peace Fellowship, included articles on issues ranging from U.S. health care policy to political repression in Burma.

Seasoned religious liberals say there is no mystery to the question of why today's religious right is stronger than today's religious left. "They've got more money," said the Reverend Finley Schaef, a United Methodist minister in Brooklyn who received national attention in 1986 when he invited Nicaraguan President Daniel Ortega to speak from the pulpit of his Park Slope United Methodist Church. That was during the height of a bitter national debate over President Reagan's campaign to undermine Ortega's left-wing Sandinista government, and when hundreds of North American churches violated U.S. immigration law by offering sanctuary to refugees from U.S.-backed regimes in El Salvador and Guatemala. Schaef retired in 1997, after twenty-five years as pastor of his congregation. A sign in front of his former church still welcomes "black and white, straight and gay, old and young, rich and poor to unite as a loving community in covenant with God." Schaef remains an unapologetic liberal, and sees hope in the new cooperation between churches and a revived labor movement. "The significant social action," he says, "comes from the grass roots today."[11]

8

CULTURE WARS, SOCIAL PEACE

Polarization in the Pews

Hundreds of gay and lesbian Presbyterians and their supporters solemnly marched through the aisles of the Albuquerque Convention Center, carrying a large wooden cross, repeatedly singing, "We are marching in the light of God." Hanging from the cross were white stoles—symbols of ordination—belonging to closeted gay Presbyterians who already served as deacons, elders, and ministers but were afraid to show their faces.

Many were in tears.

By a vote of 313 to 236, commissioners at the 1996 assembly of the Presbyterian Church (U.S.A.) had just approved a constitutional amendment limiting ordination to Christians who maintain "fidelity in the covenant of marriage of a man and a woman, or chastity in singleness."

"Ordination is not a right," the commissioners of the 2.7 million-member denomination ruled. "The refusal to repent of any self-acknowledged practice that Scripture calls sin bars one from office."

Conservatives charged that the gay rights crusade is a major reason for steady declines in the Presbyterian Church (U.S.A.). Membership had been falling by an average of about 30,000 per year since 1983. There were also signs that rank-and-file Presbyterians were dissatisfied with their denominational leadership. Unrestricted giving to national church programs had been declining by about 5 percent a year for the past decade.

At the Albuquerque meeting, conservative Presbyterians fought off an alternative proposal that would have allowed a local option on gay ordination, arguing that allowing some churches to call openly gay clergy would only lead to further "polarization and paralysis" in the deeply divided denomination. That prompted one gay-rights supporter to point out that the debate on the ordination of homosexuals sounded a lot like the arguments once used against the ordination of women in the Presbyterian Church. "It was said then that ordaining women was against the Bible, against nature, and would split the church."

Mainline Protestant churches have been struggling with the question of whether homosexuality is a sin for more than two decades. Advocates for the ordination of gays and lesbians say that it's a question of social justice and civil rights. Gay clergy have always been around, they say, and now is the time for them to come out of the ecclesiastical closet.

Conservatives warn of a church split if gay-rights forces win a national victory. "Our congregations will neither respect nor follow persons who flaunt their failures at sexual self-control," warned the *Presbyterian Layman,* a conservative church newspaper, writing on the eve of the showdown in Albuquerque. "If this General Assembly fails to uphold Biblical standards that undergird the Presbyterian ethos, a major schism that many of us have sought to avoid may be inevitable."

Among the 568 voting commissioners at the General Assembly in Albuquerque were two Presbyterian ministers who personify this bitter debate over sexuality and ordination.

Pastor John shepherds a Presbyterian church in the American heartland. For him, the issue was settled nearly 2,000 years ago when the Apostle Paul wrote a New Testament verse (Romans 1:24–32) making it clear that homosexual acts are "evil."

"Women exchanged natural intercourse for unnatural, and the same way also the men, giving up natural intercourse with women, were consumed with passion for one another," Paul writes in Romans. "Men committed shameless acts with men and received in their own persons the due penalty for their error."

"Homosexuality is a sin," Pastor John says. "I believe the Bible is God's word." Nevertheless, he says his opposition to gay clergy doesn't mean he dislikes or condemns gay people. "Every time someone takes a stand on this issue they're called homophobes, but they are just standing on the Bible as God's word. I have homosexuals in my church and I'm comfortable with them, just like I'm comfortable with people with other sins, sins of heterosexual behavior. We wouldn't ordain a heterosexual who is cheating on his wife, or someone who was a thief."

Pastor Tim, who leads a Presbyterian church in San Francisco, also has homosexuals in his church, and uses the same Bible as Pastor John. But he comes up with very different conclusions about gays and lesbians. "I don't buy the argument that there is no other way to interpret Scripture than to go by what it says," he says. "Scripture should have authority for

Presbyterians, but it is our right to interpret Scripture in the light of its historical context and our life experience."

○

Conflicts arising over moral issues will continue to spark divisive debates within American religion and society, although there are signs that the people in the pews are growing tired of polarization over hot-button issues like abortion, euthanasia, feminism, and gay rights.

Although these issues are also divisive in the broader society, they carry special import to believers because they touch on concerns religion has traditionally addressed—sexuality, family, life, death, social justice. These religious conflicts become more entrenched than mere political fights because participants find it hard to resolve moral and religious battles by negotiation and compromise. They often feel that truth—often ultimate truth—is at stake. Those working for a truce in the culture wars suggest that if opposing camps just get together and learn more about each other, these issues will stand a better chance of resolution. Although attempts to mediate contentious issues have achieved some success, some studies show that greater contact with ideological opponents can actually intensify polarization. Meeting the opposition can confirm one's views rather than dispel them.[1]

Abortion, euthanasia, feminism, and gay rights have become the great battlegrounds of the culture wars. Sociologist James Davison Hunter defines these wars as a battle over the meaning of America and its institutions, such as the family, education, law, and politics. Though surveys indicate that liberals are more likely to be secular than conservatives, these struggles frequently take place between and among religions, not just between the forces of belief and unbelief. As we saw with the Presbyterians in Albuquerque, contentious positions can be embraced and condemned by believers in the same denomination. Liberal Catholics and Southern Baptists may favor abortion rights, while conservatives within the more liberal United Methodist Church may oppose legalized abortion. These cultural conflicts cut across age groups. Researchers Barry Kosmin and Seymour Lachman found little evidence that the culture wars are pitting the young against the old. "Rather than being a generational battle, the culture war over gender and family issues involves a clash of values that divides within generations," they write. "It pits believers in personal autonomy and right-based individualism against communitarians who advocate the common good and take issue with the unencumbered sovereignty of the individual."[2]

Groups that a few decades ago were considered "secular," such as Jewish young adults and the gay community, show new signs of religious commitment. They do not park their identity at the curb when setting off on a religious journey. The movement of gays petitioning for acceptance in mainline denominations is one sign of religious interest and commitment by homosexuals. As to gay marriage, liberal Quaker meetings were holding homosexual ceremonies long before more secular activists took up the cause. The gay-oriented Metropolitan Community Church, a denomination blending evangelical beliefs with liturgical worship and liberal theology, is in the forefront of the campaign for homosexual marriages.

Weakening denominational identity and the rise of political advocacy groups in religious bodies only add to the polarization. The alternative to the culture wars is avoiding conflict, putting on a polite facade, and hoping that these issues will go away. At most denominational conventions, both strategies seem to be at work, causing gridlock between warring camps. James Hunter notes that unless there is a change in the "environments of public discourse . . . demagoguery and rhetorical intolerance will prevail." In all of these conflicts—secular or religious—there is a tendency among those who take a centrist position not to speak up, and for the media and other public institutions to reflect more extreme positions.[3]

Surveys show that most Americans are not as sharply polarized as the think tanks, the media, activists, and leaders on either side of the liberal and conservative divide. Studies show Americans do not want abortion outlawed, but neither do they wholly approve of abortion on demand. Since such ambiguity is not conducive to sound bites and political campaigns, it's no surprise that those with clearly defined positions receive the most attention.

Challenging the "Secular" Media

It was the first Sunday after the Rodney King verdict, and the smoke was just clearing from riot-torn Los Angeles. Far from the violence in South Central, a reporter and photographer from a major metropolitan daily set out to visit African-American churches, to write a religious reaction story to the Rodney King riots and the alleged racism in the Los Angeles Police Department.

Their first stop was Bethel Baptist Church, a large, inner-city African-American congregation. They called ahead and told the pastor what kind of story they imagined, stressing that they wanted to contrast the peace in their community with the violence in South Central. They arrived at the church about an hour before the service began and were ushered into the pastor's study. He and several deacons greeted them graciously and offered them coffee.

Both the reporter, a full-time religion writer, and the photographer had been to the church before, and had written a long, positive story about the role of the church in the black community and the successful social service programs it had begun. On this morning, they talked with the pastor about the difference between his community and South Central—about why one erupted in violence and the other remained peaceful. For one thing, there was a solid black middle class in this community, and lots of home ownership among African Americans. Churches and other community groups were strong and had done grass-roots work to promote ethnic and religious understanding. The reporter already knew all this, and his "bias" going into this story was that he intended to write a positive story.

After about a half-hour interview, the pastor excused himself to get ready for the service. Before leaving he asked the two journalists to stand in a circle with him and his deacons in prayer, asking God to help them find the truth in their reporting.

Inside the packed sanctuary, the red-robed choir was swaying and rocking to spirited gospel music. So was the entire congregation of nearly 1,000 worshipers. The reporter interviewed some late-arriving members of the congregation, caught the beginning of the pastor's sermon, and quietly left with the photographer for the next black church they planned to visit that morning.

They were just about to the sidewalk when one of the ushers came running out after them. "Media people," he yelled. "Pastor wants to see you." Grabbing them by the arm, the usher escorted them back into the rollicking sanctuary, up the center aisle to the foot of the stage. "We've got some folks visiting us today from the media," the pastor said, his voice rising with anger when he said those last two words—*the media*. "Come on up here and say hello to the folks."

Once they got up on the stage, the mood abruptly changed. Gone was the gracious, prayerful pastor. "These gentlemen are from the *white media*," he began. "And they want to know why all the brothers in Los Angeles are so angry."

Holding a cordless microphone, the pastor began walking around the two journalists, stirring up his rage and the anger in his congregation.

"White media!" he yelled. "Why do you wait until the riots start before coming to talk to our community? White media! Do you think all the brothers in our community are breaking into stores and stealing TV sets? White media! Look at all the brothers out there before your eyes. Why don't you write about them?"

Of course, they *were* there to write about them, and they *had* been to that church before, but none of that mattered. These two white males were reduced to symbols of oppression that Sunday morning, caught up in the rising resentment of the media by two of its least trusted constituencies—the church and the black community. Like two stage props, they were forced to stand before the congregation for five minutes before slipping away and heading back to their car.

They didn't mention the incident in the story they wrote in the Monday morning paper. "Black churches struggled to make sense of the Rodney King verdicts yesterday," their story began, "while vowing a new crusade against racism and social injustice."

———— o ————

Secular journalists and people of faith find themselves on the front lines of the culture wars. There are many reasons for the gulf between reporters and religionists. Reporters are supposedly secular. They traffic in facts. Religionists walk a spiritual path, traveling by faith. Reporters want breaking news; religionists seek eternal, timeless truth. Religionists submit to hierarchy and higher authority, institutions that reporters deeply distrust. Religionists delve into nuanced theological debate. Reports seek sound bites and a snappy lead paragraph.

Despite all these differences, there are signs of rapprochement between the secular media and purveyors in the sacred. **In the new millennium, newspapers will make greater efforts to provide intelligent and informed coverage of religion—if only because it makes good business sense.** In the 1980s and 1990s, more newspapers woke up to the fact that religion is something of deep import to their readers. Television, except for some recent efforts by the Public Broadcasting Service, still appears clueless about how to cover religion.

There have been numerous studies of religion coverage in the secular press. Like all studies, their conclusions vary greatly, depending on how the questions are posed, who is asked, what aspect of "the media" is examined, and who pays for the study. One infamous survey of the East Coast "media elite" found rampant secularism among journalists.[4] Another one studied the beliefs of religion reporters and religion editors at secular papers and found a high degree of religious commitment.[5] Some studies examined whether the media writes "positive" or "negative" stories, slippery categories at best. They looked at the number of stories about religion, using various definitions of a "religion" story. One study, for example, didn't consider the Branch Davidians and their 1993 standoff in Waco, Texas, as "religion stories."[6] Other surveys asked clergy and other experts to rate the quality of religion coverage. Anyone who knows a lot about anything is usually unimpressed by how it is covered in the mainstream media. These studies also asked religious leaders whether they liked how they were portrayed in the media, as if the job of reporters was to make them look good. Few people like they way they are portrayed in the media, including people in the media.

American newspapers have been writing about religion since the first edition of the first American newspaper, *Publick Occurences,* reported on September 25, 1690, that Christianized Indians at Plymouth gathered to thank God for a plentiful crop.[7] In the 1720s, critical coverage cf Puritan leaders Increase and Cotton Mather was featured in the *New England Courant.* A century later, James Gordon Bennett and his *New York Herald* revolutionized many aspects of American journalism—including the idea that religion should be covered as news. For the rest of the century, American newspapers ran lively and frequent coverage of the evangelical and Pentecostal revivals sweeping the nation, peaking with the deluge of coverage of the 1925 Scopes "Monkey Trial" in Dayton, Tennessee, when schoolteacher John T. Scopes was charged with violating a law against teaching evolution in the state's public schools.

In his book *Unsecular Media: Making News of Religion in America,* journalist and historian Mark Silk said "Bennettian religion writing," lively and often critical, ended with the rise of the Saturday church page, when newspapers discovered that churches would pay money to advertise their services. Wrapped around the church ads was news of bake sales, pulpit changes, and a "Sermon of the Week" from local clergy. "Disinclined to bite the hand that fed it," Silk writes, "the coverage of religion became increasingly bland and promotional."[8]

This began to change in the 1950s, with church involvement in the civil rights movement, and in the 1960s, when John F. Kennedy's Catholicism became a presidential campaign issue and the Second Vatican Council brought new attention to the Roman Catholic Church. Another watershed event was in 1976, when presidential candidate Jimmy Carter mentioned that he was "born-again" and mystified most of the nation's political reporters. Within a few years, the emergence of the Moral Majority and the New Christian Right made religion in America a "big story" involving politics and other national issues. Meanwhile, the nation's Roman Catholic bishops began issuing a series of controversial pastoral letters condemning U.S. nuclear weapons policies and the injustices of capitalism.

Political correspondents and feature writers had trouble figuring out what was behind all this strange new religious activism. Newspaper editors realized they needed quality reporting on the religion beat. Specialists were trained from existing staff, or hired from seminaries and religious studies programs. Fellowship programs like the University of North Carolina's Program in Religious Studies for Journalists were founded to improve understanding among reporters and editors. Religion writers sought to examine how religion is related to social and ethical issues, a trend evident on many Saturday religion pages now titled "Religion and Ethics." Leading this movement toward quality religion sections in the 1980s were Jeanne Pugh of the *St. Petersburg Times* and Joan Connell of the *San Jose Mercury News*. Other newspapers, the *Los Angeles Times, New York Times,* and the *San Francisco Examiner and Chronicle,* downplayed religion pages but devoted major resources to making religion a page-one story.

In the 1990s, religion reporting began to reflect the decentralized and pluralistic complexion of the American spiritual scene. There were fewer stories on denominational politics and more stories on the noninstitutional side of religion—spirituality and ethics. Meanwhile, the Religion Newswriters Association reported a sharp increase in the number of members reporting on religion at secular newspapers. Seminaries began offering courses on journalism, and journalism schools started classes on religion reporting.

Despite all this improvement, many problems remain when it comes to newspapers and their coverage of religion. Because the media views conflict as a major category of news, and because of the notion that sex sells newspapers, abortion, feminism, battles over gay rights, and clergy accused of sexual abuse get more than their share of coverage. Stories about conflict are much easier to write than subtle, nuanced accounts of religious conversion, stories about spirituality, or discussions of the content and history of religious belief. Though minority faiths like Buddhism get lots of positive coverage, stories about Muslims often focus on the most militant Islamic factions. One of the worst examples of this was the initial coverage of the 1995 bombing of the Oklahoma City federal building, when the suspected bombers were erroneously reported as dark-haired, bearded men of "Middle Eastern" or "Arabic" heritage.[9]

All of the progress of the last two decades should not obscure the fact that compared to other subjects, religion is still woefully undercovered by the media. Although active membership in the Religion Newswriters Association climbed to nearly 200 by 1997, that left well over 1,500 daily newspapers with no religion specialist. Religion journalists themselves still routinely criticize the media for underplaying the importance of the subject. Most say there is little outright hostility to religion in newsrooms, but they perceive indifference and illiteracy concerning the importance of religion among their editors and colleagues. This neglect of religion is fed by the fear of offending or of being too controversial on issues that are close to their readers.

In his analysis of religion reporting, Mark Silk questions the prevailing wisdom that reporters and religionists find themselves in opposing camps in the culture wars. Religion reporters, like most journalists, reflect the "cultural perceptions and stock sentiments" of the people they cover. Newspapers, and especially television, often reduce their subjects to stereotypes. They love to tell people what they think they already know. "When the news media set out to represent religion," Silk writes, "they do not approach it from the standpoint of the secular confronting the sacred. They are operating with ideas of what religion is and is not."[10] High on that list of ideas is that "good" religion (Mother Teresa, soup kitchens, interfaith initiatives) are stories about people doing good works and being tolerant toward people of other faiths. "Bad" religion (TV evangelist scandals, pedophile priests, Islamic extremists) involves religious hypocrisy, clergy in sexual and financial scandals, and fundamentalists who want to "impose" their beliefs on others.

In the future, look for more diverse coverage of religion. Fortunately, the call to provide journalists with better education on religion comes at the right time. The arrival of world and new religions in North America will force reporters to gain access to and show familiarity with a wide range of religious cultures.

Decentralized religion is harder to cover. One reason the news media, especially television, loves to cover the travels of Pope John Paul II is that he is a newsmaker who can legitimately claim to speak for millions of people. The media loves personalities. Widespread coverage of the pope's 1998 trip to Cuba (only tempered in volume by the Monica Lewinsky/Bill Clinton sex scandal) was made more irresistible by spinning the story as a "standoff" with another world superstar—Fidel Castro.

Any problems that newspapers have covering religion pale in comparison to the lack of resources television and radio commit to the religion beat. Broadcast news got off on the wrong foot in the 1920s when radio news networks decided that religion was not a subject to cover but a "public service" to be provided and otherwise ignored. That gave broadcast journalists no opportunity for objective, critical coverage of religion. Early radio and TV networks would only give free time to mainline denominations, which snubbed spiritual fringe groups, including the rising American evangelical movement. That forced fundamentalists,

Pentecostals, and others to develop their own media networks and to become the powerhouses of religious broadcasting we saw with the rise in the 1970s and 1980s of Jerry Falwell, Pat Robertson, James Dobson, and others.

In the 1990s, some news organizations, such as ABC, the Public Broadcasting Service (PBS), and National Public Radio, created full-time staff jobs devoted to religion coverage. Peter Jennings, senior anchor at ABC News and the editor of *World News Tonight,* admitted ABC News has a long way to go. "I have only recently come to understand how complicated and inadequate and occasionally horrifying media coverage of religion has been," he said. "I would venture that in the overwhelming majority of newsrooms in America there is an appalling ignorance of religion and faith."[11] Few local television news organizations have hired religion specialists. PBS has done a better job, with its impressive work of Bill Moyers on religion and spirituality, ranging from his conversations with mythologist Joseph Campbell to programs exploring the Book of Genesis. In 1997, PBS launched a new *Religion and Ethics NewsWeekly* program anchored by former NBC reporter Bob Abernathy.

Network television's attitudes about religion may be summed up in a remark made by Tom Brokaw, the network anchor at NBC News, during a question-and-answer session with students at the Graduate School of Journalism at the University of California at Berkeley. It was the fall semester of 1997 and the school had just offered its first course on religion reporting. Asked to comment on how well NBC covers religion in America, Brokaw replied, "We don't even come close to covering it. I suppose in part because we think it's kind of a self-contained little arena. The people that are most affected by it kind of already know about it."

Brokaw made that remark the day after a half million evangelical Christian men gathered at a Promise Keepers rally in Washington, D.C., one of the largest demonstrations ever held in the nation's capital.

Seeking Common Ground

The meeting that day in Washington in the spring of 1997 was something of an anomaly: Jim Wallis of *Sojourners* magazine, a bastion of the Christian left, and other mainline church leaders were sitting down with conservative evangelicals and discussing school vouchers, abortion, welfare reform, and other hot-button issues. The meeting, called "The Church Steps Forward: A Christian Roundtable on Poverty and Welfare Reform," was held in the wake of federally mandated changes that would affect all congregations ministering to the poor.

"When a hurricane is coming and you are passing out sandbags, you don't ask if the person sitting next to you is liberal or conservative," said Wallis. With his evangelical theology and preaching style, and history of social justice and anti-war activism, Wallis seems well-suited for bridge building.

Wallis discovered the power and appeal of common-ground efforts when he started his organization, Call to Renewal, to challenge the religious right. On a U.S. tour with the new group in the fall of 1996, he found that abortion foes and abortion rights advocates could actually sit down and talk to one another about how dramatically to reduce the 1.5 million abortions performed each year without getting into fights about enacting constitutional amendments "that everyone knows will never pass anyway." In Colorado Springs, evangelicals agreed with gay rights supporters that family disintegration stems more from heterosexual family breakdown than from any influence by radical homosexuals.

Without changing his commitment to issues of social action and peace, Wallis tried to enlarge the conversation on faith and social issues to include the Christian Coalition, the National Council of Churches, and the Catholic Alliance, a sister organization of the Christian Coalition. Forming new alliances, Wallis said, creates a new kind of spiritual unity.

"This new table of Christian unity is possible only as we seek to find the common ground that has been hidden by our divisions," he adds. "If we don't, a new period of division awaits us, perhaps not along denominational and constituency lines but along social and cultural cleavages. Instead of helping to resolve society's deepest conflicts, the church would likely ratify them."[12]

o

In the new millennium, there will be a renewed effort to find common ground between religious groups in conflict over abortion, welfare, and other social controversies.

In religion, as in politics, most activists and organizations want to avoid being identified with the extreme right or left. As noted earlier, the Christian Coalition has sought to broaden its base and address issues outside the traditional evangelical orbit. Groups as diverse as the Catholic Church and American Muslims also seek the political and social center. Although the Catholic Church has taken strongly conservative positions on abortion, euthanasia, and birth control, it has also opposed the death penalty and criticized welfare cuts. Muslims have much in common with conservative Christians in their opposition to abortion and pornography, but they have taken liberal stands on immigration and welfare issues. Keith

Fournier, president of the Catholic Alliance, an offshoot of the Christian Coalition, sees welfare reform and community development as the basis for a new kind ecumenism between the religious left and right.

Signs of a rapprochement are everywhere, even at the upper echelons of American Protestantism. For example, something amazing happened in the spring of 1996, although it received very little attention in the news media. Putting aside five decades of mistrust, conservative evangelical leaders began a dialogue with the nation's liberal Protestant establishment. Their ecumenical overture was a speech by the Reverend Don Argue, president of the National Association of Evangelicals, before the top policy-making body of the National Council of Churches, the nation's largest umbrella group of Protestant, Orthodox, and Anglican churches. "This is a very significant day in the life of the National Council of Churches," said Bishop Melvin Talbert, the NCC president. "The National Association of Evangelicals was organized to oppose the ecumenical movement. They've always been against the NCC."

In a way, it was President Clinton and Pope John Paul II who brought the two groups together. Argue, whose organization represents 42,500 evangelical congregations with about ten million people across the United States, met the Reverend Joan Campbell, the general secretary of the National Council of Churches, at a White House prayer breakfast. Then, during a papal visit to New York City, Campbell and Argue found themselves locked together in a waiting room before a meeting with the pontiff. Argue and Campbell started talking and realized that they liked each other. They were already working together on the Religious Alliance Against Pornography, and hoped their two institutions could join forces through charity work and overseas relief efforts. Just before the NCC meeting in Chicago, they dined together in Campbell's home in New York City. "A friendship has happened," Campbell said. "There has been a real bonding."

Evangelicals and mainline Protestants parted ways earlier this century over disputes about the authority of the Bible, access to network radio and television time, and theological liberalism in U.S. seminaries. In response, the National Evangelical Association was formed in 1942, followed two years later by the National Religious Broadcasters. Both groups have grown rapidly in recent decades with the rising political power of conservative evangelicals.

Argue said many evangelical leaders remain wary of mainline Protestant denominations such as the United Methodist Church or the Presbyterian Church (U.S.A.). The two factions remain far apart in their interpretation of Scripture or positions on abortion, but are starting to see more common goals than fundamental differences. "Moral values are at such a lull in the general population that those of us who hold to Biblical morality are being drawn together out of necessity," Argue said after his speech before the 270 assembled NCC delegates. Then the conservative evangelical leader led the mainline Protestant officials in prayer. Talbert, the United Methodist bishop from Northern California and an outspoken African-American liberal, could hardly believe his eyes. "The spirit is moving in our midst," he said, shaking his head.[13]

Some see the roots of this left-meets-right movement in the early 1990s, when abortion rights advocates and anti-abortion activists began a series of discussions and joint projects. They began to challenge their own stereotypes about each other. Anti-abortion crusaders learned that most abortion rights activists don't favor abortion as a method of birth control. "Pro-choicers", discovered that "pro-lifers" are not all blindly following authoritarian right-wing leaders. Though the common-ground movement has fairly strong religious participation, it has a tenuous constituency among evangelicals. Sociologist James Kelly said participation in the movement is likely to increase where abortion conflict is most intense, such as in the aftermath of abortion clinic violence.[14]

Bridges are also being built around other issues, spanning the gap between liberals who favor government support for families and conservatives who stress the family's moral and cultural importance. Since the 1960s, support for the "bourgeois" family has taken a back seat among liberal churches concerned with gay rights and women's issues. Efforts to forge a middle ground have emerged under mainline Protestant auspices such as the University of Chicago Divinity School's Religion, Culture, and Family Project. The growing debate over the health of the family inspired the reappraisal of family issues at other mainline theological seminaries.[15]

Welfare cuts in the late 1990s and the resulting need to reinvigorate private groups such as religious congregations, neighborhood institutions, and labor unions will create new coalitions between liberals, moderates, and conservatives. Complex issues such as cloning and other forms of genetic engineering will create other partnerships. For example, a coalition formed to oppose the patenting of animals for biomedical purposes included organizations as diverse as the Southern Baptist Convention, the United Methodist Church, and New Age environmental groups.

Religious communities do not seek common ground simply out of political expediency. Congregations provide what sociologist Peter Berger calls a "zone of freedom" by preaching transcendent values that can draw together people from diverse perspectives. It is this spiritual focus that can inspire a truce in the culture wars. Berger says one of the functions of the church is to serve as an open forum where moral and social concerns can be freely discussed. In the past, Berger adds, many national religious bodies have done the opposite, taking sides in conflicts rather than serving as mediating organizations.[16]

Recent research by sociologist John Coleman of the Jesuit School of Theology found that groups such as the interfaith Habitat for Humanity, Bread for the World, and Pax Christi often serve this unifying role, even though they take strong positions on social and moral issues. Coleman found that these groups bring together isolated individuals and groups within congregations to engage in common work. Coleman says paradenominational groups do not compete with local churches but provide outlets for a social faith, thereby defusing political conflicts in congregations.[17]

It is at the local level where America stands the best chance of putting aside political differences and coming together for social action. When the wave of church arson hit the deep South in the summer of 1996, it ignited yet another national battle between the conservative Institute for Religion and Democracy and the liberal National Council of Churches. At the local level, something very different happened that summer in religious communities across the United States.

It happened in Boligee, Alabama, a little town where Baptists, Jews, Methodists, Buddhists, Pentecostals, Mormons, and others came together from around the country to build three sanctuaries of hope from the ashes of hate. The trouble in Boligee began three days before Christmas 1995, when an unknown arsonist destroyed Mount Zion Baptist Church, the spiritual home of a 200-year-old congregation started by slaves and attended by forty of Boligee's three hundred residents. Then, on the night of January 11, two more isolated churches were destroyed by arson attacks—Mount Zoar Baptist Church of Boligee and Little Zion Baptist Church in nearby Tishabee. The church burnings in Boligee helped focus national attention on a wave of fifty arson attacks against Southern churches.

They also focused attention on the fact that these towns hidden in the woods along Interstate 59 are still deeply segregated. Greene County—where cotton was king but poverty now reigns—is more than 70 percent black. Most of the white residents live about ten miles up the road in relatively posh Eutaw, the county seat. Warrior Academy, a private school behind the Alabama National Guard building in Eutaw, is all white. The local public school is all black. Segregation is no longer enforced by law in Greene County, but there's still a black swimming pool and a white swimming pool, a black graveyard and a white graveyard, a black bank and a white bank. People take these things for granted in Greene County.

"All this attention has forced us to focus on our problems," said Spiver Gordon, a long-time civil rights activist and member of the Eutaw City Council. "The feeling here has been, 'You stay in your corner, and I'll stay in my corner, and we'll just live like we've always lived.' But now we've got folks coming in and saying there's something wrong with that."

Those folks came as members of interfaith delegations who had volunteered their summer vacations to help rebuild the churches of Boligee. Harold Confer, executive director of Washington Quaker Work Camps, who organized the effort, looked up at the muggy Alabama skies one afternoon as volunteers nailed a new roof atop a brand new Mount Zion Baptist Church.

"Presbyterians, Episcopalians, Methodists, Quakers, Latter-day Saints all worship one God—the God that called them to Boligee," he said. "They were called down here by the suffering of these people. They didn't come with Bibles and hymn books, but with hammers and hard hats. And in the process of rebuilding these churches, they've rebuilt their own unity."[18]

9

EMERGING SOCIAL ISSUES

Stewards of the Earth

John Muir, the nineteenth-century founder of the Sierra Club and savior of American wilderness, was a lapsed Presbyterian. He often railed against Christianity's belief in a single deity with a special interest in one creature, "Lord Man." During one of his sojourns in Yosemite, he came across a dead bear, and wrote in his journal, "Bears are made of the same dust as we, and breathe the same winds and drink the same waters. His life turns and ebbs with heart-pulsing like ours, and was poured from the same First Fountain. And whether he at last goes to our stingy heaven or not, he has terrestrial immortality."

Muir is part of a long American tradition of ecological spirituality, a heritage that includes the New England transcendentalists Henry David Thoreau, author of *Walden,* and Ralph Waldo Emerson, the poet and essayist who had a long correspondence with Muir. Emerson and Muir met in Yosemite, and in a letter to Emerson full of religious imagery, Muir urged the New Englander to spend more time amid the granite cathedrals of the Sierra. "Do not drift away with the mob when the spirits of these rocks and waters persuade you to closer communion," he wrote. "I invite you to join me in a month's worship with Nature in the high temples of the great Sierra Crown beyond our holy Yosemite. It will cost you nothing save the time and the very little of that, for you will be mostly in eternity."

Gary Snyder, the California naturalist, Buddhist, and Pulitzer Prize–winning poet, sees Muir, Emerson, and Thoreau as the prophets of an unacknowledged American folk religion. "Right there in our American tradition is a very interesting spiritual ecological line that is entirely ours," Snyder said. "You would never find an Emerson or a Thoreau on the European continent. They would not have evolved on that continent. Even though the transcendentalists were educated initially in the European Occidental tradition, they made another step and I think the step they made in part was a deep psychic response to the vast wilderness of this continent."[1]

○

Had John Muir lived at the turn of the millennium rather than turn of the century, he would have found many friends in organized religion. **For in the new millennium, communities of faith will draw on their vast resources and ancient traditions to become better stewards of the Earth.**

Environmental concerns have in recent years found wide appeal among religious groups that see ecological stewardship as a natural part of their teachings on creation and redemption of the world. Of course, environmentalism is embraced by secular as well as spiritual groups. But the religious factor in environmentalism is becoming more important, even to secular environmentalists. Belief, in one form or another, undergirds much of the environmental movement. One poll found that although a clear majority of environmentalists are not part of organized religion, most agreed with the statement, "Because God created the natural world, it is wrong to abuse it."[2]

Religious groups bring a "historical and spiritual grounding to the 'why' of why we need to save our environment," says Renée Rico, formerly of the Environmental Protection Agency. "Secular groups are really good at strategy and understanding how to do things. But when they try to articulate why, they often come across as shrill. When religious people talk about it, it comes across as part of a whole way of living."[3]

The National Religious Partnership for the Environment (NRPE) has linked together groups such as the Evangelical Environmental Network with Roman Catholic, Jewish, and mainline Protestant and Eastern Orthodox churches. There is more support among the laity for environmental activism than for many social issues pushed at church headquarters. Environmental action is practical and can be translated into congregational life more easily than more abstract issues. Church activists report that thousands of congregations are involved in environmental work. Clergy and laity have been trained at regional conferences, and hold workshops on urban gardens, conduct new liturgies, and examine their personal lifestyles. In Minneapolis and St. Paul, for example, families from Lutheran churches invest in small, organic farm operations.

Whereas ecological groups are often organized around a particular issue, such as saving the redwoods, religious environmental activists take a larger view, seeing the whole earth and humanity as God's sacred creation. Their focus on human and natural resources provides a connection with issues of poverty and social justice. They can also help feuding parties in ecological conflicts. For instance, the Interfaith Network for Earth Concerns in Oregon sponsored a conference on "Ethics, Economics, and Endangered Species: Finding Ecological and Ethical Integrity Together," where federal agencies met with timber, environmental, community-development, commercial-fishing, and small-woodland interests. These conflicted parties, offered an opportunity for dialogue in a safe and respectful environment, discussed concerns involving endangered species.[4]

Although environmentalism creates new partnerships among religious groups, these coalitions are sometimes threatened by theological differences. Evangelicals criticize "eco-theologians" who see the earth as divine, confuse God with nature worship, or embrace a "pagan" worldview that downplays the Judeo-Christian distinction between creator and creation. Those on the environmental religious left hold that these conservatives are too reluctant to break with the Judeo-Christian mind-set that views humanity as superior to nature, thereby justifying the exploitation of natural resources. Divisions have also emerged between Christians and other believers over what role the state should play in protecting the environment.

In a study of the National Religious Partnership for the Environment, sociologists Mark Shibley and Jonathon Wiggins found that Catholics, Jews, and evangelicals often take a "stewardship" approach to environmental concerns, stressing individual responsibility for God's creation. Mainline Protestants—at least on the leadership level—take an "eco-justice" stand linking environmental concerns with issues of social justice. Other partners take a more mystical approach that employs the ideas of "creation spirituality." These three schools of thought suggest that the common ground of religious environmentalism may be a shaky one.[5]

New Partnerships to Help the Poor

President Bill Clinton had just signed landmark legislation calling for a massive overhaul of the federal welfare system, and religious charities were bracing for a tidal wave of need. They knew welfare "reform" was political code-language for welfare cutbacks, and it suddenly seemed as though everyone was looking to the religious community for private-sector salvation.

For Rick Mockler, executive director of Catholic Charities of California, the largest religious charity organization in the nation's largest state, welfare reform was a thinly disguised "attack on the poor."

"We are not looking to replicate the role of government," said Mockler, whose agency already gets around 60 percent of its money from the local, state, and federal government. "As religious providers, we are not interested in taking over the welfare system."

Out in Kansas City, the Reverend Stephen Burger sat in his office at the International Union of Gospel Missions, a national network of 250 soup kitchens and rescue missions. Like many evangelicals, Burger was worried about restrictions forbidding religious charities from using government money "for sectarian worship, instruction, or proselytization." Burger has nothing against new church/state partnerships, but not if that means "having to make our programs like the government programs that didn't work."

"One reason faith-based ministries have worked is they demand certain adjustments in people's attitudes," he said. "That's the spiritual side. It has to do with moral issues that come with a belief structure—whether it's Catholic, Protestant, or Jewish."

o

Cutbacks in federal assistance to the needy and the shift of the welfare burden to state and local governments will inevitably make religious groups more involved in community development and helping the poor.

To even suggest that the cut in government assistance requires a greater role for religion is to spark controversy. Liberal religious leaders say they cannot fill the gap, and the government must remain the leading provider of social welfare. Conservatives argue that congregations and other private charities have always played a major role in meeting social needs—particularly before the growth of the welfare state—and they can do even more in the future.

Surveys reveal much uncertainty and doubt among religious leaders over what they can do to replace government welfare assistance. *New York Times* religion writer Peter Steinfels wrote in 1995 that the current "safety net" will, over the next seven years, add up to approximately $400 billion. This means that each of the nation's 258,000 congregations would have to contribute a little over $220,000 per year to meet the needs of the poor. More than 70 percent of these congregations have fewer than 400 members, and their average annual revenue is less than $100,000.[6] Even more modest proposals have been met with doubt and reluctance. President Clinton's call in early 1997 for congregations to "hire" people off the welfare rolls was viewed as impractical and even imposing by mainline Protestant and Catholic church leaders, who say the government is abdicating its rightful role as welfare provider.

But the bipartisan effort to cut welfare and encourage private groups to take up the slack will inevitably compel congregations to rethink how best to serve their communities. Congregations will broaden their sights beyond traditional collections of food and clothes. Larger religious structures will revamp their social statements and advocacy work to take up new and difficult roles. In her study of congregations, Nancy Ammerman found that churches do not exist in isolation, but are linked with their communities through governmental partnerships and local coalitions. The permeable boundaries between congregation and community were revealed in the growth of nonprofit corporations in Los Angeles after the 1992 Rodney King riots. The relationship is reciprocal: Government can ensure equal rights and access to care, while nonprofits, including congregations, can personalize services, since they are organized on a smaller scale and can be more responsive to client needs.[7]

Even before the cuts in welfare, religious groups were already involved in community service, not to replace the government but to address the unmet moral and spiritual dimensions of social welfare. Many of these faith-based programs are very effective. For instance, Teen Challenge, an evangelical ministry to help drug addicts, has better success rates than many secular drug treatment programs.

In studying religious efforts to fight poverty, researcher Amy Sherman finds new models of public-private cooperation. In Michigan, churches have redirected their benevolence away from handing out free groceries. Instead, members set up a mentoring program to provide clients the practical help and emotional support needed to find jobs. Welfare recipients involved in this program, called New Focus, meet weekly with their own personal budget counselor and attend regular classes teaching job and life skills. Sherman writes that these initiatives are effective because they stress long-term assistance that helps individuals develop and change rather than just providing short-term relief.[8]

Such partnerships allow congregations to design their own programs and avoid government interference that might squelch the religious nature of their ministries. Government leaders will have to learn that "the wisdom and practical experience of grassroots religious leaders can be powerfully helpful to the poor," Sherman adds. These congregations pursue the things they do most effectively, while relying on government programs for meeting needs outside their reach. For instance, uncooperative or highly dysfunctional individuals would be redirected to more specialized programs that fall outside of a typical congregation's abilities.

Black churches, long centers of spiritual solace and political action, are awakening to their potential for neighborhood development. Black churches have never strictly separated politics and faith. But often such social activism revolved around political advocacy, with candidates seeking votes from black pulpits or congregations rallying together to petition city hall for fair housing and racial justice. The new activism is local and stresses self-help. African-American congregations use their pulpits to expand job placement, encourage their own businesses and entrepreneurs, and even build low-income housing. This turn to economic self-empowerment requires clergy to mine the "social capital" embedded in their congregations. The Reverend James R. Samuel, pastor of the Little Rock African Methodist Episcopal Zion Church in Charlotte, North Carolina, saw his 1,500-member congregation as "more than a shepherd's flock. I saw it as an economic base which could be mobilized to undergird the success of every business within that congregation." Samuel compiled a directory of church members who ran businesses, and called business owners up to the pulpit to give a short pitch before the congregation.[9]

Another vehicle for community development is the growing cooperation between urban and suburban congregations. Some suburban churches have sent members to start or join urban churches, or even have relocated congregations to urban locations to respond to social needs. More significant is a movement of "twinning" urban and suburban congregations to work on community projects. This appeals to conservatives, moderates, and liberals. Robert Royal, of the conservative Ethics and Public Policy Center, writes that "reconnecting urban and suburban institutions—churches and other private associations—might restore to both sides realism and purpose."[10]

These partnerships are most common in the Catholic Church, which has a strong urban base. These twinnings often involve meeting together for prayer and discussion of how Catholic social teachings relate to local issues. Though these partnerships have evolved into larger coalitions, participants see improved communication between urban and suburban regions as the most important by-product. In New Orleans, for instance, the parish partnership program organized a series of dialogues on race in the wake of the O. J. Simpson verdict where blacks and whites could safely discuss that emotional issue.[11]

In a study of Los Angeles religious life after the 1992 racial unrest, researchers found that religious congregations played an important role in community redevelopment. Most striking was the increase of church-based nonprofit corporations focusing on entrepreneurial activities such as credit unions, work-training programs, and new businesses. Among these organizations, the researchers found that "religious conversion is viewed as empowering, in the broadest possible sense of that term," encouraging spiritual renewal, community organizing, and entrepreneurial skills.[12] Both the Los Angeles riots and the mounting toll of death and suffering from AIDS have propelled evangelicals, Mormons, and other conservative groups into community-development and health-care ministries. Often these community-development efforts carry a strong emphasis on racial reconciliation.

In the new millennium, community development and faith-based welfare programs will prosper among religious institutions, whether they are centrist, liberal, or conservative. The religious left, such as the Sojourners community in Washington, D.C., is as equally committed to religious community development as are the cultural and economic conservatives at the Heritage Foundation. Liberals value the way this work brings together different classes and races, while conservatives praise the emphasis on self-help and personal responsibility. These ministries will pose new questions and challenges to traditional understandings of the separation of church and state. There will continue to be differences concerning how much state and federal assistance is required to help run them, but there will nevertheless be a new convergence on social action in American religion.

Reading, Writing, and Religion: The Rise of Religious Schools

At the Community Christian Academy, religion is not just a single class in an otherwise secular school day. God and Jesus permeate every subject taught in this conservative evangelical school, where the instructors condemn evolution as heresy and teach history as the march toward God's final judgment.

"Why do we teach kids to read? So they can read the word of God," the principal explains. "Why do we teach kids about public speaking? So they can profess the word of God. Why do we teach kids about math? So they can be good stewards of what God gave them."

Although the philosophy at Community Christian Academy is conservative evangelical, the school promotes itself as independent and interdenominational. It draws its 950 students from churches representing thirty denominations, including Roman Catholic parishes, and nearly 200 different congregations. What brings students here is their parents' desire that their kids will come home from school at the end of the day with a clear idea of what is right and what is wrong.

"The religion taught in the public schools is relativism, which means that what is ethically correct has to do with how I feel about things, rather than what God says about it," says one teacher. "Our education is based on what God has said. You and I can decide what color we like best, but murder is wrong because God said it was wrong, not because you and I feel it is wrong."

———○———

In the new millennium, don't be surprised if a school like Community Christian Academy opens in your neighborhood. **Growing social diversity and the breakdown of many public school systems will prompt more parents to choose an educational environment where morality and religious faith are as important as biology and social studies.**

Religious bodies such as the Catholic Church, the Lutheran Church–Missouri Synod, Christian Reformed Church, Seventh-Day Adventists, and Orthodox Jews have long invested in parochial schooling. In recent years, the number of conservative evangelical schools has increased dramatically, making them major players in the private school market. Writing on the future of congregations, Lyle Schaller forecasts that within two decades at least a third of the nation's larger churches will offer Christian day-school programs.[13]

Non-Orthodox Jews have also shown rising interest in a new breed of Jewish schools. More than other religious groups, American Jews have long been wary of parochial schools, fearing they could mean a return to the ghetto and slow their acceptance in American society. But dissatisfaction with the crime and curriculum in many public schools, along with concerns that their children have little understanding of their own history and traditions, have compelled many American Jews to reconsider the value of religious education. The number of children in full-time Jewish day schools has tripled in the past thirty-five years. Though Orthodox schools are the most numerous, there has also been a flowering of Conservative and Reform movement institutions in the last decade. Some Jewish groups are even reevaluating their traditional opposition to school vouchers.[14]

The Catholic Church has long offered schools for its own faith community and as an educational resource for the larger neighborhood. Beginning in the 1970s, as public schools in poor inner-city neighborhoods deteriorated, urban Catholic schools opened their doors to non-Catholics. For instance, in New York State, minority enrollment in Catholic schools increased from 12 percent in 1970 to 36 percent in 1991. In the New York City borough of the Bronx, the minority enrollment in the early 1990s was up to 85 percent. Although these schools still retain a Catholic identity, and offer Catholic theology courses, they are not primarily seen as vehicles for evangelism. Sociologist James Coleman found that aside from their more rigorous curriculum and stricter discipline, Catholic schools have a common moral vision that fosters trust and cooperation among teachers, administrators, and parents.[15]

Episcopal priest and writer Ephraim Radner notes that religious schools have instituted reforms long advocated by public school educators. They use small classes, school-based management, structured learning of basic skills, after-school follow-up, neighborhood rootedness, and increased family involvement. Radner calls upon mainline Protestants to rethink their inactivity in parochial schooling and unqualified support for public schools, noting that religious education can be an important ministry for declining inner-city churches. Religious schools offer what inner-city public schools often cannot: "communal, cultural, and moral formation to children cast adrift in violence and hopelessness."[16] Lutheran school leader Melvin Kieschnick writes that congregations with schools often better reflect the cultural diversity of their neighborhoods.

There will be increased government interest in these schools. Although the political future of vouchers is uncertain, there has been increasing experimentation with tax-credit programs in cities around the United States. The results have been mixed. Experiments with vouchers in Ohio and Wisconsin have generated concern among public school teachers, labor unions, and church-state separationists. They argue that religious schools view the proselytizing of students as a key component of their educational philosophy; thus vouchers are seen as threatening church-state separation. The groups most involved in religious schooling—conservative evangelicals and Catholics—favor more accommodation of religion by government. But if vouchers and other forms of public assistance for private schooling are to take hold, the problem of one faith or movement dominating private sector schools will only be addressed as new private schools broaden the market and encourage religious pluralism. Although they may have fewer resources than conservative churches, Unitarian, Episcopal, Muslim, secular humanist, New Age–oriented, and other liberal and moderate congregations can and have created their own schools.

Concerns about the separation of church and state may prevent the widespread use of vouchers, at least in the near future. In the meantime, private donations, rather than public tax dollars, will become a popular way to finance religious-based education. In the wake of the local government's refusal to help fund programs at religious schools in New York and Wisconsin, for instance, contributions from private and corporate sources of support have been found.

Aside from the issue of church-state separation, public school advocates fear that allowing vouchers will downgrade public schools as private schools become increasingly accessible to the middle class. There are concerns that the common culture generated by public schools will erode as students are isolated from each other and balkanized in their own self-enclosed educational enclaves. Rather than fostering diversity and tolerance, critics charge that the growth and domination of private and religious schools will inhibit cultural interaction and interchange among races, religions, and social classes.

Some will question whether public schools can restore a sense of common culture to a nation already divided over moral, religious, and other social issues. Creating unity may also be beyond the scope of religious schools, but they can avoid contributing to cultural fragmentation by following in the tracks of Catholic schools. They may have to rise above sectarianism and narrow proselytism, and open their doors to the entire community. Doing so without undermining their religious identity will be a serious challenge to private schools in the new millennium.

In the future, the educational terrain will not only be divided between public and private schools. Home schooling will become a viable alternative among religious believers. The home-schooling movement took off in the 1980s among conservative Christians, reaching a total of 1.2 million children by 1996. Most home schoolers say that the family—even more than the church—is responsible for educating children. Many religious organizations have formed partnerships with parents involved in home schooling by developing curricula and providing support.

In recent years, the home-schooling movement has attracted non-Christian families, especially Jews and Muslims, who often do not have the numbers to establish their own schools. The Islamic Home School Association of North America was established in the late 1980s and has witnessed a "big surge of interest" among Muslim parents, says founder Janet Akremi. Muslim home schoolers, who represent converts and ethnic Muslims, often incorporate religious practices—such as frequent prayer—and Islamic perspectives into their lessons on history and science.[17]

Most American students will continue to attend public schools, and religion will have increasing influence even in these classrooms. After years of conflict and many court cases over the role of religion in the public schools, a consensus seems to be emerging that religious beliefs and values should be discussed in the classroom, as long as there is not advocacy of any one religion. After decades of conspicuous absence from textbooks and teaching curricula, the role of religion in U.S. history and society is being reintroduced.

The new approach, as pioneered by such educational reformers as Charles Haynes of the Freedom Forum, a First Amendment think tank, attempts to turn controversy into education. For instance, disputes over displaying Christmas creches in the classroom are now viewed as opportunities for educating students about the different religious holidays and the beliefs they represent. These opportunities allow teachers to assign students religious literature and music and to display religious symbols as instructional aids. Public educators are also giving students unprecedented freedom to observe their faith at school—a trend evidenced in the mushrooming of student prayer meetings and Bible clubs. These changes follow moderation among "culture warriors" on both sides. Many religious conservatives are wary of entrusting their faith to bureaucrats and have downplayed the old view that public schools should promote Christianity. Liberals, on the other hand, have gradually given more tolerance to religion, realizing that students benefit from discussions about ethics and moral values.[18]

New Clashes Between Church and State

Everyone agreed that Leland House, a forty-five-unit residential community for people with AIDS and the HIV virus, was desperately needed in San Francisco. More than 2,000 people with HIV were on a waiting list for affordable housing in the city. Nearly $10 million in local, state, and federal money had been found to open and operate the new center, which was to be run by Catholic Charities under a contract with the City of San Francisco.

Suddenly, there was a big problem. Just two weeks before Leland House was scheduled to open, Roman Catholic Archbishop William Levada refused to abide by a new San Francisco law requiring all city contractors to provide health insurance to the "domestic partners" of all employees—whether they were gay, straight, or bisexual. What began as a cooperative venture between the church and the city had turned into an ugly church-state showdown between Levada, a leading conservative in the American Catholic hierarchy, and San Francisco Mayor Willie Brown, the consummate liberal politician and author of some of the earliest gay rights legislation in the nation.

Levada called a press conference to announce his opposition to the domestic partners law. "To seek to equate domestic partnership with the institution of marriage and family," he said, "runs contrary to Catholic teaching, to the beliefs of most religious and cultural traditions, and to the basic convictions of the great majority of Americans."

Brown and gay power brokers on the San Francisco Board of Supervisors would not budge. To them, providing equal benefits for the partners of gay and straight city contractors was an issue of civil rights. Supervisor Tom Ammiano, one of the two gay members on the city board, had a pointed reply to Levada: "As someone educated from infancy through university in the Catholic tradition, I am well aware of the structures and philosophy of your beliefs," he said. "We simply disagree that these private convictions can ever justify discrimination in law."

Cooler heads prevailed. Archbishop Levada and Mayor Brown soon struck a compromise that skirted the "domestic partners" controversy. Under the deal, a "legally domiciled member" of the employee's household, including a mother, brother, or "good friend," could be eligible for health insurance benefits. This way, the church could practice what it preached about universal health coverage and play "Don't Ask, Don't Tell" with its gay employees.[19]

○

Although that crisis was averted, and Leland House opened its doors, controversies like the one in San Francisco are popping up in communities across the nation. **In the new millennium, increased religious involvement in welfare, health care, community development, and education will spark new conflicts between church and state.** At the same time, legal conflicts about new religious movements, minority faiths, and other spiritual groups will arise as more people live in communities with restrictive zoning laws.

Federal legislation allowing states to direct welfare funds to religious groups has already ignited a firestorm of opposition by those upholding a strict interpretation of church-state separation. That law did make provisions to prevent religious discrimination against people on welfare. If a recipient objected to receiving benefits at a designated religious site, the state would be obligated to provide an alternative location. Nevertheless, critics claim that evangelism often plays a part in charitable operations, so providing any government money constitutes public support for religious programs.

Faith-based welfare programs are also locked in legal conflicts with government programs. For instance, Teen Challenge, a highly successful evangelical drug rehabilitation ministry, has clashed with state agencies that question the legitimacy of religious programs and the licensing of their counselors. These conflicts may eventually lead to an alternative mode of certification, since secular programs have a hard time regulating religious approaches to welfare and substance abuse. As evidence mounts that faith-based social services can be more effective than their secular counterparts, look for more cooperation between the state and religious organizations.[20]

This shift to welfare privatization will also intensify conflicts between accommodationists and church-state separationists. Accommodationists, who are often political conservatives, question the traditional opposition to any governmental involvement with religion-based organizations, arguing that the Constitution only sought to prevent state-established religion, not to forbid religious participation in the ordering of society. Strict church-state separationists maintain that a "wall" was established by the nation's founders to protect religious groups from government intrusion and, at the same time, to prevent religious groups and their teachings from influencing government.

Observers from both ends of the political spectrum have seen growing accommodation of religious activity by public, tax-funded sources. In the 1985 case of *Rosenberger* v. *University of Virginia,* for instance, the Supreme Court allowed a state organization to fund a religious publication. The same year, the court ruled that student-led prayer at public school commencement exercises was permissible in specific instances. Observers of church-state decisions point out that the conservative majority now on the court is able to put its imprimatur on cases once considered safe by advocates of strict church-state separation.[21]

Forecasting the future of church-state relations is difficult because it will be shaped by the rulings of a small number of judges whose appointments are subject to the winds of political change. But considering the growth of religious social programs and how well they perform, the courts will probably continue to allow greater governmental accommodation of religion's new public role, while balancing concerns about public sponsorship of specific religious doctrine.

Nevertheless, the prospect of closer relations between the government and religious organizations has brought fears to the surface about how government regulations could thwart the freedom of faith groups. Conservative religious leaders fear that social policy and court rulings on volatile cultural issues may punish them for simply practicing their faith. For instance, a Christian homeowner who refused to rent an apartment to an unmarried couple was prosecuted for violating housing regulations. Concerns that cases like this may be a foretaste of judicial and legislative religious discrimination are a common theme in the conservative Christian press.

Another area of church-state conflict will be zoning and neighborhood restrictions that limit the growth and even presence of congregations. The battle between residents who want to protect the quality of life in their neighborhoods and other organizations who see a social or economic need to build in these areas has had particular impact on religious groups. Residents of middle-class and upper-class suburbs have imposed new zoning laws that limit the parking capacity and building expansions of congregations. Congregation-based social services, such as soup kitchens, are often viewed more as detriments than resources by residents who fear lower property values and a reduction in the quality of neighborhood life. The dramatic growth of evangelical storefront churches in inner-cities, especially in business districts, has transformed commercial sites into not-for-profit meccas, threatening municipalities with loss of tax revenue. Clergy say that their churches are being targeted with restrictions and denied building permits because they draw lower income minorities and engage in "unorthodox" practices, such as speaking in tongues and faith healing.

Rising visibility of nonconventional and new immigrant religions in American society will cause increasing conflict over the boundaries of "acceptable" religious practice. Conflict emerges over the Native American Church's use of peyote in religious rituals and in the practices of faiths such as Santeria, a blend of African-Cuban religion and folk Catholicism. Followers of Santeria clash with local officials over their practice of sacrificing small animals in their rituals. The Religious Freedom Restoration Act of 1993 was the outgrowth of concern by both mainstream and non-conventional religious groups that religious practices could be legally discriminated against, particularly if they are unpopular or marginal within society. In 1997, however, the Supreme Court ruled that such legislation was unconstitutional, thus increasing the likelihood of growing polarization on religious freedom concerns.

Cults: Dangerous, Deviant, or Just Different?

Marshall Herff Applewhite was the son of a Presbyterian minister, and the musical director at the First Unitarian Church in Houston. Bonnie Lou Nettles was a nurse, astrologer, and spiritualist. They met in a Texas hospital in 1972, and opened a short-lived metaphysical bookstore, the Christian Arts Center, at the church where Applewhite worked. Within a year, they were referring to themselves as the "two witnesses" mentioned in Revelation 11:3—"And I will grant my two witnesses authority to prophesy for one thousand two hundred and sixty days, wearing sackcloth."

Twenty-five years later, in the spring of 1997, their story exploded across front pages and television screens around the world in the form of Heaven's Gate, the Southern California "UFO cult." Convinced they would rendezvous with a UFO trailing the Hale-Bopp comet, thirty-nine true believers dressed themselves in identical black jeans and Nike shoes, downed a deadly mixture of seconal and vodka, and covered their heads in triangular purple shrouds. Left behind on the Internet were voluminous postings describing the history and the mix-and-match theology of Heaven's Gate—a blend of Biblical prophesy, spiritualism, *Star Trek,* and *The X-Files.*

Their own religious history recounts that in the early 1970s, Applewhite and Nettles were "two unsuspecting humans in Houston" who were "incarnated" by space aliens and transformed into "Bo" and "Peep," two shepherds from the Kingdom of Heaven. Nettles died in the 1980s, and Applewhite's message became more paranoid and apocalyptic. "We seem to only be good at attracting those who would mock us, misinterpret us, and want us to go away," he wrote. "They find fault in everything we did and do. We're not really the martyr type, but 'so be it' if it's His will."

Heaven's Gate resurfaced in the 1990s with an advertising blitz, a Web page, and a final cross-country tour. In 1993, Applewhite issued his "final offer" to anyone who wanted to join them, but no one seemed to be listening. Earth was doomed, he wrote, because "its inhabitants are refusing to evolve." Those who stayed in the cult spent years undergoing a strict regime of behavioral modification and thought control. "They had their identities stripped away," said one therapist who counseled two families with Heaven's Gate members. "They went around for months with hoods on and couldn't see each other. They had to stay in pairs. They had to engage in self-criticism. There were periods when they couldn't sleep for more than four hours. There were strange diets. They took on new names." Members were given rule books, and violations included "trusting my own judgement" or "using my own mind" and "keeping an offense to myself." Major offenses included "sensuality—permitting arousal in thought or in action." Some of Applewhite's male followers were so devoted that they allowed themselves to be castrated in a collective submission to their leader's own sexual insecurities. After struggling with his own homosexual impulses, Applewhite had already had himself sexually neutered.

"Leaders of these groups have such enormous power that their personal needs and problems become part of the group agenda," said Richard Ofshe, a professor of social psychology at the University of California at Berkeley, and a leading authority on thought reform. "They get imprisoned by their own ideology. They get depressed and angry and turn that against the group."

o

Heaven's Gate re-ignited the national debate about cults, or, in the more neutral parlance of academia, "new religious movements." **Religious cults and spiritual sects have flourished throughout American history, but the decentralization of religious authority and the speed of modern communications will encourage the growth of new movements in the coming century.**

Throughout the 1990s, waves of violence accompanied the rise of apocalyptic groups in the United States and abroad. In 1993, a standoff between federal agents and the Branch Davidians in Waco, Texas, ended when a hellish inferno engulfed David Koresh and seventy-two of his followers. Koresh's sect was an offshoot of the Seventh-Day Adventists, a religious denomination that has stressed "end-times" thinking since its founding during a previous wave of apocalyptic fervor in nineteenth-century America. Koresh taught that he was a second Christian messiah destined to unlock the mysterious "seven seals" in the Book of Revelation, the apocalyptic final chapter of the New Testament. But the violence surrounding David Koresh did not end in Waco. On the second anniversary of the federal raid on the Branch Davidians, Timothy McVeigh, a disgruntled Army veteran inspired by antigovernment rhetoric and right-wing Bible prophesy took revenge for the U.S. attack on the Branch Davidians by blowing up the federal building in Oklahoma City, killing 167 men, women, and children.

In the 1990s, this apocalyptic blend of violence, prophesy, and politics was not limited to "Christian" sects. In Japan, twelve subway riders died and thousands were injured in a nerve-gas attack unleashed by Aum Shrini Kyo, a cult that mixed Buddhist teachings with an apocalyptic scenario that envisioned the end of the world between 1997 and the year 2000. In Canada and Europe, a series of murder-suicides took the lives of seventy-five members of the Order of the Solar Temple, who believed death would bring them new life in a place called Sirius.

All contemporary cult tragedies and mass suicides are measured against the events in Jonestown, Guyana, on November 18, 1978, when more than 900 followers of the Reverend Jim Jones perished in the People's Temple mass suicide and murder. People's Temple and the horrors of Jonestown forever changed the way America looks at cults, sects, and new religious movements. Once viewed as more curious than dangerous, public opinion about new religious movements had already begun to change in the late 1960s and early 1970s when large numbers of young people joined groups such as the Hare Krishna movement and the "Moonies," the Unification Church of the messianic Korean sect leader, the Reverend Sun Myung Moon. After Jonestown, however, offbeat sects and new religious movements were viewed with extreme suspicion and alarm. Everyone, including

the news media, seemed to be looking for "another Jonestown." Leading
the crusade against these groups were often former members and the parents of current members. From such a perspective, all cults are bad, since
they deceptively seduce members, or "victims," into their ranks.

According to the anti-cult movement, the "marks of a destructive cult"
include charismatic leadership claiming divinity or special power; brainwashing through sophisticated techniques of coercive influence and mind
control; deceptive recruitment and fundraising; dramatic changes in diet,
sleep patterns, and privacy; alienation from friends and family; financial,
physical, and sexual exploitation; totalitarian attitudes promoting an "us
versus them" syndrome; and isolation from the outside world and relocation to remote areas.[22] This might seem cut and dried, but defining
which groups are truly dangerous is not so simple.

Those on the other side of the cult question argue that Jonestown,
Waco, and Heaven's Gate have spawned public paranoia and intolerance
toward new religious movements, prompting America to turn its back on
a long tradition of religious liberty. Show me a cult, they say, and I'll show
you somebody else's religion. "Before Jonestown, the word 'cult' had
mildly negative connotations associated with the occult," said one seasoned observer from this camp. "Now the word is synonymous with sinister, murderous brainwashers."

This more sympathetic approach to new religious movements has won
many allies in the academic community. Such scholars point to research
showing that actual "brainwashing" does not occur in most new religious
movements. The small and often declining memberships and rapid
turnovers of followers suggest that such former members were not brainwashed or subjected to long-term, damaging mind-control. They also
charge that anti-cultists have not backed up their critique with proper
social scientific research. Critics of the anti-cult movement also say the
early histories of today's mainstream religious denominations show that
concerns about mind-control could just as easily be leveled against their
enthusiastic and devoted founders. Most religions start off in an intense,
"cultic" manner and often clash with the rubrics and manners of their surrounding culture.

In December 1997, the entire issue of the *Review of Religious Research*
was devoted to analyzing how the media portrays new religious movements, and the contributing scholars were not impressed. "It would seem
that, in most cases, the only story sufficiently 'newsworthy' about these
religious groups must involve some diabolical plot to subvert the innocent, engineered of course by a crazed maniacal 'cult' leader who secretly
schemes to amass limitless power," writes sociologist Stuart Wright, a

sociologist at Lamar University. "Are the intents, beliefs, and actions of diverse collectivities of groups representing a multitude of sundry religious traditions so easily reduced to a facile storyline or imbecilic made-for-TV movie?"[23]

Defenders of new religious movements say that the anti-cult movement can be more authoritarian than the groups they profess to monitor. Take the case of Barbara, an idealistic twenty-year-old from upstate New York and a devoted member of Reverend Moon's Unification Church. Two years after joining the Moonies, Barbara was snatched off the street by deprogrammers hired by her parents. Kept against her will, she was subjected to twelve days of intense "exit counseling" by a team of anti-cult activists.

"They just kept talking about how the church is phony and how everyone is lying and manipulating people," she said. "They were just trying to downgrade it, saying that it's just a money-making organization and that people are kept from the outside world, which I know is not true."

Barbara was shipped to an anti-cult safe house in the Midwest for more deprogramming, then returned to her parents' home in New York for the Christmas holidays. Once at home, she called the local Unification Church to arrange for rescuers to drive by her parents' house. Then she slipped away.

"It was a hard thing to do, but there was nothing I could say to make my parents understand," she explained. "What makes me want to invest my life in this church is my understanding of God, spiritual reality, and my quest for an ideal. I was really impressed that there was a group of people actively trying to create a new world and become better people."

Before her parents hired the radical deprogramming team, Barbara was also seen by a "non-coercive counselor," one who does not believe in kidnaping. He told her parents something they did not want to hear, that their daughter was a "sincere ideological convert."

"Barbara was one of those Moonies who really believe their religious experience is best expressed in the theology of the Unification Church," he said. "They don't require constant group reinforcement to get them to stay in the church."

Defenders of new religious movements say groups such as the Unification Church can move in more "benign" directions over time—though public pressure by critics may help inspire them to mellow. They argue that the Hare Krishnas have lost much of their isolationist, communal orientation as the second generation of members have opted for more independent lifestyles. They also cite the Worldwide Church of God and the Family (formerly the Children of God), noting they have dismantled much of their authoritarian leaderships and have gravitated toward a more mainstream religious identity in the 1990s. Judging by their small memberships, it seems unlikely that the new religious movements that have raised controversy in the last three decades will become major religions, at least in the way that the Mormons and Jehovah's Witnesses have in recent times.

There may be more growth among what sociologist Rodney Stark and William Bainbridge call "audience cults." Such groups and teachers have a following of people who may support group teachings but have little connection with followers or leaders. Paula Nesbitt writes that the "growth of the Internet's World Wide Web holds important implications for a sizable growth trend in audience cult participation over the next several years."[24] For example, people may simply link into the home page of Osho International, the group of followers of the late Bhagwan Shree Rajneesh, the Indian guru who generated fierce controversy in the 1980s at his communal city in rural Oregon, but never become intimately involved in the organization.

Some scholars view new religious movements more as laboratories of social innovation than emerging or influential religious forces. In this view, new religious movements are societies in miniature that generate patterns of new thinking and action. For example, sociologist Susan Palmer studied converts in several new religious movements and found they offer young women rites of passage through difficult periods of transition. In the more insulated environment of a new religion, members gain some distance from their culture and are given the space and time to form their own values.[25] New religious movements have also introduced innovations to the wider society. Phillip Lucas writes that Seventh-Day Adventists were often ostracized as a cult, but since the nineteenth century have been at the forefront of innovations in medicine and diet.[26]

In 1996, the battle between new religious movements and the Chicago-based Cult Awareness Network (CAN) took a bizarre turn when individuals associated with the Church of Scientology purchased the anti-cult group's name, logo, and telephone hotline. CAN had been forced into bankruptcy following a series of lawsuits, many of them by members of the Church of Scientology or by lawyers who were Scientologists. CAN and its executive director Cynthia Kisser had been among the nation's most-quoted critics of abusive and authoritarian cults and sects. Her silencing came a year after the Scientology magazine *Freedom* devoted a special issue to the anti-cult group. The magazine called CAN "the serpent of hatred, intolerance, violence, and death," and proclaimed that "the time has come to do something about the Cult Awareness Network."[27]

Although many new religious movements may not be as dangerous as they are portrayed by anti-cult activists and the popular media, authoritarian styles of leadership can nevertheless be abusive for the followers. Canadian scholars Irving Hexham and Karla Poewe note that new religions with no connections to major religious traditions establish their own moral system and create their own standard of values "that they see as transcending all previous moralities. In many cases these values may be perfectly reasonable, indeed admirable. But cut loose from historical roots, they can easily become bizarre and socially destructive."[28]

As the new millennium unfolds, critics and defenders of cults, sects, and new religious movements all need to address the problem of religious violence and abuse. Unlike the situation in much of the world, both sides of the cult controversy in the United States agree that unconventional religious groups should not be restricted by law. Yet a major challenge for all democratic societies will be how to identify the dangerous and violent tendencies within the religious community without jeopardizing religious freedom, or stigmatizing groups just because they are different. Religious groups themselves can act as powerful alternatives to abusive religion by modeling communities that encourage the use of reason and independent thinking, by valuing self-respect rather than unquestioning obedience and conformity.

Millennial Fever: New Age Vision, Old-Time Religion

Harold Camping and José Arguelles don't know each other. They certainly don't agree on the finer points of theology and cosmology. But their stories speak volumes about the American obsession with the end of the world and the coming of a new dawn.

Harold Camping is a veteran Bible teacher and radio evangelist, a founder of Family Radio, one of the world's largest Christian radio networks, which broadcasts on dozens of American radio stations and around the world in ten languages via short-wave radio. Since its founding in the 1950s, Family Radio has quietly preached a fairly standard brand of evangelical Christianity, a mix of religious music, Bible commentary, and Christian call-in. That suddenly changed in 1993 when Camping startled his listeners by revealing his own detailed timetable to Judgment Day. On his *Open Forum* radio show and in books entitled *1994?* and *Are You Ready?* Camping predicted that Christ would return between September 15 and 27, 1994.

José Arguelles is an influential New Age theorist, the "galactic messenger" who brought the world the Harmonic Convergence, a 1987 instruction that told 144,000 spiritual seekers and aging hippies to climb mountains, hold hands, and usher in a New Age of peace and harmony. In 1995, after years of relative obscurity, this former art historian and popularizer of ancient Mayan prophecies resurfaced to hold a press conference to announce the end of time as we know it. According to Arguelles, the future of the world hinges on whether it gets rid of the exceedingly popular Gregorian calendar, which much of the world has been following since Pope Gregory XIII imposed it in 1592.

After receiving messages from Pascal Votan, a Mayan god-king buried beneath the pyramids and magic mushroom fields of Palenque, Mexico, Arguelles came up with a new calendar with thirteen twenty-eight-day months. His calendar, based on the moon and the female menstrual cycle, was said to be more in tune with the cycles of nature. Since the new year would have 364 days, the entire planet gets an extra holiday—the Day out of Time—to keep things on track with the earth's rotation around the sun.

This will truly be a New Age, Arguelles said, because the old, unnatural calendar caused humanity to declare war, worship materialism, and pollute the planet. Arguelles, who played a flute before his proclamation and wore a "Crocodile Dundee"–style hat over his long, graying hair, warned that unless humanity embraces the new calendar, there will be "total planetary collapse" by the year 2000.

Back in 1995, when he held his press conference, Arguelles said he was hopeful. We will all know cosmic consciousness is upon us, he predicted, because money and government will be abolished worldwide by 1997.[29] Of course, 1997 came, went, and we still have money. We still have government. We also still have Harold Camping on the radio, despite his prediction that Christ would return in September of 1994, and at two later dates that passed with no apparent Apocalypse.

Just a month before Arguelles made his prediction, Harold Camping sat in his cluttered office near the Oakland International Airport. At seventy-three, his faced was deeply lined, and a strand of white hair fell down upon his forehead. It had been months since September 1994, but Camping was unfazed by his failure to pinpoint the beginning of the end. "Wonderfully, I was wrong about that," he said. "You know, I'm like the boy who cried wolf again and again and the wolf didn't come. This doesn't bother me in the slightest. For those who are believers, it is a no-lose, win-win situation. A lot of people have looked at their lives and how they stand up before God, and have shaped up their lives. A few people did stupid things—like thinking they didn't have to go to work because Christ was going to come. But if the Lord doesn't come, fine. We'll just keep living our lives for Him."[30]

○

Prophecies about the end of time and the beginning of a new dawn will flourish around the year 2000 as Christians, spiritualists, and secularists search for meaning in the millennium.

Date-setting is such an old problem that the Bible warns against it. "False messiahs and false prophets will appear and produce signs and omens, to lead astray," the gospel of Mark warns. "But about that day or hour no one knows . . . only the Father."

Just two years before the millennium, *U.S. News & World Report* released the results of a poll showing that 67 percent of Americans believe the world will come to an end or be destroyed, an 8 percent increase from a survey the magazine conducted just three years earlier. Two-thirds of those surveyed also believed Jesus would someday return.[31] These findings, along with the wave of high-profile apocalyptic sects making headlines throughout the 1990s, appear to back up predictions by sociologists and church historians that the days leading up to the year 2000 would spawn a new wave of date-setters, doomsayers, and millennial fervor.

Of course, doomsayers have always been around, and have always found a following among poor, marginalized people hoping for better times in the hereafter. Many of today's apocalyptic stirrings have their immediate roots in the 1970s, when author Hal Lindsey wrote the best-selling book of the decade, *The Late Great Planet Earth*. It used Biblical prophecy to explain how Israel recaptured Jerusalem in 1967, and predicted a Soviet invasion of the Middle East, leading to the battle of Armageddon.

More than three decades later, in February 1998, President Clinton's latest military buildup against Sadam Hussein and Russian warnings against a possible U.S. attack had Christian millennialists sounding the trumpets again. They also came out with a new line of products to help usher in the end times.

As U.S. military forces headed toward the Persian Gulf, a New York company known as Prophecy Partners, Inc. issued a new video movie ($29.95) and novel ($19.95) entitled *Apocalypse,* once again telling the story of a final military showdown in the Israeli valley of Armageddon. "The timing of the release of this unprecedented evangelical movie is staggering, with Boris Yeltsin now warning of World War III," the company's press release proclaims. "What many people don't realize is that today one single event, in one day, is all it would take to plunge us into the Apocalypse."

Many of today's doomsayers are Christian "premillennialists." They follow a relatively new strand of Bible prophecy that sees the Antichrist at work in the world, making things worse and worse. In their view, even the churches are corrupt. Before the Antichrist is revealed in the flesh, they believe, Jesus will "rapture" true believers up to heaven. They will escape seven years of intense earthly "tribulation" and disaster that culminate in the end of the world. At the end of the Great Tribulation, the battle of Armageddon breaks out, with Christ fighting the Antichrist. Satan is bound and kept out of the way for 1,000 years. After the 1,000 perfect years comes the Last Judgment. People go to heaven or hell, and human history ends.

This "millennium," the thousand years of blessedness following Armageddon, has little to do with the "millennium" of the calendar, the arrival of the year 2000. Nevertheless, they have become hopelessly mixed up in the popular imagination and the mind of the media. "Millennial expectations throughout the ages have been generated from all manner of systems, some numerical, some hermeneutic, some visionary, some supposedly empirical and scientific, and some downright hallucinatory," writes Stephen Jay Gould.[32] About the only way to connect "the millennium as apocalypse and the millennium as calendrics," Gould writes, is to read a lot into the cryptic statement of St. Peter that "one day is with the Lord as a thousand years, and a thousand years as one day"(2 Peter 3:8).

This longing to find meaning in the year 2000 reaches far beyond the realm of Christian doomsayers and New Age visionaries. Missionary organizations and mainstream religious denominations, including the Roman Catholic Church, have launched ambitious, multimillion-dollar proselytizing plans aimed at the year 2000. These plans carry with them varying degrees of apocalyptic fervor, based as they are on the prophecy in the Book of Matthew, Chapter 24, Verse 14, that "this gospel of the kingdom shall be preached in all the world . . . and then shall the end come."

Americans of other faiths, as well as those with no apparent religious inclination, are also captivated by "end-times" thinking. There is renewed interest in messianic Judaism, the prophecies of the French mystic Nostradamus, and the apocalyptic stories of the Hopis, Mayans, and other Native American Indians. This vision of a future age of peace, harmony, and higher consciousness—the archetype of a New Eden arising from the ashes of global cataclysm—is found in most cultures and religious faiths.

For Christian premillennialists, this New Eden can only follow the Great Tribulation and is open only to a select group of true believers. Most New Age spiritualists, however, envision a more universal era of blessedness, and don't necessarily require great catastrophes to usher in the new dawn. For Christian apocalyptists, the Battle of Armageddon and the Great Tribulation are predetermined and unavoidable. According to the vision of the New Age Apocalypse, however, humanity has a more active role in determining the future. Through meditation or other action in the world, mankind can influence the unfolding of the Apocalypse. Religion scholar Catherine Lowman Wessinger calls this New Age twist on the millennial vision "progressive messianism," and traces it back to the teachings of Annie Besant, an early leader of the Theosophy movement.[33]

Apocalyptic thinking in the 1990s is by no means limited to religious movements. It is increasingly visible in the nation's political and economic life. When it comes to doomsaying, American-style, it has become increasingly difficult to tell where the secular stops and the spiritual starts. Before launching the war against Iraq, George Bush invited evangelist Billy Graham into the White House for spiritual guidance. "These events," Graham warned, "are happening in that part of the world where history began, and, the Bible says, where history as we know it will end. I believe there are some spiritual forces at work—both good and evil that are beyond our comprehension."

During his presidency, Ronald Reagan showed a particular fascination with the form of apocalyptic prophecy popularized by Hal Lindsey and many of Reagan's political supporters on the religious right. In his famous "evil empire" speech to the National Association of Evangelicals in 1981, Reagan said, "There is sin and evil in the world, and we're enjoined by the Lord Jesus to oppose it with all our might." In a television interview with evangelist Jim Bakker during Reagan's 1980 presidential campaign, the Republican candidate predicted, "We may be the generation that sees Armageddon."

In the new millennium, two important forces will fuel apocalyptic fervor—the mass media, and the decentralization of religious authority. Many doomsayers alive at the end of Christianity's first millennium were no doubt silenced by the church, or simply had no way of getting their message beyond their immediate village. Today, no one has a monopoly on spiritual truth. Television and radio evangelists are free to spread instantly the prophecy of any doomsayer who strikes their fancy around the globe via radio, television, satellites, and the Internet.

In 1998, a small Taiwanese group, God's Salvation Church, moved to Garland, Texas, and received worldwide attention when its leader, Hengming Chen, predicted that God would appear on March 25 on channel 18 of every TV set in the world, and that UFOs would later appear in Gary, Indiana, as Asia was devastated by nuclear war. God did not appear, but James Lewis, an authority on new religious movements and author of *The Gods Have Landed,* was not surprised by Chen's prophecy. "There have always been millennial themes in UFO circles," Lewis said, "with technological angels saving modern society and powerful space brothers replacing the redemption of God."[34]

As a new millennium unfolds, a search has begun for new ways to envision the Apocalypse, to find new meaning and inspiration in the great millennial myth. Robert Smith, a professor of New Testament studies at Pacific Lutheran Theological Seminary, said growing numbers of mainstream scholars are taking another look at the Book of Revelation, including radical proponents of liberation theology. Whereas "fundamentalists see Revelation as unveiling the precise details of God's timetable for the last days of planet earth," Smith writes, liberationists see in the book "an unmasking of the structuring of power in our world." He writes, "The ruling economic and political systems favor the rich, the powerful, and the well-connected. In New Testament times the system which dominated the cities and countries where Christians lived was the Roman Empire." According to the liberationists, the beast of the Apocalypse "has its counterpart and continuation today in the international political and financial system of the industrial world."[35]

Other nonfundamentalist visions of the Apocalypse come from psychologists and spiritualists. Some see these stories of the end times as archetypal alerts of the collective unconscious, even as a kind of early-warning system to turn humanity away from the path of destruction. Psychologist Kenneth Ring's research into "near-death experiences" has documented numerous cases of death-bed visions strikingly similar to the great apocalyptic myths. Citing individual prophecies of a global cataclysm followed by a new era of universal love and world peace, Ring suggests that humanity may be subconsciously preparing for a collective near-death experience.

We may never know how these apocalyptic stories arise, but that mystery does not prevent us from keeping an eye on how they are interpreted in the new millennium. Whether these stories are divine signals or psychological projections, they deeply affect our soul, our society, our planet. Regardless of what sociological, psychological, or theological explanation we prefer, our understanding of the end may be inseparable from its unfolding. Prophecy *can* be self-fulfilling.

POSTSCRIPT

PERSONAL FAITH, PUBLIC LIFE

FAITHFUL READERS WILL RECALL Steve and Julie, the "church shoppers" struck by the spiritual power and lively music of Pentecostal worship who later joined a less intense Southern Baptist congregation. One might think that after six years in conservative evangelical circles, Steve's social and political views would have shifted to the right. Think again.

"Actually, I was more conservative *before* I became a Christian," he says. "Now I am more middle of the road. I used to have a Rush Limbaugh attitude, but now I'm more accepting of other people. Part of it is being less driven by material things. I used to put value on a person depending on what their job was or how much money they made."

That change of heart also changed Steve's vocation. After getting a degree in business administration, he tried to start his own small business. As his faith matured, business no longer moved him. He prayed about it, talked to people he respected, and decided to change careers. "I started to ask myself if I just wanted to chase the dollar," he says, "or pursue something that helps other people." His friends and family pointed out that Steve had always been great with kids, so he went back to school to get a teaching credential to help students with learning disabilities. Today he works with some of the most difficult kids around—autistic children and others with severe disabilities. "Today I was kicked five times and spat on four times," he quips. "I love it!"

Steve's new faith has changed his politics. He no longer supports the death penalty. "It was so sudden," he recalls. "About two years ago I was driving in my car listening to some conservative talk radio guy. There was about to be another execution in Texas and they were going on and on

about how the electric chair was too good for this guy, about how someone should rape him and string him up just like he did to his victim. As I
was listening, I heard myself saying things like that in the past, and suddenly realized Christ would never say something like that. I didn't think
about it much during the rest of the day, but that night I was sitting up
and couldn't sleep. I started to pray, not even knowing what was on my
mind, and suddenly I just started weeping. Really weeping. Then I flipped
on the TV set and the first thing I heard was a report that they'd just exe-
cuted the guy. Ever since that night, I've been against the death penalty."

○

Spirituality and religious belief are not private matters. They inevitably
flow into the social and political arena. For centuries, religious faith has
inspired believers to compassion while giving others an excuse to battle
those with different backgrounds and beliefs.

In the coming century, the dizzying diversity of American religion will
make public expressions of faith ever more complex. Relations between
church and state are already delicate, but what of clashes between the government and American mosques? What about the tensions inside public
school classrooms where Christians, Jews, Moslems, Buddhists, and secularists must all take the same social studies test? What are the long-range
social implications of Christian megachurches, the privatization of welfare, biotechnology, and the computer revolution? Megachurches will
influence American society whether or not they form political action committees. They will open more Christian schools, educating an entire generation with evangelical ideas about how the world was created and how
it will end. Welfare providers will shift to local communities and faith-
based organizations with markedly different perspectives on the causes
and solutions of social ills. Scientific advances in genetic engineering,
cloning, fetal medicine, and euthanasia will clash with the moral teachings of some faiths but will be embraced by other religious groups. Rev-
olutions in information technology will either bring together people of
different faiths or build new electronic walls. In the future, new sources
of personal and "secular" spirituality—from mystical environmentalism
to apocalyptic politics—will challenge society. For better or worse, our
ideas about God, spirit, and creation will influence everything from how
we help the poor to whether we go to war.

At the same time, many of the larger crusades to instill religious values
in American society have failed to inspire people. Liberal and radical religious voices call for a social gospel that would bring Americans closer to
their vision of peace and justice—and are met with downsized govern-

ment, rising privatization, and little interest by people in the pews. More moderate proponents dream of a common moral vision and a new sense of national unity—and are confronted by the fortress of American individualism and the rise of special interest politics. Conservative evangelicals envision a "Christian America"—and are rejected by the American people's fear of authoritarianism in any form.

There's a different story at the local level. Leaders of grass-roots community development groups, religious schools, and other faith-based organizations are not just talking about diversity and multiculturalism; they are practicing it. Some will argue that all these new social groups rising from religious sources threaten national unity. Perhaps. But these associations encourage participation in the democratic process. Religious groups give citizens a way to fulfill important social roles. Rising localism does not mean that larger social movements are doomed in the new millennium. But the success of national movements will depend on how well they draw on the experience of congregations and local coalitions of faith.

AFTERWORD

PEOPLE OF FAITH have struggled with the temptations of the market-place since the dawn of the Judeo-Christian tradition. Two thousand years ago, the Bible tells us, an angry Jesus stormed into the Jewish temple in Jerusalem, where merchants sold animals for sacrifice, and kicked over the tables of the money changers.[1] Throughout Christian history, materialism and greed have challenged the Christian ideals of generosity and compassion—from the commercial interests backing the Crusades to the corrupt sale of papal indulgences. That corruption and abuse helped inspire the Protestant Reformation, which in the eyes of many historians and sociologists rose hand in hand with the growth of capitalism.[2]

So perhaps it should come as no surprise that in the twilight of the millennium, when the marketplace reigns supreme, millions of Americans are shopping for faith. It has been said that the business of America is business, and it often seems that the religion of America is consumerism. What mysterious power holds sway over the citizenry? Is it God, or television? Look around any town or city in America. What great temples have risen in your lifetime—churches, or shopping malls?

Religion both reflects the surrounding culture and offers another vision of how we should live. It is within this never-ending dance of the material and the spiritual that we understand religion, and perhaps ourselves. In this book we have tried to present a balanced and comprehensive overview of the complex interplay between faith and culture, of how this interplay inspires the personal search, the communal gathering, and public life on the edge of a new millennium.

Often we have tried to understand all this through the metaphor of the marketplace. One of the components of consumerism is choice, and whether one shops in Safeway or the spiritual supermarket, the options can be overwhelming. Shopping for faith can trivialize religion or empower the spiritual search. Viewing religion as a kind of cafeteria—a few bites of Zen meditation washed down with Gregorian chant and topped off with the latest self-help book—can leave one hungry in the end. Personalized religion can be like a personal stereo, like all those people walking around the cities of America wearing headphones, following a private beat. It's a great way to block out those around you, but only you hear the music. On the other hand, the free marketplace of spirituality can be life saving to those raised in an abusive or alienating religious climate, or for those with no religious upbringing. It can help them find an authentic spiritual path, or rediscover the essence of one they thought they already knew from traditions passed down across generations.

Some of the spiritualities we've discussed may seem hopelessly generic, or extraordinarily esoteric. Many Americans agree with that sentiment and have traded in their seeker status for involvement in distinct communities of faith, particularly as they settle down and raise a family. Yet even those who have joined more traditional congregations often sample the wares of the spiritual marketplace. Some shoppers eventually find beliefs and practices so compelling that they buy the whole package and join a more comprehensive faith. The cacophony of competing truth claims in America today does not spell the demise of serious religious faith. Rather, the competition resulting from many faiths can strengthen religious identity and inspire spiritual innovation in traditional congregations.

Rather than spark interfaith conflict, American religious pluralism can defuse tension. With so many faith groups interacting in the public square, tolerance—if not always interfaith understanding—makes more sense than religious warfare. Despite the talk of "culture wars," the new pluralism creates more than two sides to any social controversy, discouraging an us-versus-them mind-set. Likewise, the growth of religious consumerism does not necessarily mean social uninvolvement. Traditional congregations and spiritual self-help groups provide entry points for greater community involvement and social action.

Some will argue that a religious future based largely on local congregations, consumerism, and fragmented spiritualities that cater to individual needs is no future at all. Yet barring social or natural catastrophes, few alternatives appear on the horizon. Without a doubt, the future will be more religious. Many secular researchers now conclude that religious practices and beliefs are "good" for individual health and community well-being. Americans are a practical people, and many will no doubt find in this another kind of "good news." Nevertheless, there is always the danger that religion will lose its transcendent power when domesticated into something healthy and practical.

Personal responsibility will be a key concern in the American religious future. We seem to have countless spiritual and moral options. Information technology puts vast and tempting worlds of knowledge and entertainment at our fingertips. Biotechnology lets us control the process of life itself, allowing us to "play God." At the same time, the declining role of government and the breakdown of centralized religious authority make social and moral ethics a matter of individual choice, not externally imposed laws.

Strong religious communities with traditional teachings will survive and adapt, particularly those that combine ritual and spirituality. But religious communities that allow the flowering of personal spiritual experience—whether they be Pentecostal congregations or meditation support groups—may enjoy the brightest future. Shopping for faith may not be easy, and it may threaten the religious powers that be, but this uneasy mixture of practicality and personal faith will mark American religion in the new millennium.

NOTES

INTRODUCTION

1. Greeley, Andrew M., *Religious Change in America* (Harvard University Press, Cambridge, 1989).

2. Gallup, George H. Jr., *Religion in America: 1996 Report* (Princeton Religion Research Center, Princeton, 1996).

3. Kosmin, Barry, and Lachman, Seymour, *One Nation Under God* (Harmony Books, New York, 1993).

4. Associated Press, "Poll Says 71 Percent Believe in God," *San Francisco Chronicle,* Dec. 22, 1997, P. A7.

5. Hertzberg, Hendrik, "The Narcissus Survey," *New Yorker,* Jan. 5, 1998, P. 28.

6. Tickle, Phyllis A., *Rediscovering the Sacred* (Crossroad, New York, 1996), P. 17.

CHAPTER ONE

1. Hammond, Phillip E., *Religion and Personal Autonomy* (University of South Carolina Press, Columbia, 1993).

2. Roof, Wade Clark, *A Generation of Seekers* (Harper San Francisco, San Francisco, 1993), P. 70.

3. Hammond, *Religion and Personal Autonomy,* Pp. 139–166.

4. Lattin, Don, "Far from the Maddening Crowd," *Common Boundary,* Mar.–Apr. 1992, P. 34.

5. Lattin, Don, "Big Sur Monk a New Age Pioneer," *San Francisco Chronicle,* Dec. 24, 1993, P. A1.

CHAPTER TWO

1. Cox, Harvey, *Fire from Heaven* (Addison-Wesley, Reading, Mass., 1995).

2. Bloom, Harold, *The American Religion* (Simon & Schuster, New York, 1992).

3. Tickle, Phyllis A., *God-Talk in America* (Crossroad, New York, 1997), Pp. 117–118.

4. Berger, Peter L., *A Far Glory* (Free Press, New York, 1992), P. 147.

5. Patch, Rashid Raymond, "Sufi Symposium Sees More Traditional Islam," *Gnosis*, Summer 1997, Pp. 8–10.

6. Lattin, Don, "Witches Staking Claim to Halloween as Sacred Holiday," *San Francisco Chronicle*, Oct. 24, 1996, P. C1.

7. Lattin, Don, "Driven (and Drawn) by Different Drums," *Salt Journal*, Nov.–Dec. 1997, Pp. 8–15.

8. Dellinger, Drew, "Creation in Common," 1996.

9. Raschke, Carl, in *Spirituality and the Secular Quest* (Crossroad, New York, 1996), Van Ness, Peter H., Ed., P. 220.

10. Evenson, Laura, "Soulful Books Give Readers Insight, Make Best-Sellers," *San Francisco Chronicle*, Dec. 25, 1996, P. A1.

11. Lattin, Don, "Therapists Turn from Psyche to Soul," *San Francisco Chronicle*, Mar. 17, 1994, P. A1.

12. Roof, *A Generation of Seekers*, Pp. 133–148.

13. Kantrowitz, Barbara, "The Search for the Sacred," *Newsweek*, Nov. 28, 1994, Pp. 56, 61.

14. Van Ness, Peter H., Ed., *Spirituality and the Secular Quest* (Crossroad, New York, 1996).

15. Joe Holland, in *Spirituality and Society: Postmodern Visions* (State University Press of New York, 1996), Griffin, David Ray, Ed.

16. Thomas, L. Eugene, and Eisenhandler, Susan, Ed., *Aging and the Religious Dimension* (Auburn House, Westport, 1994).

17. Tickle, *God-Talk in America*, P. 47.

18. Simpkinson, Charles, Wengell, Douglas, and Casavant, Mary Jane, Ed., *Graduate Education Guide: Holistic Programs and Resources Integrating Spirituality and Psychology* (Common Boundary, Inc., Bethesda, Md., 1994).

CHAPTER THREE

1. Reuters News Service, "Promise Keepers Sacks All 345 Staff Members," Feb. 20, 1998.

2. Lockhart, William H., "Defining the New Christian Man," unpublished paper presented at Society for the Scientific Study of Religion, Nashville, Nov. 8–10, 1996.

3. Jorstad, Erling, "New Wave of Women's Spirituality Books Focus on Gender Differences," *Religion Watch,* Feb. 1996, P. 3.

4. Anonymous, "Back to the Future," *Presbyterian Layman,* Jan.–Feb. 1994, P. 2.

5. Lattin, Don, "Christian Doubters Call Sophia a Pagan Goddess," *San Francisco Chronicle,* Mar. 3, 1994, P. A1.

6. Nash, Laura, "The Nanny Corporation," *Across the Board,* Fall 1994, P. 3.

7. Laabs, Jennifer J., "Balancing Spirituality and Work," *Personnel Journal,* Sept. 1995, P. 60.

8. Gahr, Evan, "Spirited Enterprise," *American Enterprise,* July–Aug. 1997, P. 53.

9. Lattin, Don, "Hark! Hollywood Angels Take Wing," *San Francisco Chronicle Sunday Datebook,* Dec. 15, 1996, P. 42.

10. Tickle, *God-Talk in America,* P. 121.

11. Rothman, Stanley, "Is God Really Dead in Beverly Hills?" *American Scholar,* Spring 1996, Pp. 272–279.

12. Garcia, Guy, "Rock Finds Religion," *New York Times,* Jan. 2, 1994, P. 1L.

13. Strausbaugh, John, E., *The Birth of the Elvis Faith* (Blast Books, New York, 1995), P. 13.

14. Lattin, Don, "Physics, Mystics and the Essence of Things," *San Francisco Examiner,* Feb. 9, 1986, P. B1.

15. Tabliabue, John, "Pope Bolsters Church's Support for Scientific View of Evolution," *New York Times,* Oct. 25, 1996, P. 1.

16. Wilber, Ken, *The Marriage of Sense and Soul: Integrating Science and Religion* (Random House, New York, 1998), P. 3.

17. Hawes, Peter, "Casting a Wider Net," *Common Boundary,* Nov.–Dec. 1995, P. 32.

18. Clayton, Philip, "Computers and the Spirit," *Common Boundary,* Nov.–Dec. 1995.

19. Cimino, Richard P., "Scientific Breakthroughs Playing a New Role in Theology," *Religion Watch,* May 1991, Pp. 1–2.

20. Cimino, Richard P., "Health-Spirituality Connections Grow, Encountering Religious Traditions," *Religion Watch,* Dec. 1995, Pp. 1–2.

21. Hotz, Robert Lee, "Brain Could Affect Religious Response," *Los Angeles Times,* Nov. 1, 1997, P. B4:5.

22. Thomas, Gary, "Doctors Who Pray," *Christianity Today,* Jan. 6, 1997, P. 20.

23. Culligan, Kevin, "Are We Wired for God?" *America,* Mar. 22, 1997, Pp. 23–24.

24. Barnette, Martha, "Body and Soul," *Allure,* Sept. 1996, P. 258.

25. Graham, Barbara, "Meditating on Prozac," *Common Boundary,* Sept.–Oct. 1995, P. 24.

26. Delbanco, Andrew, and Delbanco, Thomas, "A.A. at the Crossroads," *New Yorker,* Mar. 20, 1995, P. 58.

PART ONE POSTSCRIPT

1. Tocqueville, Alexis de, *Democracy in America,* Book 1, Chapter 15 (Knopf, New York, 1945).

2. James, William, *The Varieties of Religious Experience* (American Penguin Library, New York, 1982), P. 115.

3. Bellah, Robert, *Habits of the Heart: Individualism and Commitment in American Life* (HarperCollins, New York, 1986), P. 77.

CHAPTER FOUR

1. Trueheart, Charles, "Welcome to the Next Church," *Atlantic Monthly,* Aug. 1996, Pp. 37–58.

2. Stevenson, A. Russell, "Megachurches Prove That Theology Matters," *Presbyterian Layman,* Sept.–Oct. 1993, Pp. 6, 8.

3. Lattin, Don, "The Word Is Marketing: Mainline Churches Seek Members," *San Francisco Chronicle,* Aug. 10, 1992, P. 1.

4. Unsworth, Tim, "Status of Protestants Under the Sanctuary Lamp," *National Catholic Reporter,* Oct. 4, 1996, P. 18.

5. Marciniak, Edward, and Droel, William, "The Future of Catholic Churches in the Inner City," *Chicago Studies,* Aug. 1995, Pp. 172–186.

6. Montali, Larry, "Catholic Parishes Take Page from Megachurches," *National Catholic Register,* Aug. 13, 1995, P. 1.

7. Lawrence, Beverly Hall, *Reviving the Spirit* (Grove, New York, 1996).

8. Rosenberg, Richard, "JCC's Soft-Sell Judaism," *Moment,* Apr. 1997, P. 35.

9. Schaller, Lyle E., *The New Reformation: Tomorrow Arrived Yesterday* (Abington, Nashville, 1995).

10. Barna, George, *Baby Busters: The Disillusioned Generation* (Northfield Publishing, Chicago, 1994).

11. Lattin, Don, "Superman of the Cloth," *San Francisco Chronicle,* Sept. 21, 1997, P. 1.

12. Smith, Brad, "Team Ministry in the 21st Century," *Next,* Feb. 1996, Pp. 1–4.

13. Barna, George, *Barna Research Group,* Feb. 28, 1996.

14. Hoge, Dean, Johnson, Benton, and Luidens, Donald, *Vanishing Boundaries: The Religion of Mainline Baby Boomers* (Westminster/John Knox Press, Louisville, 1994).

15. Roof, Wade Clark, *A Generation of Seekers* (Harper San Francisco, San Francisco, 1993).

16. Miller, Donald G., *Reinventing American Protestantism* (University of California Press, Berkeley, 1997).

17. Finke, Roger, and Stark, Rodney, *The Churching of America* (Rutgers University Press, New Brunswick, 1992).

18. Lattin, Don, "Irreverent Book Views U.S. Religion Through Economic Lens," *San Francisco Chronicle,* Nov. 6, 1993, P. A6.

19. Warner, R. Stephen, "Work in Progress Toward a New Paradigm for the Sociological Study of Religion in the United States," *American Journal of Sociology,* Mar. 1993, Pp. 1044–1095. For more on rational choice theory and its scholarly critics, see, Young, Lawrence A., Ed., *Rational Choice Theory and Religion* (Routledge, New York, 1997).

20. Hoge, Dean R., Zech, Charles E., McNamara, Patrick H., and Donahue, Michael J., *Money Matters: Personal Giving in American Churches* (Westminster John Knox, Louisville, 1996).

21. Cimino, Richard P., "Women Religious Leadership Facing Mainline Decline, Conservative Growth," *Religion Watch,* Nov. 1995, P. 2.

22. Lattin, Don, "A Church Within the Church," *San Francisco Examiner,* June 1, 1986, P. A1.

23. Ruby, Walter, "Reform Versus Conservative: Who's Winning," *Moment,* Apr. 1996, Pp. 37–39.

24. Braaten, Carl E., "Theology for the Third Millennium," *A Report from the Center,* Center for Catholic and Evangelical Theology, Summer 1996, P. 4.

25. Duin, Julia, "Denomination Blends Spirituality with High Church Style," *Charisma,* Sept. 1996, Pp. 25–27.

26. Nattier, Jan, "Buddhism Comes to Main Street," *Wilson Quarterly,* Spring 1997, Pp. 72–80.

27. Dykstra, Craig, "Religion and Spirituality," *Initiatives in Religion,* Summer 1996, Pp. 1–2.

28. Jones, Alan, *Exploring Spiritual Direction: An Essay on Christian Friendship* (Harper San Francisco, San Francisco, 1982).

29. Lattin, Don, "Churches Offer Therapy for Soul," *San Francisco Chronicle,* Dec. 25, 1991, P. 1.

30. Bass, Dorothy, in *Practicing Our Faith* (Jossey-Bass, San Francisco, 1997), Bass, Dorothy, Ed., Pp. 149–162.

31. Cimino, Richard P., "Religious Orders Branching Out, Innovating," *Religion Watch,* Sept. 1997, P. 7.

32. Koenig, John, in *Practicing Our Faith* (Jossey-Bass, San Francisco, 1997), Bass, Dorothy, Ed., Pp. 149–162.

33. Ellwood, Robert, *The History and Future of Faith* (Crossroad, New York, 1988), P. 157.

CHAPTER FIVE

1. Lattin, Don, "Challenging Organized Religion," *San Francisco Chronicle,* Nov. 21, 1992, P. 1.

2. Gallup, George H. Jr., "Small Groups Playing an Important Role in Religious Experience of Many," *Emerging Trends,* Sept. 1996, P. 3.

3. Wuthnow, Robert, *Sharing the Journey* (Free Press, New York, 1994).

4. Kurien, Prima, "An American Hinduism? Hindu Americans and the Reformulation of Religious Ideology and Practice," unpublished paper delivered at Society for the Scientific Study of Religion, St. Louis, 1995.

5. O'Leary, Denyse, "Cell Churches Around the World." *Faith Today,* Mar.–Apr. 1996, P. 30.

6. Gallup, "Small Groups," P. 3.

7. Wuthnow, *Sharing the Journey,* Pp. 357–358.

8. Lattin, Don, "The Need to Cry Out," *Common Boundary,* May–June 1991, P. 17.

9. Nelson, Alan, "Mind of a Priest, Soul of a Prophet," *Intro Action,* Apr. 1997, Pp. 1–4.

10. Schaller, Lyle E., "What Will Tomorrow Bring: Four Predictions," *Clergy Journal,* Jan. 1997, Pp. 14–16.

11. Kew, Richard, and White, Roger, *Toward 2015: A Church Odyssey* (Cowley Publications, Boston, 1997).

12. San Francisco Archdiocese, *Sunday to Sunday,* Mar. 24, 1996.

13. Appleby, R. Scott, "Crunch Time for American Catholicism," *Christian Century,* Apr. 3, 1996, P. 370.

14. Baumer, Patricia Hughes, "Empowering a New Voice: The Potential for Lay Preaching," *Catholic World*, Mar.–Apr., 1994, Pp. 93–97.

15. Lattin, Don, "Activist Lerner Returns to SF to Start Temple," *San Francisco Chronicle*, Aug. 2, 1996, P. A19.

16. Lattin, Don, "Mormon Crusade Goes Global," *San Francisco Chronicle*, Apr. 8, 1996, P. 1.

17. McCarraher, Eugene, "Smile When You Say 'Laity,'" *Commonweal*, Sept. 12, 1997, P. 23.

18. Renner, Gerald, "Reshaping Church to Link to Daily Life," *Hartford Courant*, July 4, 1995.

19. Tapia, Andres, "Engaging the Marketplace," *Christianity Today*, May 15, 1995, P. 49.

20. Graham, Barbara, "The Feminine Face of the Buddha," *Common Boundary*, Mar.–Apr. 1994, Pp. 28–35.

21. Cimino, Richard, "Women Religious Leadership Facing Mainline Decline, Conservative Growth," *Religion Watch,* Nov. 1995, Pp. 1–2.

22. Zikmund, Barbara Brown, Lummis, Adair T., and Chang, Patricia Mei Yang, *Clergy Women: An Uphill Calling* (Westminster John Knox, Louisville, 1998).

23. Woodward, Kenneth L., "Gender and Religion," *Commonweal*, Nov. 22, 1996, Pp. 9–14.

24. McCarraher, "Smile," P. 23.

25. Goldman, Ari, "Hymnals Welcomed," *New York Times*, July 31, 1993, P. 10L.

26. Stokes, Allison, *Women Pastors* (Crossroad, New York, 1995), Pp. 123–159.

27. Lattin, Don, "Called by Her God," *San Francisco Chronicle Sunday*, Mar. 30, 1997, P. 1.

CHAPTER SIX

1. McClure, Vicki, UC Berkeley Graduate School of Journalism, religion reporting project, Dec. 1997.

2. Roof, Wade Clark, and McKinney, William, *American Mainline Religion* (Rutgers University Press, New Brunswick, N.J., 1987), Pp. 172–183.

3. Synan, Vinson, *The Holiness-Pentecostal Tradition* (Eerdmans, Grand Rapids, Mich., 1997), P. 294.

4. Lattin, Don, "Twenty-Two Pastors Want to Quit Methodist Church, Take Flocks," *San Francisco Chronicle*, May 1, 1998, P. A6.

5. Cimino, Richard P., "Denominational Switching Grows Among Conservative Congregations," *Religion Watch,* July–Aug. 1996, Pp. 1–2.

6. Coalter, Milton J., Mulder, John M., and Weeks, Louis B., *Vital Signs: The Promise of Mainline Protestantism* (Eerdmans, Grand Rapids, Mich., 1996).

7. Ammerman, Nancy, "SBC Moderates and the Making of a Postmodern Denomination," *Christian Century,* Sept. 22–29, 1993.

8. Ford, Marcia, "Denomination Revamps Image," *Charisma,* Nov. 1995.

9. Lawson, Steven, "Four Square Church Faces 21st Century," *Charisma,* Mar. 1993, P. 16.

10. Chandler, Russell, *Racing Toward 2001* (Zondervan-Harper San Francisco, 1992), Pp. 240–245.

11. Bellah, Robert, *The Good Society* (Vintage Books, New York, 1992), P. 187.

12. Cimino, Richard P., "The Fuzzy Future of Denominations," *Religion Watch,* Dec. 1996, Pp. 1–2.

13. Willimon, William, "Reformer and Hand-Wringer," *Christian Century,* May 15, 1996, Pp. 533–534.

14. Cimino, "The Fuzzy Future," P. 2.

15. Brubaker, George K., "Seminary Education: Real Time, Real Life," *Christianity Today,* Oct. 7, 1996, Pp. 99–134.

16. Cimino, Richard P., "Jewish Renewal Impacts Mainstream Judaism," *Religion Watch,* Dec. 1994, Pp. 1–2.

17. Jorstad, Erling, *Holding Fast/Pressing On: Religion in America During the 1980s* (Praeger, New York, 1990).

18. Wittberg, Patricia, *Pathways to Re-Creating Religious Communities* (Paulist Press, Mahwah, N.J., 1996), Pp. 19–31.

19. Finke, Roger, "An Orderly Return to Tradition," *Journal for the Scientific Study of Religion,* June 1997, Pp. 218–231.

20. Wittberg, *Pathways.*

21. Chai, Karen, "Competing for the Second Generation: English Language Ministry in a Korean Protestant Church," unpublished paper presented at Association for the Sociology of Religion, New York City, 1996; Lawrence, Beverly Hall, Ibid.; Carrasco, Rodolpho, "Expression, Not Confession," *Regeneration Quarterly,* Spring 1995, Pp. 20–22.

22. Bellah, *The Good Society,* P. 205.

23. Trexler, Edgar R., "More Than Multicultural," *The Lutheran,* Jan. 1997, P. 58.

24. Dudley, Carl, "Pluralism as an Ism," *Christian Century,* Oct. 27, 1993, P. 1042.

25. Cimino, Richard P., "How Multicultural Are the Churches: A Canadian Case Study," *Religion Watch,* Dec. 1993, Pp. 1–2.

26. Anonymous, "Buddhism and Equality," *Turning Wheel,* Spring 1993, P. 29.

27. Rosado, Caleb, "Multicultural Ministry," *Ministry,* May 1996, Pp. 22–25.

28. Ammerman, Nancy, *Community and Congregation* (Rutgers University Press, New Brunswick, N.J., 1997).

29. Lattin, Don, "Young Muslims Struggle with Tradition, Stereotypes," *San Francisco Chronicle,* Jan. 17, 1994, P. 1.

30. Hawes, Peter, "Casting a Wider Net," *Common Boundary,* Nov.–Dec. 1995, P. 32.

31. Raymond, John, *Catholics on the Internet* (Prima Publishing, Rocklin, Calif., 1997).

32. Ansk, Daniel, "Religious Frakus Debunks Myths of Anarchy on the Net," *Los Angeles Times,* Jan. 25, 1995, P. D1:4.

33. O'Leary, Stephen, "Cyberspace as Sacred Space: Communicating Religion on Computer Networks," *Journal of the American Academy of Religion,* Winter 1997, Pp. 781–806.

34. Chandler, Russell, "Dishing Out Training—From a Distance," *Current Trends and Thoughts,* Mar. 1995, P. 24.

35. Marvel, Mark, "Channel-Surfing for God," *Elle,* Jan. 1997, P. 38.

36. Kennedy, John W., "Redeeming the Wasteland," *Christianity Today,* Oct. 2, 1995, Pp. 92–102.

37. Zikmund, Barbara Brown, "What Is the Spirit Saying to the Churches?" *Ecumenical Trends,* Oct. 1996, Pp. 1–8.

38. Fernandez-Armesto, Felipe, and Wilson, Derek, *Reformations* (Scribner, New York, 1996).

39. Kozodoy, Neal, Ed., "What Do American Jews Believe," *Commentary,* Aug. 1996, Pp. 18–96.

40. Heim, S. Mark, "The Next Ecumenical Movement," *Christian Century,* Aug. 14–21, 1996, Pp. 780–783.

41. Lattin, Don, "Crusade Countdown," *San Francisco Chronicle Sunday,* July 20, 1997, P. 1.

42. Boeve, Timothy, "Ecumenism: Changing the Course of History," *Church Herald,* Jan. 1997, P. 11.

43. Henry, Patrick, "New Geometries of Ecumenism," *Theology Today,* Jan. 1997, Pp. 491–502.

44. Eck, Diana, "Neighboring Faiths," *Harvard Magazine,* Sept.–Oct. 1996, P. 38.

45. Lattin, Don, "Religions of the World Gather in Chicago," *San Francisco Chronicle,* Aug. 27, 1993, P. A1.

PART TWO CONCLUSION

1. Synan, Vinson, *The Holiness-Pentecostal Tradition* (Eerdmans, Grand Rapids, Mich., 1997), P. 2.

CHAPTER SEVEN

1. Casanova, José, *Public Religions in the Modern World* (University of Chicago Press, Chicago, 1994), Pp. 211–234.

2. Fagan, Patrick F., *Why Religion Matters: The Impact of Religious Practice on Social Stability,* Backgrounder No. 1064 (Heritage Foundation, Washington, D.C., 1995).

3. Ammerman, *Community and Congregation,* Pp. 362–370.

4. Lattin, Don, "GOP Pilgrimage to Broadcaster's Door," *San Francisco Chronicle,* July 17, 1995, P. A2.

5. Goodstein, Laurie, "A Conservative Leader Threatens to Bolt G.O.P.," *New York Times,* Feb. 12, 1998, P. A22.

6. Green, John C., "Evangelical Realignment," *Christian Century,* July 5, 1995, Pp. 676–680.

7. Brownstein, Ronald, "Evangelicals Found to Hold Largest Share of GOP Base," *Los Angeles Times,* June 25, 1996, P. A8:1.

8. Lattin, Don, "Christian Right's New Political Push," *San Francisco Chronicle,* June 12, 1992, P. A1.

9. Briggs, Kenneth A., "Is There a Religious Left?" *Common Boundary,* Jan.–Feb. 1997, Pp. 24–31.

10. Oppenheim, Carolyn Toll, "Taking Back the Torah: Jews and Social Justice," *Fellowship,* Sept.–Oct. 1996.

11. Niebuhr, Gustav, "Religious Left Draws Strength from Grassroots," *New York Times,* June 21, 1997, P. 12.

CHAPTER EIGHT

1. Wuthnow, Robert, *The Restructuring of American Religion* (Princeton University Press, Princeton, 1988), Pp. 132–134.

2. Kosmin, Barry, and Lachman, Seymour, *One Nation Under God* (Harmony Books, New York, 1993), P. 249.

3. Hunter, James Davison, *Culture Wars* (Free Press, New York, 1994), Pp. 320–325.

4. Lichter, Robert, and Rothman, Stanley, "Media and Business Elites," *Public Opinion*, Issue 4, 1981.

5. Dart, John, and Allen, Jimmy, *Bridging the Gap: Religion and the News Media* (The Freedom Forum, Vanderbilt University, 1993), P. 35.

6. Graham, Tim, and Kaminski, Steve, "Faith in a Box: The Network News on Religion, 1993," *News Report Number Four*, Media Research Center.

7. Dart and Allen, *Bridging the Gap*, P. 53.

8. Silk, Mark, *Unsecular Media: Making News of Religion in America* (University of Illinois Press, Champaign, 1995), P. 25.

9. Lattin, Don, "Muslims, Others Feel Scapegoated by Speculation," *San Francisco Chronicle*, Apr. 20, 1995, P. A11.

10. Silk, *Unsecular Media*, P. 55.

11. Jennings, Peter, "Religion and Values in Public Life," *Harvard Divinity School*, Issue 4, 1996, Pp. 14–16.

12. Wallis, Jim, "Common Ground Politics," *Sojourners*, Jan.–Feb. 1997, P. 8; Wallis, Jim, "All Together Now!" *Sojourners*, May–June 1997; Kauffman, Richard, "Leaders Pursue Unity in Fighting Poverty," *Christianity Today*, June 16, 1997, Pp. 60–61.

13. Lattin, Don, "Mainstream Protestants, Evangelicals Come Together After Years of Mistrust," *San Francisco Chronicle*, Nov. 14, 1996, P. A1.

14. Cimino, Richard P., "Common Ground Finding Place in Churches," *Religion Watch*, Feb. 1996, P. 3.

15. Wall, John, "The New Middle Ground in the Family Debate," *Criterion*, Autumn 1994, Pp. 24–31.

16. Dorrien, Gary, *The Neoconservative Mind* (Temple University Press, Philadelphia, 1993), P. 319.

17. Coleman, John, "Under the Cross and the Flag," *America*, May 11, 1996, Pp. 6–15.

18. Lattin, Don, "Churches and Faith Rise from the Ashes," *San Francisco Chronicle,* July 12, 1996, P. A1.

CHAPTER NINE

1. Nisker, Wes, "Chan on Turtle Island: A Conversation with Gary Snyder," *Inquiring Mind,* Winter 1988, P. 1.

2. Anonymous, "American Attitudes on Creation and Earthcare," *Whole Earth Review,* Winter 1997, P. 7.

3. Baker, Beth, "Green Worship," *Common Boundary,* Sept.–Oct. 1996, Pp. 40–46.

4. Baker, "Green Worship."

5. Shibley, Mark A., and Wiggins, Jonathon, "The Greening of Mainline American Religion," *Social Compass,* June 1997, Pp. 333–348.

6. Steinfels, Peter, "As Government Aid Evaporates," *New York Times,* Oct. 28, 1995, P. A11:4.

7. Ammerman, *Community and Congregation,* Pp. 360–370.

8. Sherman, Amy L., "Get with the Program," *American Enterprise,* Jan.–Feb. 1997, P. 68.

9. Goodstein, Laurie, "From Pulpit, Pitches for the Material World," *Washington Post,* Dec. 26, 1996, P. A1:1.

10. Royal, Robert, *American Character,* Winter 1996, P. 1.

11. Zyskowski, Bob, "How Parishes Create Common Ground for the Common Good," *Salt of the Earth,* Mar.–Apr. 1996, Pp. 28–32.

12. Roof, Wade Clark, "It's in the Details," *Sociology of Religion,* Summer 1996, P. 159.

13. Schaller, Lyle E., "What Will Tomorrow Bring: Four Predictions," *Clergy Journal,* Jan. 1997, Pp. 14–16.

14. Blaustein, Rachel, "Why More Parents Are Choosing Jewish Day Schools," *Moment,* Feb. 1997, Pp. 58–62.

15. Stern, Sol, "The Invisible Miracle of Catholic Schools," *City Journal,* Summer 1996, Pp. 14–16.

16. Radner, Ephraim, "Religious Schooling as Inner-City Ministry," *Christian Century,* Mar. 6, 1991, Pp. 260–264.

17. Cimino, Richard, "Jews, Muslims Join Homeschooling Ranks," *Religion Watch,* May 1995, P. 2.

18. Felsenthal, Edward, "End of a Culture War: How Religion Found Its Way Back to School," *Wall Street Journal,* Mar. 23, 1998, Pp. A1, A10.

19. Lattin, Don, "A Compromise in the Battle for Gay Rights," *San Francisco Chronicle Sunday,* Feb. 23, 1997, P. 3.

20. Maynard, Roy, and Olasky, Marvin, "The Empire Strikes Back," *World,* July 29–Aug. 5, 1995, Pp. 13–15.

21. Jorstad, Erling, "Church-State Rulings to Encourage More Accommodation of Religion by State," *Religion Watch,* July–Aug. 1995, P. 3.

22. Singer, Margaret, *Cults in Our Midst* (Jossey-Bass, San Francisco, 1995).

23. Wright, Stuart, "Media Coverage of Unconventional Religion: Any 'Good' News for Minority Faiths," *Review of Religious Research,* Dec. 1997, Pp. 100–111.

24. Nesbitt, Paula, "Countdown to the Millennium," *Quarterly Review,* Summer 1997, Pp. 112–127.

25. Palmer, Susan, *Moon Sisters, Krishna Mothers, Rajneesh Lovers* (Syracuse University Press, Syracuse, 1995).

26. Lucas, Phillip Charles, "New Religions Needn't Be Feared," *Newsday,* Apr. 15, 1997, Pp. A41–A42.

27. Goodstein, Laurie, "Plaintiff Shifts Stance on Anti-Cult Group" and "Anti-Cult Group Dismembered as Former Foes Buy Its Assets," *Washington Post,* Dec. 1, 1996, P. A1 and Dec. 23, 1996, P. A4.

28. Hexham, Irving, and Poewe, Karla, *New Religions as Global Cultures* (Westview Press, Boulder, 1997), P. 160.

29. Lattin, Don, "New Age Showman Touts New Calendar," *San Francisco Chronicle,* Apr. 3, 1995, P. A15.

30. Lattin, Don, "The Man Who Prophesied the End of the World," *San Francisco Chronicle Sunday,* Mar. 12, 1995, P. 1.

31. Sheler, Jeffrey, "Dark Prophecies," *U.S. News & World Report,* Dec. 15, 1997, P. 62.

32. Gould, Stephen Jay, *Questioning the Millennium* (Harmony Books, New York, 1997), P. 67.

33. Wessinger, Catherine, *Annie Besant and Progressive Messianism* (E. Mellon Press, Lewiston, N.Y., 1988).

34. Lattin, Don, "Apocalypse Meets Millennium in Texas Sect," *San Francisco Chronicle,* Mar. 7, 1998, P. 1.

35. Smith, Robert, "The Prophet of Patmos and the Artist of Nuremberg," forthcoming.

AFTERWORD

1. Matthew 21:12–13.

2. Weber, Max, *The Protestant Work Ethic and the Spirit of Capitalism* (Scribner, New York, 1958).

BIBLIOGRAPHY

Ammerman, Nancy, "SBC Moderates and the Making of a Postmodern Denomination," *Christian Century*, Sept. 22–29, 1993.

Ammerman, Nancy, *Community and Congregation* (Rutgers University Press, New Brunswick, N.J., 1997).

Ansk, Daniel, "Religious Frakus Debunks Myths of Anarchy on the Net," *Los Angeles Times*, Jan. 25, 1995, P. D1:4.

Appleby, R. Scott, "Crunch Time for American Catholicism," *Christian Century*, Apr. 3, 1996, P. 370.

Associated Press, "Poll Says 71 Percent Believe in God," *San Francisco Chronicle*, Dec. 22, 1997, P. A7.

Baker, Beth, "Green Worship," *Common Boundary*, Sept.–Oct. 1996, Pp. 40–46.

Barna, George, *Baby Busters: The Disillusioned Generation* (Northfield Publishing, Chicago, 1994).

Barna, George, *Barna Research Group*, Feb. 28, 1996.

Barnette, Martha, "Body and Soul," *Allure*, Sept. 1996, P. 258.

Bass, Dorothy, in *Practicing Our Faith* (Jossey-Bass, San Francisco, 1997), Bass, Dorothy, Ed., Pp. 149–162.

Baumer, Patricia Hughes, "Empowering a New Voice: The Potential for Lay Preaching," *Catholic World*, Mar.–Apr., 1994, Pp. 93–97.

Bellah, Robert, *The Good Society* (Vintage Books, New York, 1992), P. 187.

Bellah, Robert, *Habits of the Heart: Individualism and Commitment in American Life* (HarperCollins, New York, 1986), P. 77.

Berger, Peter L., *A Far Glory* (Free Press, New York, 1992), P. 147.

Blaustein, Rachel, "Why More Parents Are Choosing Jewish Day Schools," *Moment*, Feb. 1997, Pp. 58–62.

Bloom, Harold, *The American Religion* (Simon & Schuster, New York, 1992).

Boeve, Timothy, "Ecumenism: Changing the Course of History," *Church Herald*, Jan. 1997, P. 11.

Braaten, Carl E., "Theology for the Third Millennium," *A Report from the Center*, Center for Catholic and Evangelical Theology, Summer 1996, P. 4.

Briggs, Kenneth A., "Is There a Religious Left? *Common Boundary*, Jan.–Feb. 1997, Pp. 24–31.

Brownstein, Ronald, "Evangelicals Found to Hold Largest Share of GOP Base," *Los Angeles Times,* June 25, 1996, P. A8:1.

Brubaker, George K., "Seminary Education: Real Time, Real Life," *Christianity Today,* Oct. 7, 1996, Pp. 99–134.

Carrasco, Rodolpho, "Expression, Not Confession," *Regeneration Quarterly,* Spring 1995, Pp. 20–22.

Casanova, Jose, *Public Religions in the Modern World* (University of Chicago Press, Chicago, 1994), Pp. 211–234.

Chai, Karen, "Competing for the Second Generation: English Language Ministry in a Korean Protestant Church," unpublished paper presented at Association for the Sociology of Religion, New York City, 1996.

Chandler, Russell, "Dishing Out Training—From a Distance," *Current Trends and Thoughts,* Mar. 1995, P. 24.

Chandler, Russell, *Racing Toward 2001* (Zondervan-Harper San Francisco, 1992), Pp. 240–245.

Cimino, Richard P., "Common Ground Finding Place in Churches," *Religion Watch,* Feb. 1996, P. 3.

Cimino, Richard P., "Denominational Switching Grows Among Conservative Congregations," *Religion Watch,* July–Aug. 1996, Pp. 1–2.

Cimino, Richard P., "Health-Spirituality Connections Grow, Encountering Religious Traditions," *Religion Watch,* Dec. 1995, Pp. 1–2.

Cimino, Richard P., "How Multicultural Are the Churches: A Canadian Case Study," *Religion Watch,* Dec. 1993, Pp. 1–2.

Cimino, Richard P., "Jewish Renewal Impacts Mainstream Judaism," *Religion Watch,* Dec. 1994, Pp. 1–2.

Cimino, Richard P., "Religious Orders Branching Out, Innovating," *Religion Watch,* Sept. 1997, P. 7.

Cimino, Richard P., "Scientific Breakthroughs Playing a New Role in Theology," *Religion Watch,* May 1991, Pp. 1–2.

Cimino, Richard P., "The Fuzzy Future of Denominations," *Religion Watch,* Dec. 1996, Pp. 1–2.

Cimino, Richard P., "Women Religious Leadership Facing Mainline Decline, Conservative Growth," *Religion Watch,* Nov. 1995, Pp. 1–2.

Cimino, Richard, "Jews, Muslims Join Homeschooling Ranks," *Religion Watch,* May 1995, P. 2.

Clayton, Philip, "Computers and the Spirit," *Science and Spirit* newsletter, Winter 1997, p. 1.

Coalter, Milton J., Mulder, John M., and Weeks, Louis B., *Vital Signs: The Promise of Mainline Protestantism* (Eerdmans, Grand Rapids, Mich., 1996).

Coleman, John, "Under the Cross and the Flag," *America*, May 11, 1996, Pp. 6–15.

Cox, Harvey, *Fire from Heaven* (Addison-Wesley, Reading, Mass., 1995).

Culligan, Kevin, "Are We Wired for God? *America*, Mar. 22, 1997, Pp. 23–24.

Dart, John, and Allen, Jimmy, *Bridging the Gap: Religion and the News Media* (The Freedom Forum, Vanderbilt University, 1993), P. 35.

Delbanco, Andrew, and Delbanco, Thomas, "A.A. at the Crossroads," *New Yorker*, P. 58.

Dellinger, Drew, "Creation in Common," 1996.

Dorrien, Gary, *The Neoconservative Mind* (Temple University Press, Philadelphia, 1993), P. 319.

Dudley, Carl, "Pluralism as an Ism," *Christian Century*, Oct. 27, 1993, P. 1042.

Duin, Julia, "Denomination Blends Spirituality with High Church Style," *Charisma*, Sept. 1996, Pp. 25–27.

Dykstra, Craig, "Religion and Spirituality," *Initiatives in Religion*, Summer 1996, Pp. 1–2.

Eck, Diana, "Neighboring Faiths," *Harvard Magazine*, Sept.–Oct. 1996, P. 38.

Ellwood, Robert, *The History and Future of Faith* (Crossroad, New York, 1988).

Evenson, Laura, "Soulful Books Give Readers Insight, Make Best-Sellers," *San Francisco Chronicle*, Dec. 25, 1996, P. A1.

Fagan, Patrick F., *Why Religion Matters: The Impact of Religious Practice on Social Stability*, Backgrounder No. 1064 (Heritage Foundation, Washington, D.C., 1995).

Felsenthal, Edward, "End of a Culture War: How Religion Found Its Way Back to School," *Wall Street Journal*, Mar. 23, 1998, Pp. A1, A10.

Fernandez-Armesto, Felipe, and Wilson, Derek, *Reformations* (Scribner, New York, 1996).

Finke, Roger, "An Orderly Return to Tradition," *Journal for the Scientific Study of Religion*, June 1997, Pp. 218–231.

Finke, Roger, and Stark, Rodney, *The Churching of America* (Rutgers University Press, New Brunswick, 1992).

Ford, Marcia, "Denomination Revamps Image," *Charisma*, Nov. 1995.

Gahr, Evan, "Spirited Enterprise," *American Enterprise*, July–Aug. 1997, P. 53.

Gallup, George H. Jr., "Small Groups Playing an Important Role in Religious Experience of Many," *Emerging Trends*, Sept. 1996, P. 3.

Gallup, George H. Jr., *Religion in America: 1996 Report* (Princeton Religion Research Center, Princeton, 1996).

Garcia, Guy, "Rock Finds Religion," *New York Times*, Jan. 2, 1994, P. 1L.

Goldman, Ari, "Hymnals Welcomed," *New York Times*, July 31, 1993, P. 10L.

Goodstein, Laurie, "A Conservative Leader Threatens to Bolt G.O.P.," *New York Times*, Feb. 12, 1998, P. A22.

Goodstein, Laurie, "From Pulpit, Pitches for the Material World," *Washington Post,* Dec. 26, 1996, P. A1:1.

Goodstein, Laurie, "Plaintiff Shifts Stance on Anti-Cult Group" and "Anti-Cult Group Dismembered as Former Foes Buy Its Assets," *Washington Post,* Dec. 1 and 23, 1996.

Gould, Stephen Jay, *Questioning the Millennium* (Harmony Books, New York, 1997), P. 67.

Graham, Barbara, "Meditating on Prozac," *Common Boundary,* Sept.–Oct. 1995, P. 24.

Graham, Barbara, "The Feminine Face of the Buddah," *Common Boundary,* Mar.–Apr. 1994, Pp. 28–35.

Graham, Tim, and Kaminski, Steve, "Faith in a Box: The Network News on Religion, 1993," *News Report Number Four,* Media Research Center.

Greeley, Andrew M., *Religious Change in America* (Harvard University Press, Cambridge, 1989).

Green, John C., "Evangelical Realignment," *Christian Century,* July 5, 1995, Pp. 676–680.

Hammond, Phillip E., *Religion and Personal Autonomy* (University of South Carolina Press, Columbia, 1993).

Hawes, Peter, "Casting a Wider Net," *Common Boundary,* Nov.–Dec. 1995, P. 32.

Heim, S. Mark, "The Next Ecumenical Movement," *Christian Century,* Aug. 14–21, 1996, Pp. 780–783.

Henry, Patrick, "New Geometries of Ecumenism," *Theology Today,* Jan. 1997, Pp. 491–502.

Hexham, Irving, and Poewe, Karla, *New Religions as Global Cultures* (Westview Press, Boulder, 1997), P. 160.

Hoge, Dean, Johnson, Benton, and Luidens, Donald, *Vanishing Boundaries: The Religion of Mainline Baby Boomers* (Westminster/John Knox Press, Louisville, 1994).

Hoge, Dean R., Zech, Charles E., McNamara, Patrick H., and Donahue, Michael J., *Money Matters: Personal Giving in American Churches* (Westminster John Knox, Louisville, 1996).

Hotz, Robert Lee, "Brain Could Affect Religious Response," *Los Angeles Times,* Nov. 1, 1997, P. B4:5.

Hunter, James Davison, *Culture Wars* (Free Press, New York, 1994), Pp. 320–325.

James, William, *The Varieties of Religious Experience* (American Penguin Library, New York, 1982), P. 115.

Jennings, Peter, "Religion and Values in Public Life," *Harvard Divinity School,* Issue 4, 1996, Pp. 14–16.

Holland, Joe, in *Spirituality and Society: Postmodern Visions* (State University Press of New York, 1996), Griffin, David Ray, Ed.

Jones, Alan, *Exploring Spiritual Direction: An Essay on Christian Friendship* (Harper San Francisco, San Francisco, 1982).

Jorstad, Erling, "Church-State Rulings to Encourage More Accommodation of Religion by State," *Religion Watch*, July-Aug. 1995, P. 3.

Jorstad, Erling, *Holding Fast/Pressing On: Religion in America During the 1980s* (Praeger, New York, 1990).

Jorstad, Erling, "New Wave of Women's Spirituality Books Focus on Gender Differences," *Religion Watch*, Feb. 1996, P. 3.

Kantrowitz, Barbara, "The Search for the Sacred," *Newsweek*, Nov. 28, 1994, Pp. 56, 61.

Kauffman, Richard, "Leaders Pursue Unity in Fighting Poverty," *Christianity Today*, June 16, 1997, Pp. 60–61.

Kennedy, John W., "Redeeming the Wasteland," *Christianity Today*, Oct. 2, 1995, Pp. 92–102.

Kew, Richard, and White, Roger, *Toward 2015: A Church Odyssey* (Cowley Publications, Boston, 1997).

Koenig, John, in *Practicing Our Faith* (Jossey-Bass, San Francisco, 1997), Bass, Dorothy, Ed., Pp. 149–162.

Kosmin, Barry, and Lachman, Seymour, *One Nation Under God* (Harmony Books, New York, 1993).

Kozodoy, Neal, Ed., "What Do American Jews Believe," *Commentary*, Aug. 1996, Pp. 18–96.

Kurien, Prima, "An American Hinduism? Hindu Americans and the Reformulation of Religious Ideology and Practice," unpublished paper delivered at Society for the Scientific Study of Religion, St. Louis, 1995.

Laabs, Jennifer J., "Balancing Spirituality and Work," *Personnel Journal*, Sept. 1995, P. 60.

Lattin, Don, "A Church Within the Church," *San Francisco Examiner*, June 1, 1986, P. A1.

Lattin, Don, "A Compromise in the Battle for Gay Rights," *San Francisco Chronicle Sunday*, Feb. 23, 1997, P. 3.

Lattin, Don, "Activist Lerner Returns to SF to Start Temple," *San Francisco Chronicle*, Aug. 2, 1996, P. A19.

Lattin, Don, "Big Sur Monk a New Age Pioneer," *San Francisco Chronicle*, Dec. 24, 1993, P. A1.

Lattin, Don, "Called by Her God," *San Francisco Chronicle Sunday*, Mar. 30, 1997, P. 1.

Lattin, Don, "Christian Doubters Call Sophia a Pagan Goddess," *San Francisco Chronicle*, Mar. 3, 1994, P. A1.

Lattin, Don, "Christian Right's New Political Push," *San Francisco Chronicle,* June 12, 1992, P. A1.

Lattin, Don, "Churches and Faith Rise from the Ashes," *San Francisco Chronicle,* July 12, 1996, P. A1.

Lattin, Don, "Churches Offer Therapy for Soul," *San Francisco Chronicle,* Dec. 25, 1991, P. 1.

Lattin, Don, "Crusade Countdown," *San Francisco Chronicle Sunday,* July 20, 1997, P. 1.

Lattin, Don, "Far from the Maddening Crowd," *Common Boundary,* Mar.–Apr. 1992, P. 34.

Lattin, Don, "GOP Pilgrimage to Broadcaster's Door," *San Francisco Chronicle,* July 17, 1995, P. A2.

Lattin, Don, "Hark! Hollywood Angels Take Wing," *San Francisco Chronicle Sunday Datebook,* Dec. 15, 1996, P. 42.

Lattin, Don, "Irreverent Book Views U.S. Religion Through Economic Lens," *San Francisco Chronicle,* Nov. 6, 1993, P. A6.

Lattin, Don, "Mainstream Protestants, Evangelicals Come Together After Years of Mistrust," *San Francisco Chronicle,* Nov. 14, 1996, P. A1.

Lattin, Don, "Mormon Crusade Goes Global," *San Francisco Chronicle,* Apr. 8, 1996, P. 1.

Lattin, Don, "Muslims, Others Feel Scapegoated by Speculation," *San Francisco Chronicle,* Apr. 20, 1995, P. A11.

Lattin, Don, "New Age Showman Touts New Calendar," *San Francisco Chronicle,* Apr. 3, 1995, P. A15.

Lattin, Don, "Physics, Mystics and the Essence of Things," *San Francisco Examiner,* Feb. 9, 1986, P. B1.

Lattin, Don, "Religions of the World Gather in Chicago," *San Francisco Chronicle,* Aug. 27, 1993, P. A1.

Lattin, Don, "The Man Who Prophesied the End of the World," *San Francisco Chronicle Sunday,* Mar. 12, 1995, P. 1.

Lattin, Don, "The Need to Cry Out," *Common Boundary,* May–June 1991, P. 17.

Lattin, Don, "Therapists Turn from Psyche to Soul," *San Francisco Chronicle,* Mar. 17, 1994, P. A1.

Lattin, Don, "Witches Staking Claim to Halloween as Sacred Holiday," *San Francisco Chronicle,* Oct. 24, 1996, P. C1.

Lattin, Don, "Young Muslims Struggle with Tradition, Stereotypes," *San Francisco Chronicle,* Jan. 17, 1994, P. 1.

Lawrence, Beverly Hall, *Reviving the Spirit* (Grove, New York, 1996).

Lawson, Steven, "Four Square Church Faces 21st Century," *Charisma,* Mar. 1993, P. 16.

Lichter, Robert, and Rothman, Stanley, "Media and Business Elites," *Public Opinion*, Issue 4, 1981.

Lockhart, William H., "Defining the New Christian Man," unpublished paper presented at Society for the Scientific Study of Religion, Nashville, Nov. 8–10, 1996.

Lucas, Phillip Charles, "New Religions Needn't Be Feared," *Newsday*, Apr. 15, 1997, Pp. A41–A42.

Marciniak, Edward, and Droel, William, "The Future of Catholic Churches in the Inner City," *Chicago Studies*, Aug. 1995, Pp. 172–186.

Marvel, Mark, "Channel-Surfing for God," *Elle*, Jan. 1997, P. 38.

Maynard, Roy, and Olasky, Marvin, "The Empire Strikes Back," *World*, July 29–Aug. 5, 1995, Pp. 13–15.

McCarraher, Eugene, "Smile When You Say 'Laity,' " *Commonweal*, Sept. 12, 1997, P. 23.

McClure, Vicki, UC Berkeley Graduate School of Journalism, religion reporting project, Dec. 1997.

Miller, Donald G., *Reinventing American Protestantism* (University of California Press, Berkeley, 1997).

Montali, Larry, "Catholic Parishes Take Page from Megachurches," *National Catholic Register*, Aug. 13, 1995, P. 1.

Nash, Laura, "The Nanny Corporation," *Across the Board*, Fall 1994, P. 3.

Nattier, Jan, "Buddhism Comes to Main Street," *Wilson Quarterly*, Spring 1997, Pp. 72–80.

Nelson, Alan, "Mind of a Priest, Soul of a Prophet," *Intro Action*, Apr. 1997, Pp. 1–4.

Nesbitt, Paula, "Countdown to the Millennium," *Quarterly Review*, Summer 1997, Pp. 112–127.

Niebuhr, Gustav, "Religious Left Draws Strength from Grassroots," *New York Times*, June 21, 1997, P. 12.

O'Leary, Denyse, "Cell Churches Around the World," *Faith Today*, Mar.–Apr. 1996, P. 30.

O'Leary, Stephen, "Cyberspace as Sacred Space: Communicating Religion on Computer Networks," *Journal of the American Academy of Religion*, Winter 1997, Pp. 781–806.

Oppenheim, Carolyn Toll, "Taking Back the Torah: Jews and Social Justice," *Fellowship*, Sept.–Oct. 1996.

Palmer, Susan, *Moon Sisters, Krishna Mothers, Rajneesh Lovers* (Syracuse University Press, Syracuse, 1995).

Patch, Rashid Raymond, "A Sufi Symposium Sees More Traditional Islam," *Gnosis*, Summer 1997, Pp. 8–10.

Radner, Ephraim, "Religious Schooling as Inner-City Ministry," *Christian Century*, Mar. 6, 1991, Pp. 260–264.

Raschke, Carl, in *Spirituality and the Secular Quest* (Crossroad, New York, 1996), Van Ness, Peter H., Ed., P. 220.

Renner, Gerald, "Reshaping Church to Link to Daily Life," *Hartford Courant*, July 4, 1995, P. A1.

Reuters News Service, "Promise Keepers Sacks All 345 Staff Members," Feb. 20, 1998.

Roof, Wade Clark, *A Generation of Seekers* (Harper San Francisco, San Francisco, 1993).

Roof, Wade Clark, "It's in the Details," *Sociology of Religion,* Summer 1996, P. 159.

Roof, Wade Clark, and McKinney, William, *American Mainline Religion* (Rutgers University Press, New Brunswick, N.J., 1987), Pp. 172–183.

Rosado, Caleb, "Multicultural Ministry," *Ministry,* May 1996, Pp. 22–25.

Rosenberg, Richard, "JCC's Soft-Sell Judaism," *Moment,* Apr. 1997, P. 35.

Rothman, Stanley, "Is God Really Dead in Beverly Hills?" *American Scholar,* Spring 1996, Pp. 272–279.

Royal, Robert, *American Character,* Winter 1996, P. 1.

Ruby, Walter, "Reform Versus Conservative: Who's Winning," *Moment,* Apr. 1996, Pp. 37–39.

San Francisco Archdiocese, *Sunday to Sunday,* Mar. 24, 1996.

Schaller, Lyle E., "What Will Tomorrow Bring: Four Predictions," *Clergy Journal,* Jan. 1997, Pp. 14–16.

Schaller, Lyle E., *The New Reformation: Tommorow Arrived Yesterday* (Abington, Nashville, 1995).

Sheler, Jeffrey, "Dark Prophecies," *U.S. News & World Report,* Dec. 15, 1997, P. 62.

Sherman, Amy L., "Get with the Program," *American Enterprise,* Jan.–Feb. 1997, P. 68.

Shibley, Mark A., and Wiggins, Jonathon, "The Greening of Mainline American Religion," *Social Compass,* June 1997, Pp. 333–348.

Silk, Mark, *Unsecular Media: Making News of Religion in America* (University of Illinois Press, Champaign, 1995), P. 25.

Simpkinson, Charles, Wengell, Douglas, and Casavant, Mary Jane, Ed., *Graduate Education Guide: Holistic Programs and Resources Integrating Spirituality and Psychology* (Common Boundary, Inc., Bethesda, Md., 1994).

Singer, Margaret, *Cults in Our Midst* (Jossey-Bass, San Francisco, 1995).

Smith, Brad, "Team Ministry in the Twenty-First Century," *Next,* Feb. 1996, Pp. 1–4.

Smith, Robert, "The Prophet of Patmos and the Artist of Nuremberg," forthcoming.

Steinfels, Peter, "As Government Aid Evaporates," *New York Times*, Oct. 28, 1995, P. A11:4.

Stern, Sol, "The Invisible Miracle of Catholic Schools," *City Journal*, Summer 1996, Pp. 14–16.

Stevenson, A. Russell, "Megachurches Prove That Theology Matters," *Presbyterian Layman*, Sept.–Oct. 1993, Pp. 6, 8.

Stokes, Allison, *Women Pastors* (Crossroad, New York, 1995), Pp. 123–159.

Strausbaugh, John, E., *The Birth of the Elvis Faith* (Blast Books, New York, 1995), P. 13.

Synan, Vinson, *The Holiness-Pentecostal Tradition* (Eerdmans, Grand Rapids, Mich., 1997), P. 294.

Tabliabue, John, "Pope Bolsters Church's Support for Scientific View of Evolution," *New York Times*, Oct. 25, 1996, P. 1.

Tapia, Andres, "Engaging the Marketplace," *Christianity Today*, May 15, 1995, P. 49.

Thomas, Gary, "Doctors Who Pray," *Christianity Today*, Jan. 6, 1997, P. 20.

Thomas, L. Eugene, and Eisenhandler, Susan, Ed., *Aging and the Religious Dimension* (Auburn House, Westport, 1994).

Tickle, Phyllis A., *God-Talk in America* (Crossroad, New York, 1997), Pp. 117–118.

Tickle, Phyllis A., *Rediscovering the Sacred* (Crossroad, New York, 1996), P. 17.

Tocqueville, Alexis de, *Democracy in America*, Book 1, Chapter 15 (Knopf, New York, 1945).

Trexler, Edgar R., "More Than Multicultural," *The Lutheran*, Jan. 1997, P. 58.

Trueheart, Charles, "Welcome to the Next Church," *Atlantic Monthly*, Aug. 1996, Pp. 37–38.

Unsworth, Tim, "Status of Protestants Under the Sanctuary Lamp," *National Catholic Reporter*, Oct. 4, 1996, P. 18.

Van Ness, Peter H., Ed., *Spirituality and the Secular Quest* (Crossroad, New York, 1996).

Wall, John, "The New Middle Ground in the Family Debate," *Criterion*, Autumn 1994, Pp. 24–31.

Wallis, Jim, "All Together Now!" *Sojourners*, May–June 1997.

Wallis, Jim, "Common Ground Politics," *Sojourners*, Jan.–Feb. 1997, P. 8.

Warner, R. Stephen, "Work in Progress Toward a New Paradigm for the Sociological Study of Religion in the United States," *American Journal of Sociology*, Mar. 1993, Pp. 1044–1095.

Wessinger, Catherine, *Annie Besant and Progressive Messianism* (E. Mellon Press, Lewiston, N.Y., 1988).

Wilber, Ken, *The Marriage of Sense and Soul: Integrating Science and Religion* (Random House, New York, 1998), P. 3.

Willimon, William, "Reformer and Hand-Wringer," *Christian Century*, May 15, 1996, Pp. 533–534.

Wittberg, Patricia, *Pathways to Re-Creating Religious Communities* (Paulist Press, Mahwah, N.J., 1996), Pp. 19–31.

Woodward, Kenneth L., "Gender and Religion," *Commonweal*, Nov. 22, 1996, Pp. 9–14.

Wright, Stuart, "Media Coverage of Unconventional Religion: Any 'Good' News for Minority Faiths," *Review of Religious Research*, Dec. 1997, Pp. 100–111.

Wuthnow, Robert, *Sharing the Journey* (Free Press, New York, 1994).

Wuthnow, Robert, *The Restructuring of American Religion* (Princeton University Press, Princeton, 1988), Pp. 132–134.

Young, Lawrence A., Ed., *Rational Choice Theory and Religion* (Routledge, New York, 1997).

Zikmund, Barbara Brown, "What Is the Spirit Saying to the Churches?" *Ecumenical Trends*, Oct. 1996, Pp. 1–8.

Zikmund, Barbara Brown, Lummis, Adair T., and Chang, Patricia Mei Yang, *Clergy Women: An Uphill Calling* (Westminster John Knox, Louisville, 1998).

Zyskowski, Bob, "How Parishes Create Common Ground for the Common Good," *Salt of the Earth*, Mar.–Apr. 1996, Pp. 28–32.

LIST OF LINK PAGE HEADINGS

The following words are highlighted in the CD-ROM text as hyperlinks. Where indicated, some of the words may be found *under* a different word or term, for example, Enneagram (under New Age) means that Enneagram will be found on the New Age link page.

ACLU (under Separation of Church and State)
AIDS
Affirmative action
Alcoholics Anonymous (under Self-help groups)
Americans United for Separation of Church and State (under Separation of Church and State)
Angelica, Mother (under Televangelism)
Angels (under Spirituality)
Anglicanism
Apocalyptists (under Millennialism)
Arguelles, Jose (under Millennialism)
Billy Graham Evangelistic Association (under Evangelicalism)
Bioethics
Born again (under Evangelicalism)
Born-again Christians (under Evangelicalism)
Buddhism
Buddhist (under Buddhism)
Campbell, Joseph (under Spirituality)
Campus Crusade for Christ (under Evangelicalism)
Catholic (under Catholicism)
Catholicism
Celestine Prophesy (under New Age)
Cell group churches
Celtic spirituality (under Spirituality)
Center for Evangelical and Catholic Theology (under Renewal groups)
Charismatic Episcopal Church (under Anglicanism)
Children of God (under New religious movements)
Christian Broadcasting Network (under Televangelism)
Christian Coalition (under Religious right)
Christianity Today (under Evangelicalism)
Chopra, Deepak (under Spirituality)
Church of Jesus Christ of Latter-day Saints (under Mormons)

Church of Scientology (under New religious movements)
Civil rights
Clinton, Bill
Common Boundary (under Spirituality)
Common-ground movement
Creation spirituality (under Spirituality)
Cult Awareness Network (under New religious movements)
Dead Sea Scrolls
Eastern Orthodox (under Eastern Orthodoxy)
Eastern Orthodoxy
Ecumenism
Enneagram (under New Age)
Episcopal Church (under Anglicanism)
Episcopalian (under Anglicanism)
Evangelical (under Evangelicalism)
Evangelical Episcopal Church (under Anglicanism)
Evangelical Episcopal Church International (under Anglicanism)
Evangelicalism
Farrakhan (under Islam)
Feminist spirituality (under Spirituality)
Focus on the Family (under Religious right)
Fox, Matthew (under Spirituality)
Gallup Organization
Gallup poll (under Gallup Organization)
gay spirituality (under Spirituality)
Gnostic (under Gnosticism)
Gnosticism
Greek Orthodox (under Eastern Orthodoxy)
Graduate Theological Union (under Seminaries)
Hare Krishna (under Hinduism)
Hartford Seminary (under Seminaries)
Harvard Divinity School (under Seminaries)
Health and healing
Heaven's Gate (under New religious movements)

INDEX

A

Abbot, Elliot, 38
ABC, 152
ABC News, 152
Abernathy, Bob, 152
Abortion issue, 136, 145, 153, 155
Accommodationists, 170
Addiction, psychopharmacology versus self-help programs for, 47–48
Affirmative action programs, 109, 110, 127
African Americans: church activism and, 134, 162–163; Islamic, 111; megachurches of, 60–61; men's movement of, 33; Rodney King verdict and, 146–148; search for spiritual roots of, 24; strict practices and, 66; women clergy and, 88–89
African-American Pentecostals, adoption of liturgical worship by, 70
Aging, secular spirituality and, 29
Akremi, Janet, 167
Alabama church burnings, 140, 156–157
Alcoholics Anonymous (AA), 48, 80–81
Alliance of Confessing Evangelicals, 68–69
Allure, 46–47
American Academy of Family Physicians, 45
American Civil Liberties Union, 138
American Jewish Congress, 138

Americans: individualistic spirituality of, 9–16, 49–51; religiousness of, 1–5
Americans United for Separation of Church and State, 138
Ammerman, Nancy, 98–99, 110–111, 134, 162
Ammiano, Tom, 169
Anderson, H. George, 115
Angelica, Mother, 115
Angels, popularity of, 38
"Angels on the Web," 111
Anglicanism: decline of, 126; spiritual virtuosos in, 105–106. *See also* Episcopal Church
Antichrist, 180
Antidepressants, 47
Anti-nuclear activism, 140
Antiochian Evangelical Orthodox Mission, 96–97
Apocalypse, 179
Apocalyptists: cults and, 173–174; millennial, 177–182; prevalence of, 179
Apostolic succession, 120
Appleby, R. Scott, 85
Applewhite, Marshall Herff, 171–172
Are You Ready? (Camping), 177
Argue, Don, 154–155
Arguelles, José, 177–178
Artificial intelligence, 43
Assemblies of God: authority-based leadership in, 91; and awakening of experiential spirituality, 17–18; growth and appeal of, 66, 126
Association for Church Renewal, 119

217

CD-ROM INSTRUCTIONS

Systems Requirements

Windows PC

- 386, 486, or Pentium processor-based personal computer
- Microsoft Windows 3.1, Windows 95, or Windows NT 3.51 or later
- Minimum RAM: 4 MB for Windows 3.1; 8 MB for Windows 95 and NT
- Available space on hard disk: 4MB Windows 3.1; 8 MB Windows 95 and NT
- 2X speed CD-ROM drive or faster
- Netscape 3.0 or higher browser or MS Internet Explorer 3.0 or higher

Macintosh

- Macintosh with a 68020 or higher processor or Power Macintosh
- Apple OS version 7.0 or later
- Minimum RAM: 12 MB for Macintosh
- Available space on hard disk: 6MB Macintosh
- 2X speed CD-ROM drive or faster
- Netscape 3.0 or higher browser or MS Internet Explorer 3.0 or higher

Note: This CD requires Netscape 3.0 or MS Internet Explorer 3.0 or higher. You can download these products using the addresses below:

Netscape: *http://www.netscape.com/download/index.html*

Microsoft Internet Explorer: *http://www.microsoft.com/ie/download*

Getting Started

Insert the CD-ROM into your drive. Launch your Internet browser. Use File . . . Open from within the browser to open the Shopping for Faith icon on your CD drive, and then double-click the Index.html folder (Index.html may come up automatically on the Macintosh). You will see an opening screen with the book cover and two buttons. From this screen, you can click on either the Start or Help button. The Start button will lead to the Main screen.

Moving Around

From the Main screen, if you have installed one of the required browsers listed previously, you will see two frames. The frame on the left-hand side contains a navigational toolbar with buttons. From this toolbar you can click on the buttons to get to the linked text that will then appear in the frame on the right-hand side. Parts One, Two, and Three contain the chapters and postscripts for each of those parts. The other sections are designated with their own individual buttons. You can use the Back button on your browser to get back to the previous screen at any time.

Keywords button: This is a convenient list of all of the linked terms that appear throughout the text of the book. If you prefer not to see the terms in context, you can go to the links directly from this list.

In Case of Trouble

If you experience difficulty using the *Shopping for Faith* CD-ROM, please follow these steps:

1. Make sure your hardware and systems configurations conform to the systems requirements noted under "Systems Requirements."
2. Review the installation procedure for your type of hardware and operating system. It is possible to reinstall the software if necessary.
3. You may call Jossey-Bass Customer Service at (415) 433-1740 between the hours of 8 A.M. and 5 A.M. Pacific Time, and ask for Jossey-Bass CD-ROM Technical Support. (It is best if you are sitting at your computer when making the call.) Before calling, please have the following information available:
   - Type of computer and operating system
   - Version of Windows or Mac OS being used
   - Any error messages displayed
   - Complete description of the problem.
4. To report a broken link, email the Service Department at The Link Library directly at *service@thelinklibrary.com.*